Lion Woman's Legacy

THE CROSS-CULTURAL MEMOIR SERIES
Available from The Feminist Press

I Dwell in Possibility, a memoir by Toni McNaron
The Seasons: Death and Transfiguration, by Jo Sinclair
Fault Lines, by Meena Alexander

Lion Woman's Legacy

An Armenian-American Memoir

Arlene Voski Avakian

Afterword by Bettina Aptheker

THE CROSS-CULTURAL MEMOIR SERIES

THE FEMINIST PRESS
at The City University of New York
New York

Published 1992 by The Feminist Press at The City University of New York,
311 East 94th Street, New York, NY 10128
Distributed by The Talman Company, 150 Fifth Avenue, New York, NY
10011

95 94 93 92 6 5 4 3 2 1

Library of Congress Cataloging-in-Publication Data
Avakian, Arlene Voski.
   Lion woman's legacy : an Armenian-American memoir / Arlene Voski
   Avakian ; afterword by Bettina Aptheker.
      p.   cm.
   ISBN 1-55861-051-0 : $35.00. — ISBN 1-55861-052-9 (pbk.) : $14.95
   1. Avakian, Arlene Voski. 2. Armenian Americans—Biography. 3.
Feminists—United States—Biography. I. Title.
E184.A7A8 1992
973'.049199202—dc20
[B]   91-14302
                                                                        CIP

This publication is made possible, in part, by public funds from the New
York State Council on the Arts. The Feminist Press would also like to thank
Mariam Chamberlain for her generosity.

All photographs courtesy of Arlene Avakian. Far left cover photo is the
author and her grandmother.
Cover design: Lucinda Geist
Text design: Paula Martinac

Printed in the United States of America on acid-free paper by McNaughton
& Gunn, Inc.

To the voices of resistance—
the silent and those raised in defiance

Acknowledgments

I wrote this memoir to show how a particular life is shaped, in part, by cultural and social forces. Because I was interested in the development of consciousness, I tried, as much as possible, to recreate my response to events and people in my life as I understood them at the time. The people who appear in this work are characterized from this perspective, as their histories are filtered through my memory. I wanted to tell the truth with this narrative, but I understand that my truth is only one of many.

Without the women's liberation movement, this work would never have been conceived or undertaken. By giving me an understanding of women's roles in our culture, the women's movement has touched my life and changed it profoundly. I owe a debt to those brave and angry women of the second wave of feminism who recognized women's oppression and had the courage to confront it in society and in their own lives. The civil rights and black power movements, whose spokespeople articulated some of what was wrong in America and gave me an awareness of both my whiteness and my ethnicity, have been equally important in the development of my consciousness.

This book, which began as a dissertation, owes its life to John H. Bracey, Jr., and Johnnetta B. Cole, who convinced me that autobiography was an appropriate vehicle for expressing my concerns about ethnicity, race, and feminist theory. Being neither famous nor old enough to be a "proper" subject for an autobiography, at first I was plagued with the problem of thinking "So what?" and depended on an army of readers to tell me that someone other than me cared about the details of my past. I will always be grateful to John Bracey, who, the day after I had given him a chapter, always called to say, "Keep going." Lorna Peterson's unwavering enthusiasm was a constant reminder that my life did matter, and Joanne Kobin helped me to see I could be a "real writer." I will never forget Bettina Aptheker's praise, which came at a particularly difficult period. Also deserving of thanks in helping to move the work along are: Lisa Baskin, Mary Bowen, Judy Davis, Howard Kobin, Sara Lennox, Alec Martin, Dale Melcher, Leah Ryan, Ruth Thomasian, and Marea Wexler.

As *Lion Woman's Legacy* moved from a dissertation to a book, I had additional help from my friends. Lee Edwards and Irma McClaurin Allen suggested ways to cut the original six hundred pages. More readers—Elizabeth V. Spelman, Clare Coss, Louise Murray, Jay Kidd, Kim Townsend, Sue Thrasher, and Margaret Randall—helped me to continue to believe in the book's value. From the day she suggested I write an autobiography to the time the final manuscript went into production, Johnnetta B. Cole has been both steadfast and, as is her wont, an activist in her support of this book.

Reclaiming my ethnic identity would not have taken the form it did without my intimate and intense interaction with Martha Ann Ayres, a "WASP" who was willing to fight with me. I cannot adequately express my gratitude to her, both for the fights and for her empathy. I trust that we will continue to fight and love each other for many more years.

Finally, I thank my grandmother, who survived and passed the story of that survival on to me.

Chapter 1

*I*t was Easter Sunday, 1954, and my family and I were coming out of church. I had on the new clothes I had made for the occasion and high heels. I wore lipstick but no other makeup. My legs were shaved, but my eyebrows remained untweezed.

The church, the Holy Cross Armenian Apostolic Church, on 187th Street between Audubon and St. Nicholas avenues in Manhattan, was just around the corner from the Presbyterian church where my cousin Susan was probably standing at that very moment waiting to shake hands with the minister, as was the custom in "regular" churches. In our church the congregation had no such opportunity, since the priest who officiated at the three-hour, highly ritualistic ceremony—conducted in ancient Armenian—merely disappeared behind the ornate altar after the service.

My time in church hadn't inspired me, nor did I feel any particular relationship to the God whose resurrection it celebrated. The point of going to church on Easter Sunday was to try to become an American. Regular church attendance is as common among Armenians as it is with other groups, but my parents rarely went to church. The only time they went with any regularity was on Palm Sunday because, as my mother reminded us every year, she liked to have the palms that were given out to the congregation in the house for the year. Palm Sunday and the dry fronds that for me bore no resemblance to any living plant were fine, but going to church on Palm Sunday was not enough. As I understood it, real Americans went to church every Sunday or, at the very least, every Christmas and Easter.

Years earlier, in an attempt to be the best kind of American, I

1

had tried regular church attendance. Since I was about nine or ten years old at the time, this meant going to Sunday school. For a few Sundays I walked to church with my grandmother, who did attend regularly, though the practice did not seem to make her any less "old country." The class consisted of coloring pictures of Bible scenes for what seemed an eternity. Then we were marched into the old, dark, incense-laden church for the last half hour of the long service.

The Sunday school classes always came into the church at the point in the service when the choir sang the "Lord's Prayer." I was glad that this hymn, which I considered a universal Christian song, was sung in our church, but our version would never have been recognized by an American. The meaning remained the same, but the prayer, of course, was sung in Armenian to a melody that sounded nothing like what Americans knew as the "Lord's Prayer."

Not only was this hymn wrong, but everything about the church was. The ancient Armenian language used for church services sounded as if it might be understood, but it was unintelligible to me. That our priest used an even stranger form of a language, peculiar enough as it was, was not the only thing about church that bothered me. The altar was adorned not with pictures of a sweet Jesus surrounded by little children or his apostles but with two paintings that horrified me, though my eyes were drawn back to them repeatedly during the service. In the middle of the altar was a picture of the crucifixion with blood dripping from Christ's hands and side. The other painting was a bust of Christ with more blood from the thorns cutting into his forehead. The emphasis was clearly on his suffering rather than his glory.

The priest, too, looked like nothing I had seen in magazines or books. The black suit or the simple black cloak of the American minister was replaced by an ornate brocade cape worn over a black gown. A huge gold cross, jewelled and filigreed, hung on his chest. At various points during the service a brocade curtain was drawn across part of the altar and the priest disappeared behind it, emerging after a few minutes carrying a scepter and wearing a high, brocaded, brimless hat. The one good thing about our priest was that he was clean shaven and had short hair. Sometimes on special occasions—and these were usually times when the whole family went to church—the archbishop presided. His flowing white hair and long white beard, which reached down to his chest, made him look like some familiar depictions of God, but nothing at all like what priests were supposed to look like. Even the pope didn't look like our archbishop.

I could have endured Sunday school, despite the fact that it was boring and my classmates and the teacher were disturbingly Armenian looking, if it had not culminated in our being marched into that church with that priest to the strains of that "Lord's Prayer." It soon became clear to me that the road to becoming an American, at least as I had defined it in 1949, did not lie in attending this church. That approach seemed hopeless. The whole experience made me feel more Armenian and less American.

Why couldn't we go to the "regular" church around the corner? My cousin went there and she was as Armenian as we were. My mother told me it was not our church but where "they" went. I recognized her use of they. It meant "wrong." But that church looked like heaven to me. Although I had never been inside, I knew it had to be different from our church. For one thing, it wasn't called the Holy Cross American Apostolic Church. It was an American church that had Presbyterian in its name. I didn't know what that meant, but I had heard of it. What was really important was that Americans went there, and it was of some Christian denomination. I knew it was important to be Christian—certainly, to be American meant to be Christian.

Before my short Sunday school experiment, I had longed to be Catholic. Catholics, it seemed to me, had a lot going for them. Two of my favorite movies, *The Bells of St. Mary's* and *Father Flannigan's Boy's Town* had big stars in them, and they were about Catholics. And not only were Catholics recognized as Americans, but they were treated specially. Every Thursday afternoon our school lost half of its students: Catholic kids were actually allowed to leave school for catechism. Not only did they get to leave school, but it was clear that the teachers did not do anything important while they were gone. For me, however, becoming a Catholic was out of the question. Most of the Catholics in my neighborhood were Irish, and my mother was very clear about the fact that they, like Presbyterians, were wrong. They had too many children and were lazy, dirty, and stupid—nothing like the characters played by Bing Crosby, Ingrid Bergman, and Pat O'Brien. There was also, according to my mother, something wrong with their religion itself, but she was not clear on that point. I knew I could not pursue my dream because being Catholic was something you and your family were, not something you became.

By 1954 my admiration for Catholicism had faded, but my attempts to become American had become more intense. If attending church regularly was not going to work, there was one last thing to try. I could convince my parents to go to church on holidays—American holidays. Christmas presented a major problem since Armenians, different as always, celebrate Christmas on the sixth of January. Going to church on December 25 would be fruitless, and, besides, we were pretty American around Christmas. We always had a big tree and presents. Christmas dinner was at the home of my father's brother, Uncle Alex, and his wife, Aunty Goharik, whose large fieldstone and frame house in Westchester County was filled with many relatives, who brought presents to put under the tree. Best of all, Aunty Goharik always made a turkey for dinner. Of course, we also had stuffed grape leaves, rice pilaf, and Armenian pastries for dessert, but the highlight of the dinner, at least for me, was Uncle Alex carving the turkey—very American.

Easter, on the other hand, presented a perfect opportunity to make use of church. Amazingly, Armenian Easter fell on the same day as "regular" Easter. (My Greek friends were not so lucky since the orthodox church followed a different calendar. I was surprised that they did not seem to be bothered by this difference.) I began to plan early because there was a lot to get done. The first thing, to get my parents to agree to go to church, went fairly easily, though they were surprised at my request, since my only interest in church had been a few weeks of Sunday school and my request for a Bible that Christmas. Every real American had a Bible.

The second part, getting our clothes, proved to be very difficult. Americans did not go to church on Easter wearing any old clothes. They went to church in Easter outfits. Yes, my mother explained, we would go to church if I wanted to, even though it would make the preparations for the Easter dinner more difficult, but new clothes were out of the question. I argued that Easter outfits were an American institution; wasn't that clear from the Easter Parade that happened every year right here in New York City on Fifth Avenue in front of not just a church but Saint Patrick's Cathedral (more evidence of Catholic power)? It was to no avail. I tried again with the fact that big stars, Judy Garland and Fred Astaire, had marched in front of this very cathedral in the movie *Easter Parade,* but as I spoke I knew it was a lame argument; my mother hardly ever went to the movies and had no interest in big stars. What was an institution for me, and obviously for the rest of America, the movies, was to my mother only ostentatious display. It was something "they" did, not us.

What we did for Easter was to get palms from church and make them into little crosses that we wore on our coats. We also ate special foods. While we did not observe Lent with meatless dishes as other Armenians did, we never ate meat on the Friday before Easter. The meal began with the traditional egg fights. A bowl of dyed hard-boiled eggs sat in the middle of the table. Some of the eggs were the familiar pale yellows, purples, blues, pinks and oranges; dyed with egg coloring we bought at the grocery story like everyone else. Others were a deep reddish-brown, dyed by boiling them with onionskins my mother got from the greengrocer who saved them for the Armenians and Greeks in the neighborhood. We all would choose an egg and test it for its strength by tapping it on our front teeth. We would then go around the table tapping each other's eggs. The egg that broke all the others was the champion, and we saved it until the next round. The eggs were eaten wrapped in soft *lavash*, a very thin bread, with fresh dill, scallions, and parsley. When everyone had finished their eggs, those who wanted a second helping could also have another try at beating the champion egg. This time the winning egg would be saved for the Easter meal, which also began with an egg fight.

The most important thing about Easter, though, was Easter dinner. Weeks before, my grandmother would begin to bake her specialty, *khata*, a buttery, flaky pastry. No one in the family made *khata* like my grandmother, so she made them not only for our dinner but also for family members who would not be with us for Easter. Days before the feast she would prepare the course coming after the eggs, either artichokes or stuffed mussels. Both dishes took enormous amounts of time to prepare. The mussels had to be cleaned and opened. They were then stuffed with many pounds of finely chopped onions that had been cooked slowly with rice, pine nuts, and currants. Once the mussels were stuffed they were cooked in a mixture of lemon and olive oil. My grandmother made enough so that each of us could have four or five. The mussels were never eaten with a fork or spoon but by using one half of the shells to scoop out the delectable stuffing. While the artichokes were not quite as time-consuming, it seemed to me that my grandmother sat at the kitchen table for hours trimming dozens of artichokes, reaching into the cactuslike vegetables to scoop out the chokes, and then cooking them with potatoes and small white onions in olive oil and lemon.

The day before Easter my mother would begin to prepare her specialty, Persian pilaf. This dish was never made with rice that we bought at the store, but rice from Persia, kept in big jars and used only on special occasions. My uncles, who had an Oriental rug importing business, made arrangements with their suppliers to send us rice with each shipment of rugs. We didn't get our rice in an ordinary way, but wrapped in bales of rugs. My mother also made leg of lamb—we always had lamb on Easter—and spinach and eggs. All our energy went into the preparation of food for Easter, none of it into what we would wear.

Even if I had to accept the fact that my mother and father were going to church on Easter in their old clothes, that didn't mean I couldn't have a new outfit. Choosing clothes I wanted had been a battle for the last few years. I wanted lots of the clothes my friends wore—what my mother called "cheap." She bought me a few "good" clothes from Best and Company, Lord and Taylor, or B. Altman. These shopping trips downtown had been fun when I was younger, but they became increasingly frustrating as I approached my teens. I didn't want "timeless classics"; I wanted what was in style right now. In desperation, I took up sewing and made skirts out of yards and yards of cheap cotton, and I saved my allowance and babysitting money for see-through blouses with puffy sleeves and little black ties at the throat. I was prepared to make my Easter outfit. Luckily, I had won the stockings and high heels argument the previous year and was making headway on makeup. Unlike some of my cousins, I was allowed to shave my legs and wear lipstick, but wearing other makeup and tweezing my eyebrows would have to wait "until I was older."

I was reasonably satisfied with how I looked on that Easter Sunday in 1954. Yet, as I stood on the steps of the church surrounded by people who were praising the resurrection of Christ in Armenian, few of whom looked as if they had given much thought to their Easter outfits, I realized that these people would never look or act like people in *Life* magazine, the *Saturday Evening Post*, or on the silver screen. America was around the corner in the Presbyterian church, and going to the Holy Cross Armenian Apostolic Church was not the way to get there.

As if reading my thoughts, a young man in his twenties approached me. He asked my name, and, when I replied with a name that had the characteristic "ian" at the end, he responded that I certainly didn't look Armenian. He went on to explain that I was too tall, too narrow in the hips, too light, and I didn't have a big enough nose or enough hair to look like a real Armenian. His comments were meant as a compliment, and I took them as such: they made my day. It was possible to come from these people and "pass." And it was clear, too, that I was not the only Armenian who put a premium on looking American.

Chapter 2

I consciously began my campaign to become an American toward the end of my elementary school years, but the process of assimilation had actually been started by my parents when I was born and named Arlene Voski. According to Armenian tradition, the first female child should be named after the father's mother. My parents decided that, since I was born in America and would probably live in this country all my life, they would give me an American first name and use my grandmother's for my middle name. My parents were following the lead of older family members who had emigrated to the United States. My father's Uncle Mesrop and his wife, Aunty Manoush, renamed their children when they emigrated from Persia. There was precedent too for American names in my mother's family. Uncle George's name had been Americanized when he came here as a young child, and he and my aunt, my mother's sister, had named their three sons George, Howard, and Edmond.

While my first name was Arlene, the emphasis, it seemed to me, was on my middle name, Voski. Arlene was the name they had given me to face the world, but Voski was who I was to my family and in the neighborhood. The language of the streets, like that of our house and family, was usually Armenian. We lived in the center of the Armenian community in New York City, Washington Heights. As a very young child, my journey into the world centered around shopping with my mother. In the 1940s in New York City there were no supermarkets, not even for Americans. Shopping for food was done in small, specialized stores. We made frequent trips to the Greek bakery for round, fluffy loaves of *pideh* or rolls. If we wanted rye or pumpernickel bread, we went to the Jewish bakery. Fish came

9

from the fish market, where live fish swam in the big tank in the window; we got vegetables and fruits from the greengrocer, the same one who saved the onionskins for my mother at Easter time. For a special treat we went to the Jewish delicatessen for cold cuts, hotdogs, sauerkraut, and pickles. Once a week we went to Zarifian Brothers, the grocery store where my mother bought meat, canned goods, and staples.

As a young child my weekly trips to Zarifian Brothers with my mother were pure joy. It was our store. The people in it were like the people at home, buying the kind of food we ate and speaking our language. It even smelled right, wonderfully fragrant with olives and cheeses. The small store was generally crowded with women whom my mother knew.

The wait was usually long, as the women slowly read their lists to one of the brothers who picked the items off the shelves. I waited anxiously for one of the women to request something on the top shelf so I could watch one of the Zarifians get out the long stick with a claw on the end, expertly grasp a can or box, and drop it into his hand. They also dished out spoonfuls of olives or pickled vegetables and sometimes gave me a taste, or they cut hunks of cheese from the big wheels in the glass case. Meat was kept in the walk-in refrigerator, and sides of lamb were brought out and the roast or chops cut off while we waited. Meanwhile the women talked with each other, always in Armenian. I wonder now about what information was exchanged at the grocery store, how topics under discussion in our community might have been shaped by the women waiting their turn at Zarifian Brothers. I wonder, too, if anyone ever spoke English there. Did non-Armenians, *odars*, ever wander into the little store? It seemed as unlikely to me as seeing an *odar* sitting in our living room.

Until I began to bring my friends home after school in the fifth or sixth grade, not many *odars* came into our home. The two exceptions were my aunts Vera and Sonia, who were English and Russian, respectively. It was amazing that my father's two brothers had married *odars*, but, as far as I could tell, they were as much a part of our family as anyone else. Aunt Vera and Uncle Vaghoush lived with us for a short time when they moved to the United States from England. Aunt Sonia, too, moved in with us when she emigrated from Persia after her husband died. She and her daughter, Mary, lived with us, while her two sons, Leopold and Peter, lived with Uncle Alex and Aunty Goharik. Aunt Vera's English accent and non-

Armenian ways (using Windex to clean windows instead of vinegar and water, for example) clearly identified her as an *odar*. But Aunt Sonia, who spoke English with a very heavy Russian accent and was also fluent in Armenian, did not seem like an *odar* at all. I had identified *odars* as Americans.

There were two things about Aunt Sonia that distinguished her from the other women in the family, though they did not make her American. One was that she had long and often heated debates with my father and uncles, using words I had never heard before. None of the other women spoke up during these discussions, and perhaps that is why I was curious about them. When I asked my mother what Aunt Sonia and the men were talking about, she told me with a wave of her hand that it was just talk. While this talk was clearly not something "they" did and therefore not automatically wrong, I sensed that something about it was not right. My mother disapproved not so much of the conversation but of Aunt Sonia's part in it. It was "men's talk"—probably politics—and women did not discuss such things. The other thing about Aunt Sonia that made her different from the other women in the family was that she called herself an artist. She painted, not just to fill the time after her children were grown, but because she was an artist. Aunt Sonia had ideas of her own and was willing to argue about them with men, and she had an interest that was totally unrelated to her children. These were unusual qualities in a woman, to be sure, but they were certainly not attributes that other women of the 1940s and 1950s— American women—possessed either. They did not make Aunt Sonia any more like an *odar* than her Russian accent. Aunt Sonia was strange.

There was one thing, however, that made her more like what I imagined *odars* to be: the way she used the city. Although she was a newcomer to this country and spoke English very badly, Aunt Sonia regularly went to the museums. No one else in the family ever went downtown for anything but shopping, with the one exception of my grandmother, who took me to Radio City Music Hall for the Christmas and Easter shows. While it was unusual for my grandmother to love Radio City as she did, she could argue that she was just taking her granddaughter out for a holiday excursion. Aunt Sonia, on the other hand, went alone and often. Though Aunt Sonia and Aunt Vera had strange ways, they were my uncles' wives and therefore were accepted.

Little in my life was confusing during my preschool years. Like my parents, my life was spent within the womb of the extended family. My only other contact was with the Armenian community in our neighborhood. Our apartment was always full of people; at various times from five to twelve people lived in our five rooms. When men were out of work or when people came from Persia or Turkey, they moved in with us until they were able to get settled. But contact with the family was just as intense whether or not we actually lived under the same roof. I made the rounds of visits with my mother or grandmother and spent weekends with relatives. My only playmates were my cousins.

My most vivid memory of these visits is of the ritualistic drinking of Turkish coffee. It was always offered when people dropped in and rarely refused. Everything about Turkish coffee was special. It was made in a gleaming brass *jezveh*, a wide-bottomed, long-handled, coverless pot. The pulverized coffee and sugar were boiled together until they were thick and foamy. My mother always made the coffee, carrying the steaming *jezveh* out of the kitchen on a round brass tray. The thick bittersweet coffee was carefully poured into small cups that had absolutely straight sides. The shape of the cups was crucial to the telling of fortunes, which was as important as the drinking of the coffee. Because the coffee and the water are boiled in the same pot, Turkish coffee has a thick sediment that collects at the bottom of the cup. When the coffee is finished, the cup is turned over on its saucer, turned three times to the right, and not touched until completely cool. When the time was right my grandmother would choose one of the cups, turn it over, and peer into it, studying the patterns that the sediment had made. Some patterns formed delicate and intricate shapes; others had fallen into a thick mass, which always looked foreboding to me. As my grandmother held the cup, everyone was silent, waiting to hear what she ''saw.'' My mother didn't believe in the fortunes, but my grandmother had a reputation for always ''telling the truth.'' There were some days, however, when she would not agree to tell fortunes and some people whose cups she never read, for reasons known only to her.

She was clear on one thing though. It was forbidden to tell children's fortunes. I wasn't allowed to drink the coffee either, though I pleaded with her to let me dump out the coffee and turned my cup over too. But tradition prevailed, and I never had my fortune told. By the time I had reached the age when I was old enough to both drink the coffee and have my cup read, like my mother, I didn't want any part of that foolishness. Also the drinking of Turkish coffee and the ritual surrounding it had become very confusing to me. By that time I had heard about the Armenian genocide and what my grandmother had suffered "at the hands of the Turkish devils." I had also heard comments about Turks from other family members that made them seem like they were evil incarnate. Uncle Ashot was adamant that a Turk would never cross his threshold. Yet the focus of many afternoons was the drinking of Turkish coffee, and some of our favorite foods were Turkish.

One of my favorite places to visit was Aunty Lucy's house. Her husband, my father's uncle, had come to New York City from Persia to join his brothers in the family Oriental rug importing business, Avakian Brothers. According to my mother, Aunty Lucy had not wanted to leave her home in Persia, and it was clear from her behavior that she was unwilling to accommodate herself to this country. Aunty Lucy lived and died in the eight-room apartment on 193rd Street and Wadsworth Avenue that Uncle Hagop had rented when they first arrived. Though she lived in America for more than fifty years, she refused to speak one word of English, even when it meant being unable to communicate with some of her grandchildren. Two of them, Rita and Susan, lived with Aunty Lucy when her son Hemeyak and his wife, Lucy (known in the family as "little Lucy"), moved in with her. During the years that they lived together the usual tendency of the children of immigrants to teach their elders the ways of the new land was reversed. Rita and Susan learned enough Armenian for minimal communication with their grandmother, but Aunty Lucy learned no English, at least she never let anyone know she had any understanding of it.

There was little about this country that Aunty Lucy liked or trusted. Shortly after their arrival, Uncle Hagop died, and after that she rarely went out of the house. Zarifian Brothers delivered most of the food she needed, and family members did her other shopping. Aunty Lucy was very particular about the food she ate, and she refused to believe that American meat was edible. Before she and Uncle Hagop left Persia, their nephew, Alex, had come to the United States for a visit. He returned to Persia with stories of the wonders of America, including the fact that meat was kept fresh for weeks at a time. When Aunty Lucy moved here she insisted that meat kept that long without salting would surely be rotten, and she became a vegetarian. Explanations of the process of refrigeration were to no avail. During her time in this country Aunty Lucy ate meat only twice, when Alex, feeling responsible for her refusal to eat red meat, bought live lambs and had them slaughtered for her.

For me as a young child, however, the only strange thing about Aunty Lucy was that the Armenian she spoke sounded different from that of my parents, though I had little trouble understanding her. I would sit in her ample lap in the summer and drink hot tea out of a tall, thin glass in an ornate silver holder, while the rest of the family had iced tea or other cool drinks. There was something comfortable about Aunty Lucy and her apartment: the highly polished mahogany furniture, the brilliant silver coffee service, and the candy dishes filled with salted pumpkin seeds, roasted chickpeas, and pistachio nuts. The floor of every room except the kitchen was covered from wall to wall with a Persian rug, even the two bathrooms and the long hall that ran from one end of the large apartment to the other. Her house was her country. She hadn't wanted to emigrate, and she would keep as close to her own ways as possible. There was no ambivalence in Aunty Lucy.

As I grew older, I lost the security of Aunty Lucy's lap. My relationship with her diminished as I lost fluency in Armenian. My desire to be American was as strong as Aunty Lucy's refusal, and by the time I was in my late teens we barely understood each other.

I am not sure that all the members of the family were comfortable with Aunty Lucy's insistence on maintaining Persian-Armenian traditions, but her position in the family demanded that they cater to her wishes nonetheless. My father's family was organized around a strict hierarchy that was obvious even to a young child. The father in each family held major decision-making power over business as well as private matters, since all males in the family were on the board of directors of the family business, and many of them worked at Avakian Brothers. As a woman, Aunt Lucy had no power in the business, of course, but she was deferred to respectfully by all family members.

While Aunty Lucy and Uncle Hagop, and after his death Uncle Mesrop, were at the top of the hierarchy, and everyone in the family was deferential to them, older brothers also held positions of authority. As a younger brother, my father was just below Uncle Alex. During the Great Depression, Uncle Alex, in consultation with Uncle Mesrop, of course, decided that my father should move to Cleveland and sell Avakian Brothers' rugs through a concession in a department store. My father, who was in his thirties, married, and the owner of a small restaurant, complied with his brothers' decision.

There was little of that kind of hierarchy in my mother's family. My mother, the youngest, freely disagreed with her brother, sister, and even her mother, though my uncle, her brother, was pampered by all the women. When my grandmother was in her thirties, however, her sister did exercise significant authority over the family. Turvanda Donigian was eighteen years older than Elmas, my grandmother, and was living in New York City when my grandmother and her three children were able to leave Turkey for the United States. Arsenic, Elmas's oldest daughter, had fallen in love with a young Armenian man and wanted to stay in Turkey to marry him. Elmas felt she could not make the decision to leave Arsenic behind without consultation, despite the fact that she had been responsible for the survival of the family for the eleven years since her husband's departure. Since her father, all of his brothers, and her brother-in-law were dead, she wrote to her older sister Turvanda for permission for Arsenic's marriage. Turvanda replied that Arsenic must come to America because she had decided her niece was to marry her son George, regardless of the fact that they were first cousins. My grandmother complied, and when the family arrived in New York City Arsenic went directly to Turvanda's house, while the rest of the family went to live with my grandmother's other sister until they could find the means to get a place of their own. Over the years, as Turvanda grew older, no other woman emerged to become head of the family. There were some men of my mother's generation in the family, and the women deferred to them, but there was not the strict hierarchy of my father's family.

While I was aware of this hierarchy as a very young child, I was bothered neither by it nor by the women's deference to men. Until my cousins Rita and Susan moved to Washington Heights from California when I was around ten years old, I was the only child of the Avakian clan and duly pampered by my paternal kin.

But when I was six and a half years old my brother was born, and my life changed. I do not recall how I learned that my mother was pregnant, but the memory of hearing that the baby was a boy is clear. I was in the living room with Daisy, who was my favorite cousin. The phone rang, and my grandmother ran to answer it, anxious no doubt to hear news of my mother, who was having a long labor. We could hear from the excitement in my grandmother's voice that my mother was all right and that the baby had been born. My grandmother hung up the phone and burst in to the living room. It was a boy!

I can't remember that either Daisy or I responded. My grandmother left the room, and we heard her dialing the phone to convey the news to Aunty Ars. I sensed that disaster had struck. During my mother's pregnancy I sometimes thought about having another child around and even looked forward to it. But in none of my fantasies had the baby taken the shape of a boy. I turned to Daisy and asked her what I was going to do. She said nothing. She merely shrugged her shoulders. Even Daisy, who was ten years older than I, could not help me.

I also remember going to the hospital to bring my mother and the baby home. I was in the back of our 1936 Chevy with my grandmother, while Aunty Ars sat up front with my father. Weeks before the birth my mother and I had planned that I would hold the baby on the ride home. When we got there Aunty Ars and my father went to get my mother, and my grandmother and I waited. When my mother finally appeared and handed the bundle that was my brother, Paul Khosroff, to me, I hesitated. I did not want to hold this baby. My grandmother's arms shot out and she took him. Sitting next to them I felt for the first time a circle of intimacy from which I was excluded. Later that day, while the family celebrated the homecoming, I went into my parent's room where the baby lay in his crib. I looked at him for a long time wondering why he had to have been a boy and whether I would ever love him.

A few months later I saw my mother and grandmother in the dining room bending over my brother, totally absorbed. The closed circle I had sensed on the day we brought him home now included my mother. I stood apart watching them and saw the circle as double-edged. I couldn't get in, but it was also clear to me that he couldn't get out. I felt compassion for my brother who was, after all, only a baby. But the circle, closing me out and him in, was too powerful for me. The compassion faded, and I felt mostly hatred and jealousy.

My father and I sometimes spent time together on weekends, when it seemed to me that we were outsiders together. But he was not home often enough to ease my jealousy, and the circle that had enclosed my brother never enveloped me. I took more trips to relatives' homes. My cousin Daisy, who had been with me when I heard about my brother's birth, lived only a few blocks away, and I often went to her house after school. Her mother, Aunty Vart, made the best *simits* (a crisp, buttery cookie with sesame seeds) in the family. When I came in we went directly to the kitchen, and she would go to the cupboard where she kept a tin, which miraculously was always full of *simits*. She put two on a plate—always two, and I knew not to ask for more—and I ate them as slowly as I could, picking the sesame seeds off the plate with a wet finger when they were gone. When Daisy came home from high school we either listened to her Billie Holiday records or went to her room to talk. Later in the afternoon Aunty Vart would ask if I wanted to stay for dinner, and I always said yes.

I particularly loved going to my mother's sister's house in New Jersey for the weekend. Aunty Ars had three boys and told me that she had always wanted a girl. I became her daughter. Though she worked full-time in a clothing factory and cooked, cleaned, and ironed for her family, Aunty Ars always had time for me. She cooked all my favorite foods, read to me in the broken English that I loved, and, as I remember it, agreed to anything I suggested, including sleeping with her.

As my brother grew older, he stayed within the circle, never making the visits I did. This was partially because the family had changed. People were moving out of the neighborhood to the suburbs. When I was fifteen and he was nine, we, too, moved to New Jersey, and he couldn't walk over to a relative's house and make it his own as I had done. But he had not begun to do this even before we left the neighborhood. He stayed at home with my mother and grandmother, where he was their king, or *pasha* as my grandmother called him.

Chapter 3

I began the process of moving away from the orbit of family and the Armenian community when I entered public school, but it took years before I became fully aware of my non-Armenian surroundings. I remember little of those early school years because I wasn't fluent in English and because of the separation between school and the rest of my life. The only contact I had with non-Armenians was during school hours. Afterwards, I came home to my mother and grandmother and was content either to play alone or make the round of visits to relatives as we had done before.

Yet, when I saw that I was one of the few children who walked home from school alone, I decided it was time to make some friends—American friends. Excited by the prospect, I told my mother about my decision. She looked at me for a long time and then told me to be careful: it was clear that there was danger in associating with people who were not blood kin. I was undaunted, however, and began to talk to the other children in school with the goal of making a friend.

My first conquest was Carol Capps, who, with her long, blond banana curls, seemed just right to me. When she asked me to come to her house after school, I ran home for lunch and excitedly told my mother, who had to think about it for the rest of the afternoon. Just before she put dinner on the table I asked her again, and she said yes, but I could go only for an hour. I felt a kind of triumph as I not only walked out of the school yard with a friend but was on my way to her house to play.

When we got to her apartment I found it very different from what I was used to. Carol had her own key and opened the door to an empty apartment. I had never had a key. I had never even used one. Someone was always home at my house. If my mother were out shopping, my grandmother was home. But Carol's mother wasn't out shopping or visiting relatives; she worked. Aunty Ars was the only woman in our family who worked, and that was only because her sons were in high school.

The apartment, too, was like another world. There were no Oriental rugs on the floors, no candy dishes filled with goodies. And it smelled different from the homes of my family. When I came home from school or went to one of my relative's houses at three o'clock in the afternoon, something was usually simmering on the stove or meat was marinating on the counter, filling the apartment with the smells of onions, olive oil, tomato sauce, lamb. We didn't stop in the kitchen for something to eat but went directly to Carol's room, where she began to show me her clothes. Carol Capps had nylon stockings. I could hardly believe it and asked her if she ever wore them. She looked at me as if I were crazy and told me that of course she did, every Friday when she went to temple. I came home with the news of Carol's nylons, not to ask for some of my own—that I did not do for many years—but simply to relate an amazing fact. I was informed by my mother that Carol was Jewish and that Jews had such things.

My next friend was more familiar. Thalia Marmarinos was Greek. Her mother was home when we got to her house after school, and there was the smell of food in the apartment. Through my friendship with Thalia I also met Athena, whose family had changed their name to Andrews, although there was little about them that wasn't Greek. Athena's mother also was home when she got there, also spoke English with difficulty, and was usually cooking. The Andrews's apartment looked and smelled like Greece itself.

While I knew that my Greek friends, like me, were different from Americans, it seemed easier to be Greek than it was to be an Armenian. We learned about Greece in school. It was the cradle of our civilization, of democracy. I also remembered, from the time Aunt Sonia had taken me downtown, that Greeks were represented in the Metropolitan Museum of Art. Whole rooms were full of Greek sculpture. Even the drugstore had pictures of Greeks on the walls, and, although they looked strange in their togas and sandals, they were Greeks and somehow related to Thalia and Athena.

Being Armenian, on the other hand, was not so clear, even in Washington Heights, where there was a large Armenian community. Greeks, German Jews, Romanians, and Irish populated the neighborhoods and ethnic identity was of paramount importance. When you met someone new you were immediately asked about your nationality if your name did not clearly indicate your origins. I dreaded hearing the question "What are you?" from other kids because when I answered "Armenian" the response was either a blank stare or more often another question, "What's that?"

I was hard put to answer what an Armenian was. It was who I was and what I had known all my life, but how could it be defined? I knew that my mother came from Turkey and my father from Persia, but they were definitely not Turks or Persians. Where was Armenia on the map? I asked my mother, and she told me that it was in the northeast corner of Turkey, part of what was called Russia—I don't remember hearing the name Soviet Union until I was in college. Though I knew that my father had lived in Russia and that Uncle Alex had fought in the Russian army, I knew that we were not Russians. Nothing about being an Armenian was clear. When I couldn't answer what I was clearly the next question was usually, "Well, what religion are you?" The answer to this question meant more confusion. The Holy Cross Armenian Apostolic Church was as mysterious as my country of origin. Was I Catholic? Protestant? I could only answer that, as my mother had told me, our church was like the High Church of England. Though I had no idea what that meant, it usually stopped the questions.

The only non-Greek friend I had in elementary school was Rachel Herzberg, whose parents were Jewish immigrants from Germany. Like that of my Greek friends, Rachel's nationality and religion were evident. It was somewhat problematic to be Jewish ("real" Americans weren't Jewish) but people didn't ask Rachel what she was as they asked me. I was clearly a minority among minorities.

I knew other Armenian children. There was Elise Najarian at school. Our mothers were friends, and she was in my class. She was very shy and timid, not the kind of friend I had decided I wanted-ed. And there were, of course, my cousins. Aunty Lucy's granddaughter Susan and I became good friends when she moved to the neighborhood. We had a tacit agreement that we were not going to be "feminine" like her older sister Rita. We convinced our mothers to buy us dungarees—they had to be Levi's, not exactly a household name in the early 1950s—and we saved our money for garrison belts, thick black leather belts with brass buckles. The dungarees were rolled up and worn with one of our father's white shirts. As soon as we came home from school we changed into our "real" clothes. Susan and I were also great baseball fans and went to the games every Ladies' Day, paying our quarter for the bleachers and then sneaking into the better seats. Though my school friends also wore dungarees and garrison belts, I was a real "tomboy" only with Susan.

The other setting where I met Armenian children was at dancing school. My mother wanted me to have both dancing and piano lessons so that, as she frequently told me, "I would grow up to be a flower, not a weed." I was excited by the prospect of both lessons. I asked my mother if I could go to the dancing school Thalia attended. She took tap and had shown me her black patent leather shoes with the huge metal taps on the soles. "No," my mother said. "Tap was common." I would take ballet from Madame Seta, whose son was a lead dancer in the Ballet Russe. Despite my disappointment over not being allowed to take tap with Thalia, I happily went to my first lesson at Madame Seta's.

I was upset by both the teacher and the students. Not only was Madame Seta a stern, old woman who barked commands to us in her Russian-Armenian accent, but all of the students in the class were Armenian. After about six months at Madame Seta's I wanted to quit. I would rather have no dancing lessons than be in this school with this teacher and these students. I wanted to work to be like everyone else, and the first step was to avoid being surrounded by Armenians.

My goal was thwarted at every turn by my mother, who reminded me constantly that I was an Avakian, which meant I would do nothing that was common but have only "the best." My piano lessons underscored that message. I would not have a piano teacher like my friends but would go to music school. One day after school my mother and I took the subway down to 125th Street and walked over to the Juilliard School of Music, where I was to have my "audition." My mother waited in the hall when I was called into a large room with the largest grand piano I had ever seen. There were three people sitting at a long black table, and one of them asked me to play. I had never had a lesson, but my cousin Daisy had taught me to play the melody to "Beautiful Dreamer," so I sat down at the piano and picked out the notes with one finger. They thanked me, ushered me out of the room, and we went home. To my surprise, they called the next week to say that I had been accepted and my teacher was Miss Hull. We went to meet her on a Tuesday, which would be my regular lesson time. In addition to my private lesson, I found out from Miss Hull that I would also be required to go to a theory class on Saturday mornings. It all seemed ominously different from what my friends were doing.

After a few months of enduring the theory class in which I was the only beginner and was regularly humiliated, I asked my mother if I could leave Juilliard and get a piano teacher. My mother would not hear of it, despite our almost daily arguments when it was time for me to practice. Yet, just when it seemed impossible to get out of going to Juilliard I had some unexpected help from Miss Hull, whom I did like a bit even though I would never tell my mother that. She held a recital for her students at her apartment in Greenwich Village.

My mother wondered aloud on the long subway ride there why a nice woman like Miss Hull would live in such a nasty place. When we got to her small apartment it was already crowded with her other students, all older than I and some looking dangerously "arty" with long hair and beards. One thing was clear though. They were all playing very difficult music. Their books were black with notes. When it was my turn I played my little piece and thought I had done quite well. I hadn't missed a note and had used the pedals correctly. I had even thought about how I was holding my hands while I was playing, but, instead of the applause the others received after their performances, I heard laughter. Miss Hull stood up and admonished her students, saying that they had all begun by playing that piece, and she gave me a round of applause. But the point that I had been trying to make with mother was well made that afternoon. I was in the wrong place. Soon after the recital I left Juilliard and got a piano teacher.

The next great battle with my mother was over which high school I would attend. By the sixth and seventh grades I had begun to feel comfortable with my small group of friends. Thalia, Athena, and Rachel were my constant companions, that is, as much as my mother and the family would permit. My mother allowed me to be with my friends three out of five weekday afternoons. But her response to my pleas to be with my friends on the weekends was consistently negative. She was incredulous that I would even consider friends to be as important as family. How could I, she wondered, think of disappointing my aunts and uncles by not going to visit them? My mother's message was clear: friends might be a nice diversion, but family is all important.

During my last year in elementary school my mother began to talk about high schools. I had assumed I would go to George Washington, the large public high school three blocks away from our apartment. All my friends except Rachel, who had chosen another city high school because she showed talent in art, were going there. My mother wanted me to go to Barnard or Hunter. I knew only that these schools were not for "ordinary" students, that they were out of the neighborhood, and that they were for girls only. My friends, however, were going to George Washington, and that was where I was going to go. The battle was set, and I intended to stand my ground.

By 1951 I was twelve years old and had become adept at arguing with my mother. I was fully prepared for the now familiar argument that she wanted only the best for me. George Washington was for ordinary, even common, people's children. This time I pressed her to tell me what she meant by "common." It was then that she told me that half of the student population of the school was "Negro." I was shaken by this news.

Although my family had not assimilated entirely into American culture, they had understood very well America's racial code and had transmitted it to me. As early as my preschool years, I had learned to be a *white* American. A very special treat was going downtown with my mother, but I had mixed emotions about the bus trip, which went through Harlem. Because everyone on the street was Negro—even the billboards advertising familiar products looked so different to me, with Negro people drinking Coke or smoking Lucky Strikes—it felt as if we were in another country. It made our trip like a special adventure.

I was also afraid, but my mother was sitting right next to me, and I was viewing the scene from the protection of the bus. The strongest emotion I can remember was sympathy for the dogs on the street. I loved dogs, and, even as young as I was, I knew that something as good and lovable as a dog could not be Negro. The dogs, then, had to be white, and I felt sorry for them because they belonged to Negro people and had to live surrounded by Negroes. By the time I went to kindergarten the fear that I had felt on the bus with my mother was firmly entrenched and focused on black men. On my way to school in the mornings I passed a Negro man, who was often sitting on the stoop of the building. I think he was a janitor. I can see his shape but not his face. I was friendly with the janitor in our building; I was afraid of the cellar there but not the janitor. He was white. I cannot remember ever walking down the side of the street where the black man sometimes sat, whether he was there or not.

My friends and I did not have the same fears about other non-whites. We were, in fact, very friendly with a few boys in our class who had recently emigrated from Puerto Rico. We invited them to the weekly dances at the Greek church and spent many hours learning the mambo, cha-cha-cha, and merengue from them while we tried to teach them the lindy. We knew that some people thought that Puerto Ricans were dangerous, but our friends seemed very much like us. They and their parents had come from another country. They spoke another language at home and ate "different" foods. In fact, they seemed to have some advantages over Armenians. Although I wasn't sure where Puerto Rico was, I did know that it was a country that stood on its own; it wasn't a corner of Turkey or a part of Russia, like Armenia. And the language they spoke was Spanish. There was nothing mysterious about that. Negroes, on the other hand, weren't immigrants from anywhere that I knew about, and they were, it seemed to me, nothing like me or any of my friends.

I decided that, even though I may have some misgivings about going to school with Negro students, George Washington was still where I wanted to go to high school. I told my mother, and myself, that I wasn't going to associate with Negro students. I had my own friends, and they were all Greek. I also told my mother that there was no way she could make me go to Hunter or Barnard. I was not going to school if I couldn't go to George Washington. She asked me what I meant, and I told her that I would simply not go to school, that she had no control over me once I left the house. If she let me go to George Washington, I promised I would come home for lunch every day. I won.

My victory, however, was not complete. I went to George Washington, a regular school with my regular friends, but we were in different classes. My attempt to be ordinary had been foiled. To my chagrin, I found that I was in the honor class, a class set apart for good students. I would try to take care of that.

Chapter 4

*T*hough I would never admit it to my mother, there was much about George Washington High School that was intimidating to me, and I wondered during the first few weeks of school whether I had made a mistake in going there. I had known that the school was huge, but the experience of going to school with six thousand students was overwhelming. Even in 1952 George Washington was something of a fortress. Student monitors guarded the doors at all times to insure that only students, teachers, and other school personnel entered. Visitors were escorted to the office, where they could get an authorized pass only if they had legitimate business. The movement of students within the school was also tightly controlled. If students were caught roaming the halls without a pass during classes, they would be punished. Order was maintained by teachers with the help of students, who, in order to graduate, were required to earn a number of service points in addition to accumulating academic credits. Monitoring the doors, halls, and lunchroom were only a few of the many service jobs for students. After school, however, there were no monitors to control what happened, and, as I remember it, there was at least one fight every day outside the gates of the building. Although I never approached the fights, I heard that some were the result of Puerto Rican and Negro gangs.

The fights, the gangs, and the rumors of switchblades and zip-guns were part of my environment, but they were in the background, and I made good the assurances to my mother that I would not associate with "those people." Although half of the students at George Washington were Negro and Puerto Rican, my classmates, as in elementary school, were mostly the children of European and

Middle Eastern immigrants. My contact was mostly with other honors and college prep students. It was as if there were two distinct schools housed within George Washington.

I saw the "other" school only during typing and gym class. Although a number of us from the honors class were in typing, we were in the minority. The back row was occupied by boys wearing leather jackets—a sure sign in my neighborhood in the early 1950s that they were "hoods." Their hands never touched their typewriters; instead, they beat out rhythms on their desks. Occasionally, the teacher screamed at them to stop their tapping. They shrugged their shoulders, stopped for a while, then slowly and quietly began again. Sometimes the teacher sent them out of the room, and I wondered how they negotiated the halls without a pass, but they were so mysterious to me that I had no real concern for their welfare.

The gym class was three or four times the size of the typing class, which was already larger than the honor classes. Sports designed for a handful of players were redesigned to accommodate forty to fifty people on each side. A few students participated, while most of us stood around and talked. The several gym teachers, like the typing teacher, ignored those of us who did not take part. About once a month we had dancing class, and I welcomed the opportunity to see Negro girls dance and to copy their steps. Although my friends and I considered ourselves good dancers and spent most afternoons practicing, we knew we were outdone by our Negro classmates. As much as we wanted to improve our dancing, however, we never asked them for help, not only because we were in awe of their abilities, but because we just didn't speak to Negro students.

I made one exception to this unspoken rule at my service job at the pool. Of the four students who worked at the pool, taking attendance and giving out suits and towels, I was the only white. Though I was uncomfortable at first, I soon looked forward to spending time with Madeline, one of my co-workers, and I discovered that Madeline was a loyal friend. One day, as I was on my way from the office to the pool to take attendance, I was stopped by four Negro girls, who accused me of having marked them absent the previous week. All the stories I had heard about Negro and Puerto Rican girls carrying razors flooded my mind, and I stood paralyzed with fear. They told me that were I ever to mark them absent again, they would beat me up, and one said that maybe they should give me a taste now of what I would get if I didn't do what they said. Just at that moment Madeline walked over and said, "She's okay." Miraculously, they left. That class had perfect attendance for the rest of the term, and my friendship with Madeline deepened.

Shortly after this incident Madeline asked me to come to her house after school, and I was surprised by the otherwise normal gesture of friendship. Madeline was my friend at the pool, but though I really did like her, I had never considered the possibility of a relationship with her outside of work. I asked her nervously where she lived and realized from the address that it was in Harlem. The fears I'd had about that "other country" as a young child on the number 3 bus with my mother were still with me. I told Madeline that I would have to ask my mother and would let her know. I counted on the probability that my mother would not let me go, and she did not disappoint me. Nevertheless, I felt obliged to argue with her. Knowing there was no possibility of visiting my friend, I could easily be indignant that my mother was so strict and narrow-minded. And there was a part of me that was genuinely upset that my friendship with Madeline had limits. Mostly, I wished that Madeline were white or, at least, that she didn't live in Harlem. When I told her that my mother would not let me go to her house, I tried to let Madeline know that I really had wanted to visit her, but I was not very convincing. Our friendship cooled. It never occurred to me to ask her to come to my house.

Though clearly I was set apart from Negro students at George Washington, I was also attending a different school than most of my friends. Only Athena Andrews was in the honor class with me. I toyed with the idea of doing badly enough to be dropped from the class, but I knew my parents would be furious with me if I did. They always expected me to do well in school and assumed I would go to college. I, too, thought college was an attractive idea, though I had only a vague idea of what it was about. Besides, I liked some of my teachers and the smaller classes for honors students. And, although I wanted to be ordinary, I didn't want to be dumb. One day in French class I became aware that I had some choice about how well I learned. We were working on vocabulary in pairs, and Athena was my partner. When we came to a word neither of us knew, I realized that I didn't have to try to guess what it meant from its context or its similarity to an English word. I could just say I didn't know what it meant, and I did. Athena, who had no qualms about being a "brain," did what I had previously done and guessed the meaning correctly. I asked her how she knew what the word meant, but I didn't even listen to the answer, which I already knew. I became less and less adept at learning French. I would stay in the honor class, but I had found a way to be less than exceptional.

My urge to be like everyone else was intensified by something that happened when I was fourteen years old. As far back as I can remember, my grandmother had said on occasion that she would tell me her story, but only when it was time. As I grew older and became more insistent, she only shook her head and retreated into what seemed a deep and mysterious sorrow. But when I was fourteen, she told me of her life.

She began by telling me about my grandfather and their life together in Kastemoni, Turkey. I was used to her familiar description of him as the most wonderful, intelligent, and kind man in the world, but this time her praises were embellished with how well he had provided for her and their three children. As she described her house, the servants she had, and how wonderful their life had been, it seemed that the story I had waited so long to hear was going to be just another tale of how much better everything was in the old country, or, as my family called it, "the other side." Aunty Ars and Uncle George occasionally told my cousins and me how, on the other side, vegetables grew to be much bigger than in this country. Lemons were as large as grapefruit, and cabbages were so huge that only one would fit in the cart. Now I listened to my grandmother with some of the same skepticism my cousins and I had about the wonders of Turkey.

Her story lost its idyllic quality, however, when she told me that one day my grandfather was taken away to be in the Turkish army, and she never heard from or saw him again. Sometime later she came home from church on a Sunday to find that the doors of her house had been sealed. She went to the town square, where all the other Armenians, whose homes had been similarly barred, had already assembled. Town officials were there to tell them that they would soon be sent into the interior of the country, and that until that time they would have access only to one room of their homes. The police commissioner, who had been a friend of my grandfather's, wanted to help my grandmother. He advised her to become a Turk—to renounce Christianity and become a Moslem. Although he warned her of the great danger she and her three children faced, she said she could not give up her religion and would face the consequences with the rest of her people.

The day for their departure came soon. My grandmother and

her children were exiled with other relatives, all women and children, since all the Armenian men in the town had suffered the same fate as my grandfather. My grandmother said she was lucky to have been assigned to a kind soldier, yet, although the journey was not impossible, she and the others were taken to a place so "barbaric" that the people who lived there had never heard of Christians. Despite their lack of "civilization," however, they treated my grandmother and her family fairly well. She and her relatives were given one room and provided with some food, but the women were very fearful nonetheless. Some nights they would hear noises outside, and they would crouch in the corner until they could no longer hear anything. One night the noises were so persistent that they stayed there until morning, only to find that a bird had gotten caught in the chimney.

After some time two soldiers came and took my grandmother's eight-year-old son away to make him, she said, into a Turk. She left her two daughters in the care of her relatives and bartered the few pieces of jewelry she had managed to bring with her for Turkish clothes and set out to where she thought her son had been taken. She found him in a detention camp for Armenian boys. She walked to Kastemoni to ask for help from the police commissioner who had warned her of the impending danger. He told her that he could help her only if she would become a Turk, and this time she agreed. He arranged for her son's release from the camp, as well as the return of her daughters and other relatives from exile.

Although they were all reunited in Kastemoni, life was very difficult. My grandmother was outraged that her neighbors spied on her to make sure the family was performing Moslem prayers at the appropriate times of day. They were also very poor, and she earned money by going out into the countryside to sell pins, needles, and other sewing necessities. Years later Uncle Charlie, my grandfather's nephew, heard about their fate and sent money so that my grandmother and her children might come to America.

When she had finished, she sat back, relieved, it seemed, to have finally told her story. "That is my story, *yavroos* (meaning darling), she said, "and I want you to tell it to the world."

I didn't want to tell it to anyone. I was sorry that I had heard it. My grandfather had been taken away and had disappeared. My grandmother, aunt, uncle, and even my mother had been sent into a barbaric land alone to survive as best they could and then were

forced to become Turks, practicing a strange, uncivilized religion,
Why? Why had those horrible things happened to them? My grandmother explained that the Turks were devils who hated Armenians, but the whole thing was totally incomprehensible and horrible
to me. Why would I want to know about people who were unknown
to most of the world, who were hated so much when they were
recognized that they were forced to leave their homes and to give
up their religion, who were even killed. I was sorry that my grandmother had told me her story. I was sorry that I had asked her to
tell it to me. I didn't want to know it. It was bad enough to be
unknown, strange, and different from everyone else, but it was un-
bearable to be despised. I would forget it.

Superficially, it was easy not to think about my grandmother's
story. No one else in the family ever talked about it. My mother
had been in the apartment when my grandmother was talking to
me, but she had stayed out of the dining room, where we were sitting. She never asked me about it, and I had the sense that she did
not approve of my grandmother's telling me her story. My uncle
talked about hating Turks, and there were occasional comments from
other family members about the "Turkish devils," but, then, my
family had negative opinions about many groups of people. Their
hatred of Turks was especially confusing. We seemed to be so connected to Turkey ourselves. The "other side" was, after all, Turkey. Some of our favorite foods were Turkish. It was a very special
occasion when my grandmother made *atleakmak,* a Turkish meat
turnover. She would make them, one at a time, and my mother
would bring them into the dining room. We'd eat them, moaning
all the while about how wonderful they were, and, even from her
rather poor vantage point in the kitchen, my grandmother always
knew exactly how many *atleakmaks* each of us had eaten. We danced
Turkish and Armenian dances to Turkish music, and the men of
the family played *tavloo* (backgammon) for hours on end, shouting
the numbers in Arabic after each roll of the dice. Older family members were fluent in Turkish and spoke it whenever they didn't want
children to understand what they were saying. And the coffee that
provided the focus for our afternoon rituals was Turkish coffee.

How could it be that my family could hate what was so intimately woven into the fabric of their lives? The *atleakmaks,* the *tavloo,* the music, and the coffee were very real, but the story my
grandmother had told me was remote and unbelievable. Could it
be that she had made it up? Why didn't anyone else talk about it?

Although I had serious questions about what she had told me, I didn't discuss them with anyone. Maybe I didn't want her story corroborated. As it was, it was something she told me one afternoon then mentioned only rarely, when she reminded me to tell it to the world. What her story did do for me at fourteen years of age was to make me even more determined to deny my difference from everyone else.

I would change my ways and try to get my family to change too. The family fights that had begun when I was in elementary school intensified. Although I had loved most Armenian food, I began to refuse to eat certain dishes and berated my mother for not serving American food—Wonder Bread, potato chips, Lipton Chicken Noodle Soup, steak and potatoes. She had nothing but disdain for these American delicacies. Americans were stupid about many things, and food was no exception. I had learned, too, that Americans were generally not as clean as Armenians. In cooking class, for example, we washed the dish towels after drying the dishes. I came home with the news that Americans were so meticulous that they washed their towels after every use. My mother's reply was quick and sure. "They" have to do that, she informed me, because "they" don't really get their dishes clean. As for their food, it could even be dangerous. The potato chips were sure to be fried in some unmentionable grease rather than in butter or olive oil, which were the only acceptable shortenings. My father, who was in the wholesale butter and egg business, added his knowledge about the cheese that Americans ate. He brought home real cheese—five-pound bricks of Muenster, which my mother and grandmother peeled and cut into pieces and stored in a brine of saltwater. According to my father, my Velveeta, which I had convinced my mother to buy, was not really cheese at all but a "cheese food" that could be harmful if eaten in large quantities. I was sorry at that point that I had brought up the subject of food, since Velveeta's quality was now coming under discussion.

Only the hamburger deserved respect, but making it like Americans did was beyond the skills of every woman in the family. Everyone had her own formula for making this simple but elusive dish. Some put chopped parsley in the meat and breaded the patties; another mixed the meat with ice water. Some said that the meat wasn't supposed to be touched too much; others that it had to be handled roughly. Despite their attempts, everyone in the family knew that only Americans could make good hamburgers. But, except for this fluke, Americans had nothing to teach Armenians about food. An Armenian idiom summarized how the family felt about the American palate: "They don't know the taste of their own mouths."

While I considered the attempt to change my family's eating habits important, the real battle was about how much control my parents and my relatives would exercise over me. The arguments with my mother over spending time with my friends instead of going to visit relatives on the weekends now took on monumental proportions. I not only wanted to be with my friends, I also wanted to get away from my family. There were some exceptions, of course. I was still very close to my cousin Susan and I loved Aunty Ars dearly, but I began to refuse to attend many family events. I did not think very much about what my grandmother had told me, but unconsciously the knowledge that I belonged to a people who were despised contributed to my drive to get as far away from being Armenian as possible. The family, with its adherence to old world traditions, *was* Armenia.

My anger began to erupt—at my mother for her strict controls over me, at the family for demanding so much of my time, at the Turks for having done what they did to my family, and at my grandmother for having lived through such horror and for telling it to me. I vowed be like my friends. I would tweeze my eyebrows. I would wear lipstick. I would go out with boys. And, most of all, I would get away from my family as soon as I could.

My friends became my allies. The closely knit circle I was a part of in elementary school expanded to include new friends, but it remained basically intact. Though she went to another high school, Rachel had become my best friend. She was the only Jew in our group, which was still mostly Greek. It never occurred to me, at least consciously, that Rachel and I had a common history. I knew that her parents had had to leave Germany because they were Jews, but I was only dimly aware of the Holocaust. Rachel never talked about being Jewish, and she seemed to have no particular anger toward Germans. We felt sorry for our new German friend, Marjorie Bismark, because she had no father and lived with her mother and aunt, who both spoke no English and were very poor. We could never have thought of Marjorie's mother or aunt as in any way responsible for what had happened to Rachel's parents. Like me, Rachel didn't seem to have a troublesome past. Unlike our Greek friends who spoke Greek at home and seemed eager to participate in their culture, Rachel and I were trying as hard as we could to be Americans.

Our main interests were boys, dancing, and clothes. While Thalia's mother made her clothing, Rachel and I had to find ways to supplement the less than adequate wardrobes our mothers agreed to buy for us. We tried to sew, but our efforts yielded only barely presentable skirts sorely in need of belts to cover botched waistbands. Blouses and dresses were beyond our skill. One day Rachel came home from school with the news that some of her friends bought used clothing and there were some stores that sold them in Inwood, the neighborhood adjacent to ours. We ventured down Dykeman Street and found the stores. The clothing seemed dirty to us, and we could not bring ourselves to buy it, but we found one store that sold only belts—boxes and boxes of all kinds and sizes, and none over fifty cents. We spent many afternoons continuing to look at the clothing. We never bought any, but we both had a huge collection of belts.

Most afternoons we spent with Thalia, perfecting our dance steps. Dancing was the focus of our social life. Friday nights we danced to a jukebox at the Greek church, and sometimes one of us would give a party and we'd dance to records.

For most of my friends, boys functioned primarily as dancing partners. Though I was exceptional in having boyfriends, the main difference between my friends and me was that, unlike them, after the dance or the party, my current flame and I walked home together. When we reached my building, we spent a few minutes kissing, with closed mouths, of course. My only formal date was at the end of my freshman year in high school. I had been seeing Dickie, who was a senior, and he asked me to go out with him on senior night. Since there were no dances at George Washington High School, not even a senior prom, seniors chose one night when they went as a group to one of the nightclubs downtown.

How to convince my mother to let me go? Not only was this my first date, but we were going to a nightclub. And Dickie himself presented an obstacle. I knew my mother's first response would either be "no" or "what is he?" She asked the question instead of immediately telling me that I couldn't go, and I was ready with my answer, "He's Spanish, but from a very good family." Then she said no. We argued for weeks, generally over the television. My mother didn't usually watch television in the afternoon, so I was surprised to come home from school and find the television on and my mother watching the screen with a worried and serious look. During our first battle over my date with Dickie I, too, looked at the screen and saw not a game or variety show, but men sitting at tables talking and sometimes screaming at each other. I took time out from arguing to ask what that show was all about, and my mother told me that it was from Washington—some kind of hearings with a man named Joe McCarthy. She finally let me go out with Dickie. I didn't know if it was because she was so distracted by the McCarthy hearings or because my constant badgering just wore her down.

After that I did not have another date for more than a year. In the meantime, I was quite content going to dances and parties with groups of friends, whether or not I had a boyfriend to walk me home. By the time I was fifteen I was attaining a sense of self-assurance and ease with my friends, but it was not to last.

Chapter 5

*E*arly in 1954 my parents told me that they were thinking about moving to New Jersey. I was horrified. Why would they want to do such a thing? We lived in a nice neighborhood. I loved my school and my friends. My parents informed me, however, that our neighborhood was not so nice anymore since so many Puerto Ricans were moving into it. They also told me they didn't want my brother to grow up in New York City. It had been fine for me, I argued. Couldn't they wait just two more years until I graduated from high school? But they were determined to save my brother from the neighborhood, and they spent their weekends with realtors.

I didn't argue with my parents when they assumed that I would join them on their search for the new house. I was curious about what the house might look like, and, if I went, we were usually home by late afternoon so that I could still be with my friends in the evening. We always began at the real estate office where the broker talked with my parents about the kind of house they wanted. Among the questions about size, price, and location there was always one about what church they attended. My mother was usually the one to answer, "We are Episcopal." I was very confused by this lie. My mother had told me our church was like the Episcopal church, but when my parents went to church it was to the Armenian church. My mother told me that the realtors wanted to make sure that we were Christians before they showed us a house. She seemed glad that we would live in an area that didn't allow Jews. I quietly thought of Rachel. After a few weeks of looking at small houses on streets that all looked the same, I convinced my parents to leave me home when they went to look for their new house. I didn't really believe that they were going to move anyway, and I hated all the houses and the realtors with their questions.

Despite my denial, however, it happened. My parents bought a three-bedroom ranch-style house in Glen Rock, New Jersey. We moved that June. Because I'd refused to accompany them, I hadn't seen the house before moving day. Now I walked around the small rooms of perfectly measured space. There were no long hallways, no deep closets, and the low ceilings made everything seem closed in. There was nowhere to go in that house, no cozy nook to escape to. In the city, our phone was at the end of a long hallway away from the center of activity, but here it was right in the middle of the galley kitchen, with no possibility of privacy. I wanted to die. How did they expect us to live in this box? My parents seemed very content with the house; they were disappointed that it did not have a separate dining room, but they had already decided to build one.

For me there was only one positive thing about the house. I would no longer share a room with my grandmother but would have a room all to myself for the first time in my life. My brother would share the small bedroom at the back of the house with my grandmother. Given their intensely close relationship, it seemed right that they should share a room, although I did feel guilty that I would have my own room while my nine-year-old brother had to share his with an ancient woman.

I was as disturbed by the environment around our new house as I was with the house itself. The surrounding streets were divided into measured lots. A ranch house exactly like ours—or a split-level variation—sat in the middle of each lot. As far as I walked in either direction the scene was the same except for the small shopping center eight blocks away. The supermarket, drugstore, dairy, and bakery were surrounded by a parking lot. No one, it seemed, walked anywhere in New Jersey. Early in the morning men passed by our house on their way to the bus, which would take them to their jobs in New York City, and in the evening they would return. During the day only the mailman walked on the sidewalks. Even children were rarely on the street, since they each had their own little plot of land behind their house. Although there was a kind of main street in Glen Rock, the two blocks of stores, the town hall, the library, and the train station, where most of the men went to get to their jobs in the city, had nothing to offer me.

After days of roaming the streets looking for a neighborhood, I gave up. I knew there must be people my age in the town, but

I ran out of places to look for them. I understood, too, why the side-walks were empty. There was nothing to walk to. No streets lined with shops. In New Jersey people drove to shopping centers, I sup-posed, to buy their clothes and food. Here no one walked to the soda fountain to sit for an hour or more sipping a freshly squeezed orangeade and watch for friends to drop in and come over to your table.

My brother quickly found friends, as our area—I would never call it a neighborhood—was populated by young married couples and their preadolescent children. We had moved to the right place for him, it seemed, but the wrong place for me. I spent most days lying in our little plot of land in the blazing New Jersey sun trying to get a tan and wondering what kids my age would be like in this strange place. I knew very little about Ridgewood High, the school I was to attend in the next town. My parents told me that it was a very good school, so good that there was no need for an honors class. Most of the students went on to college. My parents drove me to look at it shortly after we moved, and I went back as often as I could get someone to drive me there. The large brick building with its ivy-covered walls and clock tower was surrounded by ter-raced lawns and huge trees and looked more like a college campus than a high school. When I thought about the building and the foot-ball field with neat bleachers on either side, I imagined that such a school would also have dances, proms, yearbooks, and the big football game of the year on Thanksgiving. At those times I began to think that my parents' decision to move us might have been cor-rect. It might be that here I could really become an American.

After months of anticipation, I rose early on the first day of school and dressed in the best clothes I had. I had decided to wear my fullest skirt and a new blouse that picked up the aqua in the print of the skirt, a wide cinch belt that I had found on Dyckman Street with Rachel, and my red flats. They weren't Capezios, which I could not afford, but a good copy. When I reached the bus stop I was delighted to see a group of girls waiting for the bus. They all lived in the area and seemed friendly enough. We boarded the bus, which, I was surprised to find, only went to the center of town. Af-ter a long walk we finally got to school, and I searched for my homeroom. When I got there everyone seemed to be talking to peo-ple they knew, and I sat quietly and waited for the teacher to enter. We began the day with a reading from the Bible. Although I was somewhat uncomfortable because I didn't know whether or not to bow my head during the reading or cross myself at the end, I knew that I had come to America, and I was glad.

When I returned to homeroom for the last period, I thought the day had begun well enough. My classmates had seemed very different from my friends in New York in ways that I could not articulate, but they seemed friendly, enough for the first day at least. As the bell rang, my teacher called me aside and told me to report to the office. I had been very quiet all day, dutifully listening to my teachers and even taking notes. Had I broken some rule I didn't know about? But as I walked to the office my optimism returned, and I thought that maybe the school counselor wanted to know how my first day had gone.

As I approached the door to the office, a man gruffly asked me if I was Arlene Avakian, stumbling over my last name. When I responded that I was, he told me that I had a detention. I looked at him, puzzled. A detention sounded bad, but I knew neither what it was nor why I had it. He informed me in the same gruff voice that it was a punishment and that I would have to stay after school for the length of a class period. Before I could ask what I had done, he told me that he was going to make sure I behaved myself and that he had to teach "city kids" like me a lesson right away. He turned and left before I could ask again what I had done. I held back my tears of anger and hurt and silently cursed my parents for bringing me to such a place. When the period was over I walked the long distance to the bus alone. When I got home my mother was angry because I was home so late, but when I told her what had happened she was silent. We never talked about it again. If P.S. 189 and George Washington High School had been remote for my parents, Ridgewood High School was clearly in another world. I imagined she thought that if the people at school thought I deserved punishment I had better accept it and hope that it wouldn't happen again.

When I got to the bus stop the next morning the girls I had met the day before asked me where I had been after school. I told them what had happened, and, like my mother, they were silent. I expressed my outrage at being treated so badly. Didn't the people in the school know I had come from the honors class? They merely said that Mr. Lindenmeyer—that was the first time I'd heard his name—was awful and that everyone hated him. I sensed that, though they thought the assistant principal was too strict, they might have shared his fear of city kids. What did they think about people who lived in New York City? I wondered if they thought that

George Washington was like the school depicted in *The Blackboard Jungle*. But no one, neither the girls at the bus stop nor Mr. Lindenmeyer, had accused me of anything other than being from New York.

As the weeks wore on, I became less and less comfortable at school. I had many encounters with people who asked me fantastic questions about the city. Had I used dope? Did I sell it? I didn't even know what dope was, except that it was something bad kids used. Had I ever seen a tree before? I thought these people were really stupid. Had they never heard of Central Park or the Bronx Zoo? How could they live only eleven miles away from one of the greatest cities in the world and be so ignorant about it? I answered their questions patiently and tried my best to educate them. But they were not too interested.

My classmates' initial friendliness never went beyond that. I was not asked to anyone's house after school or to any other social events. The school did have dances, as I had hoped, but girls did not go unless they had dates. Nothing could be done in New Jersey, it seemed, without a date. Finally, after what seemed like an eternity, a boy in one of my classes asked me to one of the dances. Though it felt strange to go out with someone I hardly knew, I hoped that we would meet some of his friends at the dance.

Phil didn't seem very interested in talking to me or anyone else, and the evening grew long. Like so many of the other students, Phil had his own car, and we went to a drive-in for something to eat. While we waited for our hot dogs and root beer in silence, I thought it would be nice to hear some music and reached for the knob of the car radio. Before I reached it, Phil grabbed my hand and told me it was his car and he would decide whether we would have music. I quickly ate my hot dog and anxiously waited for him to take me home, but he had other plans. He drove down a deserted road, parked the car, and moved over to kiss me. When I resisted his advances he became furious, muttered something about me being from the city and started the car. That was my last date with a boy from Ridgewood High School. I guessed that he passed the word on that I was not the easy mark he had thought I was.

I was clearly different from everyone else, and my difference was decidedly not an asset. I began to study the other students. They didn't look like me or any of my friends in the city. They weren't all blondes, but most of the students, particularly the school leaders, had light skin, even if they had brown hair. Their names were familiar enough, but not like the names of anyone I knew: Doris Lane, Muffy Tipton, Yvonne LaGuerre, Chuck Anderson, Carol Smith, Roger Wolf. They had names like characters in the movies, not like the people in my former neighborhood. There were a few Italians, fewer Jews, and two or three Negroes. As far as I knew I was the only Armenian, and there were no Greeks.

As I walked the halls or sat in the lunchroom or study hall, I listened to the conversations around me. It seemed as if most people's mothers belonged to the Ridgewood Women's Club, and their parents seemed to know each other. Many of the girls had free use of their mothers' charge cards at the expensive store in the middle of town, and they spent their afternoons shopping for Dalton cashmere sweaters and English wool skirts. They wore the ''classic'' clothes of B. Altman and Lord and Taylor that my mother had bought for me when I was younger.

As I listened, watched, and asked questions of the few people who did talk to me, I found that those of us who came from the towns surrounding Ridgewood were considered ''lower'' than those who lived in the town. But even within Ridgewood there were divisions. Most of the school leaders lived in upper Ridgewood, the most expensive part of what I had come to realize was a town of very rich people. While many of the students who came from the towns surrounding Ridgewood were not rich, students from upper Ridgewood set the standard that most other students strove to attain. For the first time in my life I felt poor, and, though I had felt like an outsider before, at Ridgewood High I felt like an outcast.

By the end of the first term I had found a few other ''outcasts,'' and we shared our hatred of the school. Mimi Kopecky was blonde and had very fair skin, but beyond these physical attributes she had as little in common with the Ridgewood type as I did. She, too, had moved to Ridgewood from a city, but, unlike me, she carried the extra burden of living in a rented house in the center of town. Mimi's mother was dead, and Mimi lived with her father and her older brother, Freddy. Freddy was a senior at Ridgewood High, and, though he was also blonde, very tall, and good looking, he had not made it into the ''in'' crowd. Unlike us, however, Freddy was a part of a small group who were known as ''the hoods.'' I don't know what they did to deserve their reputation as bad kids, but they wore their hair long and slicked back, drove motorcycles, and usually had cigarettes dangling between their lips.

Through Mimi I met Octavius Pitzalis, Jr., known to his friends as Pitzie. He had grown up in Ridgewood, and, though his parents were very rich, he had also had problems at Ridgewood High. Pitzie's family were immigrants from Italy and ran a beauty salon in the center of town. I loved being in his house and hearing his family talk to each other in Italian. Thought Pitzie and I never talked about his Italian background, we shared our disdain for Ridgewood and its narrow-minded provincialism as well as our love for New York City. With Mimi and a few other friends in school and Pitzie after school, I was able to bear the long, lonely days. And, as often as my parents would let me, I went into the city and relaxed in the company of people I knew.

I felt like an outcast at Ridgewood High, not only around students but teachers as well. I didn't have any more problems with Mr. Lindenmeyer, but I felt as if my teachers expected very little from me. At George Washington I had special treatment because I was an honors student, while at Ridgewood my teachers assumed that I was part of the very small group of students who would not go on to college. Both situations contributed to my lack of interest in academics, and, when I was counseled to take sewing in my senior year, I did not object.

The days of being an honors student were decidedly behind me. I had striven to be average, and it seemed clear that I was. The discovery of my brother's high I.Q. and my mother's excitement about it certainly didn't help. In the 1950s numbers resulting from tests administered to school children were considered to be an absolute verification of the genetic entity of intelligence. These numbers were so powerful that they were closely guarded secrets known only to school personnel. I had always wondered what my number was, but I thought there was no way to find it out.

An Armenian woman who worked at the testing agency had noticed my brother's score. She had, of course, known he was Armenian by the "ian" at the end of his last name, and it was her habit to inform Armenian parents of their children's scores if they were particularly high. She didn't know us but asked all of her friends if they knew any Avakians and finally found one who knew my family. This woman called my mother to tell her that my brother had a very high number, though her friend did not tell her the exact figure. My mother was ecstatic and said that, if only one of her children was very smart, she was glad it was Paul because he was a boy. Although I had tried all these years to be ordinary, my heart sank when I heard that there was incontrovertible proof that, indeed, I was. This woman had worked for the agency for years, and my number had obviously not impressed her. But I agreed with my mother, it was better that Paul had gotten those genes. Boys did need to be smarter than girls.

Except for my grandmother, who maintained that she had always known that her Paul was brilliant, my family's attention to my brother intensified after they received proof of his intelligence. Even my father, who was generally not easily excited, was drawn into the plans for Paul's future. His best friend in Paris had been a doctor. Maybe Paul would like to go to medical school. My mother, on the other hand, had visions of West Point. She thought it would be wonderful if Paul became a general like President Eisenhower whom she liked because he was "such a gentleman." Paul was ten years old, and my parents were already planning his career. I was sixteen and beginning to apply to colleges, but my parents seemed unconcerned about where I would go and what I would do. My father thought I should go to a girl's school and be a teacher. I thought he was ridiculous. I liked boys, and I was not going to isolate myself from half the human population. College was a place to find a husband as well as get a degree. As for teaching, I hated school, and the thought of spending my life teaching was repulsive. My father merely shook his head and said that teaching was a good profession for a woman.

I didn't have any idea what I wanted to do, but I did know one thing about college. It was a way for me to get away from home, and I desperately wanted to do that. After Ridgewood High I was determined to go to a place that would be comfortable. I would have loved to have gone to college with some of my friends from New York City, but none of them who had decided to go to college considered going away. They would stay in the city and go to Hunter or City College.

I wanted most of all to find a college where I would be accepted, but how to find it was a real problem. My counselor at school was not much help. I sensed that, like my teachers, she didn't really think I was "college material," but she did suggest that I go to hear the various representatives from colleges that visited our school regularly. When the representative from Alfred University came to Ridgewood to talk about the small college in western New York State, he emphasized the friendliness of the campus, and I was sold. I went through the ritual of the required meeting with my counselor to discuss my choice. As she told me that Alfred had a good academic standing, I wondered if she meant "good enough for you," but I didn't really care. I told my parents of my choice, and my father raised his objection to a coed school. But I was determined, and he agreed to let me go, "if you can get in." I expected to get in and was merely waiting for graduation day when I could get out of Ridgewood High School and away from home.

Chapter 6

I was accepted at Alfred University, and, despite the fact that no one I knew had heard of the small liberal arts school in western New York (which also included the state schools of ceramic engineering and ceramic design), I knew I had made the right decision. The response of my friends and family to my choice was generally, "Alfred? Where's that?" Explaining where Alfred was located was almost as hard as trying to tell people where Armenia was, but it had none of the emotional impact. I didn't care that the town of Alfred was so small that it was hard to find on a map and that it was more than two hours away from any place that people I knew could recognize. I had chosen to go to this unknown school. My confidence was based on the assurances of Alfred's representative to Ridgewood High School that the campus was friendly and also the emphasis on friendliness in the literature I received when I wrote for an application. Alfred had also met the other criterion that was important to me and to all the women I knew at Ridgewood High—the high ratio of male to female students. Although I knew other schools had a higher proportion of males to females, Alfred's ratio of two males for every female was clearly within the acceptable range. In 1956 these numbers were important, not because they would help to determine whether schools discriminated against women but because they indicated the availability of dates.

My preparation for college consisted of building my wardrobe. The arguments with my mother over clothes had ended when I decided to get a job after school and during the summers in order to buy my own clothes. I augmented my carefully chosen purchases with clothes I made. The sewing class I had taken my senior year in high school had improved my skills, and I was now able to turn out acceptable skirts, slacks, bermuda shorts, and even a jacket.

While I was frantically sewing and looking for bargains, my mother and grandmother made me a comforter. I had told them that I didn't want it—that an ordinary blanket would be just fine—but they were convinced that I was going to the end of the earth and that it would be very cold there. They sent to Turkey for the necessary materials, despite my assurances that Alfred was not Alaska and that I was sure the dorm would be heated. My cousins in Turkey sent the raw wool that would become the filling and a large piece of patterned silk for the face of the comforter. For days the house smelled like wet wool as my mother and grandmother washed it and set it on brown paper to dry into hard matted clumps, which they spent days pulling apart until it was a huge fluffy mass. When the large, bulky comforter was finally finished, I reluctantly added it to the pile of things I was taking to college. I was sure I would be the only person at school with such a thing, but I guessed it would be warm. By September the set of plaid luggage I had bought myself was full of what I considered to be the right clothes. Although I wished I had been able to buy or make more, I was fairly confident of my collection.

My spirits were high as we set off on the eight-hour drive to Alfred. After stopping for lunch in the Catskills, we headed west into the most isolated countryside I had ever seen. As I looked out at the scene of mountains and trees with only a few houses scattered here and there, I quietly wondered what kind of place I was going to. My anxiety increased as the scene became more and more sparsely populated. What kind of people would choose to go to a school so far away from civilization? Would there be any students from New York City at Alfred or would they all be from upstate? I was grateful that my parents hadn't noticed that I had become very quiet since we left the familiar resort area of the Catskills. The lump in my throat was so large I knew I wouldn't have been able to speak had they asked me a question.

When we drove into Alfred the desolation gave way to the bustle of a small college town on the day the freshmen arrive. The town was nestled into the hills that had seemed so desolate. As I looked at them from the vantage point of the main street crowded with fashionably dressed college students, the hills seemed almost beautiful. When my father turned into the steep drive up to the freshmen dorm for women and two handsome young men approached the car, I began to feel even less apprehensive. They were football players there to help us carry things to my room. We got there just as my roommate was saying good-bye to her father. My parents exchanged glances when Mr. Lanzi, dressed in a pin-striped suit, introduced himself and said he lived in Buffalo. I was glad that my roommate was Italian and from a city, but I knew that my parents were thinking that her father was probably a gangster.

One of the young men who had been helping us brought up the last load and told us that the stores in town, including the banks, had opened that Sunday to accommodate the freshmen. Because my father wanted to open a checking account for me, we walked the short distance to the main street, and my mother and I waited while my father went into the bank. I wondered why I needed to have a checking account, but it seemed to be the thing to do; the small bank was crowded with freshmen and their parents. When he returned, my father handed me a checkbook and began explaining how to use it. My nods convinced him that I understood the process, although I did not have the faintest idea what he was talking about.

As much as I had wanted them to leave, when my parents drove away I was terrified. I was really alone for the first time in my life, miles away from anything in the least bit familiar, and the lump in my throat was back. I turned before the car was out of sight and ran into the dorm and up the stairs to the only person I knew, though I had just met her. Tina seemed so calm. She had just finished putting her clothes into her dresser and was considering whether to change for our orientation meeting. I had no idea that we were to go to a meeting and asked her how she knew about it. She picked up a schedule of events for the first few days of school from a packet of materials that looked vaguely familiar. I remembered that I too had recently received such a packet, but I had been too anxious to read. I marveled at Tina's composure and frantically searched through my suitcases for my schedule. I began to doubt whether I would be able to manage college at all, but since it was time to go I put on a fresh coat of lipstick, checked the seams in my stockings, and walked to the meeting with Tina.

Within the next few hours I had met most of the other freshman women and some of the men. To my great relief I found that many were from New York City or had only recently moved to the suburbs. Like my roommate, they had last names that proclaimed their ethnicity, and, although I was the only Armenian and I hadn't met any Greeks, I began to feel less frantic. I also met people whose names did not connote their English or German ancestry but who were, like most of the students at Ridgewood High, American. Unlike my former classmates, however, these Americans seemed to be as friendly as everyone else. As I walked out of the meeting with the green and yellow freshman beanie I was to wear Monday through Friday until the end of that school year, the freshman handbook I was required to memorize, and my new friend, Shirley Brown, my confidence about my ability to survive returned.

Shirley was born and raised in New Jersey, not the suburbs I hated so much, but the Jewish section of Newark. Assuming from her last name that Shirley was American, I asked why her parents had chosen to live there. She assured me that she was Jewish. Brown was not her real name. Her grandfather had decided, when he emigrated to this country, that it would be wise to change the family name to something that sounded neutral. Once I knew that Shirley was not an American but different like me, I felt safe, and we quickly became "best friends."

It was incredibly easy to make friends at Alfred. There were only a little over one hundred women in the freshman class, and we lived in one dormitory. I loved the old, three-story building, which reminded me of my apartment house in the city, and soon became as comfortable in "the Brick," as it was called, as I had been in New York. Within a few weeks of the beginning of school I knew everyone in the dorm by name and Shirley and I had begun to develop a circle of friends. Although none were from New York City, and most were Americans, I quickly felt at ease.

The academic side of college, however, was another matter. I had no idea how to choose courses and was relieved to find that some were required. Whole fields like philosophy were totally unknown to me, and others, like political science, were, I thought, for men. My advisor suggested that I begin to fulfill my distribution requirements, and I chose biology from the math/science group. I didn't know what geology was, and, although I had gotten grades in the nineties in both my geometry and algebra regents exams, I had decided I was terrible in math. I chose German for the required language because I had heard that Dr. Buchanan, the German professor, was very nice, and if you sat in the back row and didn't look at him he never called on you. For my elective I decided on "Introduction to Music." I loved jazz and Latin music, but I thought it was time for me to learn about "serious" music.

At the end of the first day of classes I realized that the books the professors had assigned were not given out at the end of class as they had been in high school. We had to buy them! It also became clear to me that they would cost more than I had in my checking account. My friends all had enough money for books. Their parents, it seemed, knew they would have to buy books and had given them enough money. When I called home to ask my father for the money, he said that he would send it soon and that I could use the books in the library in the meantime. I was furious with my parents for not knowing that I would need money for books and ashamed of my own ignorance. With tears in my eyes I screamed that everyone had their own books and that I needed them immediately. He agreed to send a money order the next day.

Once I had the books, however, I didn't know what to do with them. The years of trying not to be a "brain" at George Washington and the alienation I had felt at Ridgewood High left me with no idea how to study.

By mid-semester some of my grades were barely passing, though I was gaining an A in my social life. Not only did I have lots of girlfriends, I had a date every weekend. And, after a somewhat shaky start, I managed to go out with men who belonged to the "right" fraternities. During the first few weeks of school I realized that I had gone out with only Jewish men. I didn't mind dating Jews, but I was not satisfied with my dates' fraternities. Social life at Alfred revolved exclusively around fraternities because of school restrictions and town ordinances. Having a good time in the 1950s was unthinkable without drinking alcohol, but there were no bars in Alfred because the town was dominated by Seventh-Day Adventists who prohibited the sale of alcohol. Getting to the next town where there was a bar, which was used exclusively by Alfred students, required a car. People could, of course, have alcohol in their homes, but most students lived on campus. Single women students were not only forbidden to have their own apartments; they also were not allowed to be in an apartment with a man unless properly chaperoned. Getting caught more than once could mean expulsion from school, and I didn't know anyone who broke the rule. The weekly fraternity parties—duly chaperoned by a faculty couple— where students drank kegs of beer provided the social life for most of the campus.

One's choice of fraternities was, however, limited. Of the six on campus, three allowed membership only to white, Christian males. Of the three others, only a local one was nonsectarian in its membership. The other two houses had nonsectarian policies, but their members were Jewish—except the one that included two Negro members. The popular fraternities, at least as my circle of friends understood it, did not include the two Jewish houses.

I discussed my problem with Shirley, and she suggested that men thought I was Jewish. We decided that I should wear my cross, and, because most people thought she was Christian, she thought it would be fun to wear her star, although she had already begun to date a man from one of the preferred houses. The next day heads turned as we walked down the streets with our religions around our necks. That very weekend I had a date with a Christian man.

The discrimination against Jews was taken by most people on campus as a fact of life, but late in my first semester Nate Lyons, the editor of the school paper, wrote an editorial charging the school with anti-Semitism for allowing the restricted fraternities to operate on university property. I was shocked that he had dared to use the term *anti-Semitism*. It reminded me briefly of those realtors in New Jersey and my revulsion at their questions, but mostly I thought it was wrong to talk about it. I was relieved to find that Shirley was also disturbed by what Nate had written. She argued that he had only made matters worse. Now, she said, everyone would be talking about the policy of the fraternities, and now Christians who didn't mind Jews would turn against them because Nate had stirred up trouble. The man she had been dating told her that it was all right that she was Jewish because she wasn't like the others. Shortly after Nate's editorial, however, they ended their relationship.

Nate Lyons's charge of anti-Semitism also affected our discussions about sororities. Although we would not be able to pledge a house for another semester, my friends and I had begun to weigh the merits of the two sororities we were considering. There were four on campus, but two were out of the question since the girls in them were unpopular—even on that small campus we hardly knew who they were. The sisters in Theta and Sigma, on the other hand, included the few women who held leadership positions at the school and, more important for us, were the queens of the Military Ball, the Interfraternity Ball, the Winter Carnival, and the Saint Pat's Festival. We had decided one thing. We would all pledge the same sorority. For weeks we had discussed the women in the two sororities and the location and size of the houses without facing the fact that, at least for one of us, there really was no choice. Sigma did not accept Jews. Now that Nate's editorial was out, we didn't talk much about sororities anymore.

One day when we were at dinner someone brought the question up, and the discussion, which had been highly animated only a few weeks earlier, was strained. Penny Allen suddenly looked at Shirley and asked her what it was like to be Jewish. As Shirley tried to collect herself to respond, Penny said, "You must wish you were Christian." Shirley rose and said something to Penny which I didn't hear because I was too overwhelmed with what Penny had said. I wanted to put my body between Penny's and Shirley's to protect one friend from the violence of the other's comment. I followed Shirley out of the dining room and assured her that I thought that what Penny had said was awful and that I would never really consider pledging Sigma whether she was my friend or not. I lied about the last part. I didn't really know what I would have done if Shirley had not been my best friend, but she was, and I didn't want to join a sorority without her. Shirley said that Penny was no different from the man she had been dating, who had never accepted the fact that she was Jewish. There were damn few goyim who could be trusted, she added. I hoped that I was one.

While I was forced to think a little about anti-Semitism, I was oblivious to the other forms of prejudice on our quiet and "friendly" campus. Out of my freshman class of about three hundred students there were two Negro students: a man and a woman. I never asked why there were so few Negro students at Alfred. I did think that it must have been very hard for the ones who were there, particularly Norma, the only black female. While I never saw the few Negro men at Alfred with dates, all of the upperclassmen were in fraternities, and Charles Axt was president of one of the Jewish houses. The men could at least go to parties without dates. I never saw Norma on the weekends.

Despite the fact that most of the rules governing student behavior applied only to women, I generally accepted them, as did my friends. We thought our curfew times were too early, but no one thought we shouldn't have them. We never considered that it was our right to have men in our rooms or to visit a man in his apartment. Since my parents would never have agreed to let me live in my own apartment at school or anywhere else, that prohibition seemed normal. I was annoyed that I couldn't smoke on the street or wear slacks to dinner, but I agreed that men and women should act differently.

During my freshman year there were two incidents that angered me. In the second semester an "older" woman came to Alfred and was required, like the rest of us, to live in the dorm. I thought it was unfair to make her live with us, since she was in her late twenties. The school would never have required an older male to live with eighteen- and nineteen-year-olds, but since she was a woman the rules that applied to young women were not relaxed for her. The second incident concerned a friend of mine, Linda, who found out that she was pregnant and married a man from another school. It was late in the second semester, and she wanted to complete the last six weeks of school. She had already broken one rule, which applied to both male and female students: Students who intended to marry were to notify the personnel deans of their plans. Since Linda was already married, the administration agreed to overlook this infraction. The second problem was more serious. Married women were not permitted to live in the dorm, but Linda could not live off campus unless she were living with her husband. Linda's husband, who also wanted to finish the school year, did not live in Alfred. My friends and I were furious. It was awful that Linda had gotten pregnant, but we thought it was unfair to make her leave school because the administration could not decide where she could live. After many meetings with the dean of women and letters from her professors saying that even as a freshman Linda was one of their best students, the administration finally agreed to let her live in the dorm. Since she was pregnant, however, she would have to move from her room on the second floor to one on the first floor.

My only other problem with the way women were treated at Alfred was that only men got second helpings at meals. I had an enormous appetite and knew that I ate more than many men, but, despite my hunger after what I considered very skimpy meals, there were no seconds. After the first few weeks of school I tried to organize a boycott of the dining room to protest the quality and quantity of the food, but no one else seemed to care about what we ate. As it worked out, all my friends were perpetually on diets, so I ate their potatoes and bread. My parents sent me packages of cheeses and salami, but for the first semester I regularly dreamt of food, mostly stacks of *lahmajoon* (Armenian meat pies).

Except for the food, I didn't think about being Armenian much that year. The six-credit required freshmen course "Our Cultural Heritage" made no mention of Armenians, but I had never expected to hear about us in school. We learned about ancient Persia and the Ottoman Empire, "the sick man of Europe," but nothing about the massacre of Armenians that my grandmother had told me about. Yet I did a paper on the massacre. Reading the accounts of the tortures inflicted on the Armenians by the Turks, I realized that my grandmother had left a lot out of the story she told me. My grandfather was not a soldier in the Turkish army, as my grandmother had implied, but had probably been used as a pack animal until he died of exhaustion. I was moved by what I read about the massacre, but once I finished the paper I didn't think much about it. I put my grandmother's story away again. That paper, however, was the only schooolwork that had engaged me. For me and most of my girlfriends courses were something we had to take in order to be at Alfred.

The only glimpse I had that first year about what education might be about came not from my classes but from a relationship with a man whom I had begun to date toward the end of my second semester. Although Dave Robinson was in one of the preferred fraternities and was majoring in ceramic engineering, he was on the fringes of one of the small groups of students who did not participate in the general social life of the campus. Instead of dancing and playing drinking games on Saturday nights, these students gathered in someone's apartment, sometimes with a chaperone but just as often without, and talked about literature. Sometimes one of them read his or her own writing and the group then discussed it. Although I felt very inadequate at the gatherings and often wished I was at a fraternity party instead, I was also intrigued. None of these people seemed to care about being different. Women in the group clearly seemed proud of their intellectual abilities. I decided to be more careful in my selection of courses the next semester. I would also try to learn something.

I had told my parents a little about Dave, who was working his way through college because his parents could not afford the tuition. While they said nothing about the fact that he was poor, they told me I was too young to be "serious" about anybody. I should study hard and have lots of friends, by which I knew they meant dates. During my summer vacation, however, my mother began to be explicit about what it meant to be an Avakian. She explained that, while the family was not rich in this country, in Persia they had been aristocrats. The Avakians had a family seal, she told me, and had maintained a full staff of servants. In this country Avakian Brothers was one of the major Oriental-rug importing firms, and all the

Avakians—she meant the men but did not say that—were highly respected in the trade. She also recounted the many achievements of Avakians who had entered the professions: Souren, the chemist, who had identified an enzyme that bore the family name; Peter, who had gone to the Massachusetts Institute of Technology on full scholarship; his brother Leo, whose education at Juilliard was also entirely supported by scholarships and who was preparing for his debut at Carnegie Recital Hall; George, a vice president at Columbia Records; and his brother Albert, who was a filmmaker.

Her emphasis was on the Avakian family. Of her own relations, she merely said that they had been prominent in Turkey "before," by which I vaguely knew she meant "before the massacre." My grandmother, she told me, had had a large house and servants. Yet, although my mother didn't talk about it, I knew there were some real differences between the two sides of the family. Even as a child I had noticed that the Avakians' relationships were much more formal than those of the Tutuians and Donigians. There were other differences too. The language of my father and his family was slightly different from that of my mother's side of the family. More important, each side of the family ate different foods. Of course, we all ate lamb in various forms, including shish kebab, and vegetables stuffed either with ground lamb and rice and cooked in tomato sauce or with onions, rice, and currants and cooked in lemon and olive oil. While both families ate rice pilaf at least three times a week, each had a different method of cooking it. My father's family made their pilaf the Persian way, soaking it in saltwater overnight, draining, washing, and parboiling it the next morning, then drenching it with melted butter and baking it. Turkish pilaf was much less complicated to make. Thin egg noodles were browned in butter and the rice added and sauteed until the grains were coated with butter. Boiling chicken broth was added to the mixture, and the rice was simmered until done. My mother made both varieties but was renowned among the Avakians for her Persian pilaf, a concrete example to me of how much of an Avakian she really was.

I preferred not only Turkish pilaf but the other foods my mother's family made: *lahmajoon* and *atleakmak, enginar* (artichokes braised in lemon juice and olive oil), and *chee kufta* (raw ground lamb mixed with bulgur and eaten with chopped onions and parsley), which we ate only on the rare occasions when my father was not home because considered it barbaric to eat raw meat.

I vaguely sensed that the differences between Turkish and Persian Armenians went beyond those of language and cuisine. Nothing was ever said directly, but when the two sides of the family were together, which was fairly frequently, it seemed to me that members of my mother's family were somewhat deferential to the Avakians. A few times I heard Aunty Ars refer to the Avakians as *Barska Hyes* (Persian Armenians) in a tone that connoted more than national origin. One time, when I knew that she was angry at someone in my father's family, I asked her why she called them Persian Armenians. After I badgered her to tell me what she really meant, she said that Persian Armenians thought they were better than everyone else. She didn't explain why, but I wondered if their superior attitude had anything to do with the massacre that they had escaped by not having lived in Turkey. Other differences between the two families made it difficult to get any clarity on the significance of this factor. What was clear was that the Avakians had more money than the Tutuians and Donigians and that the Avakian Brothers' position within the Oriental rug trade made the Avakians prominent members of the Armenian community.

But there was more than economics involved in the status difference of the two families. My mother's brother, for example, made enough money so that his wife never had to work, and the year before my father bought our house, Uncle Ashot bought a large, older, two-story house in Westchester County. I knew it was worth more than our new five-room tract house in New Jersey, but, despite his more expensive house, Uncle Ashot was in a different category than any of the Avakians. Like many Armenians of his generation, Uncle Ashot was a photo engraver, and I knew from conversations between my parents that he belonged to a union. I didn't really know what unions were, but I gathered from the way my mother's voice curled around the word that they were something bad. My uncle's union had provided triple time for him when he worked on Sunday, and that seemed to be a good thing to me. I also heard that Aunty Ars's union had paid for her medical expenses when she developed an ulcer, and that also seemed to be a good thing. I was confused by my mother's nonverbal message that there was something wrong with belonging to a union. It was clear that they were for working people. Maybe my mother was upset because her sister and brother were workers.

Throughout the summer, without mentioning my relationship with Dave, my mother impressed upon me the kinds of people who were acceptable and those who were not. While we both knew that

Dave would probably make a more than adequate salary as a ceramic engineer, he was clearly not from the right sort of people.

But I was lonely for him that summer. I still saw my city friends, but I began to feel that I was changing and my friends were not. The change in me had something to do with being away at college. I wanted to escape what I considered to be the limits of their vision. They were content to be living at home with their parents, working at their jobs or commuting to college. I didn't have any idea what I wanted, but I was not content. Only one thing was clear in my behavior, if not also in my mind. I did not need my friends from the city as I once had. My new life focused on my friends at college, and I eagerly awaited the opening of school in the fall.

Driving to Alfred in September of 1957 with my parents, I looked out lovingly at the hills that had seemed so desolate to me the year before, and I was now as calm as Tina Lanzi had looked on that first day we met which now seemed so long ago. In my room I smiled as I made my bed with the new blanket and bedspread that I had convinced my mother to buy. My roommate for the year was Sally Henderson, who was as American as anyone could be. She was blonde, had a small, turned-up nose, and was from a small town in western New York State. Unlike most of my other friends, Sally was a serious student. I hoped that her habits would influence me, for I had decided that I would give learning a try.

My selection of courses was still based mostly on information I had gotten from my friends about which professor had a reputation for being an easy grader, but I chose "Introduction to Art History." I had heard that Dr. Klitzke was a good teacher.

What was uppermost in my mind that semester was which of the two sororities my friends and I would pledge. There was no question that we would all go to the same house, and, since Shirley had not returned to school, the discrimination policies of Sigma did not seem to be a real issue. Yet every time I thought of choosing that sorority I saw Shirley's face. I began to campaign for Theta, and we all finally decided to pledge there. Because so many of us had decided against their sorority, the women in Sigma had to decide between a very small pledge class of Christians, on the one hand, and a large, "mixed" class, on the other. Since they were a local sorority and could choose to change their rules, they opted for the large, mixed class. I felt a small and private triumph when I heard the next day that Sigma had admitted a few Jewish women.

My other focus that semester was Dave. My feelings about him

continued to be intertwined with what he and his friends represented for me—a world that was as elusive as it was compelling.
I was attracted to the idea that there was more to life than dates,
clothes, and parties, but I was mystified about what this other world
was really like. I knew it had to do with reading and thinking but
not necessarily studying for courses. Dave and his friends considered most of the faculty at Alfred to be badly trained and hopelessly conservative. Only a few of the older faculty and a handful
of young faculty, whom they considered friends, were exceptions.
Alfred had little to offer them. Part of me was content with my
friends and the social life on campus, but another part of me wanted something more. I had decided to try to be more serious about
school, but I knew that what Dave and his friends represented was
not related to studying for classes. I could only define it as something that had to do with ideas. If I tried to be more like them, I
would certainly threaten my current friendships. If I didn't learn
from my teachers, where could I turn? Certainly not to this group
of people who, I was sure, thought I was a silly coed. I felt like I
was walking a tightrope between what I was—everything they
thought one shouldn't be—and the strangely appealing life of Dave's
friends.

I got some help from my course in art history. Dr. Klitzke's view
of creative production was that it was intimately connected to the
social and intellectual currents of its time. To really understand art—
to see its true meaning—one had to study everything about the context in which it was created. For the first time in my life I was excited by an idea. I read my assignments as thoroughly as my limited
skills allowed and looked forward to Dr. Klitzke's lectures.

Two books that were assigned in my sociology class also addressed the issue of meaning in life: *The Organization Man* by Wil-
liam H. White and *The Lonely Crowd* by David Riesman. I understood
from these books that most people's lives were directed by what
others wanted, and only the exceptional few lived their lives according to their own needs. It was clear to me that Dave and his friends
were just those "inner-directed" people the books talked about. I
wanted to be like them but had no clue how to find my "inner
needs." Despite my confusion, or perhaps because of it, I became
a missionary for this new vision. I wanted my friends to come along
with me on this new way of life and urged them to be more serious.

I felt lucky that Dave was willing to be my mentor. With him
as a guide I would perhaps find my own inner direction. As our

relationship deepened, we began to discuss the possibility of marriage after we finished school. I was only too happy to keep marriage plans in the future since Dave's description of his family made painfully clear that they were poor. We talked about the differences in our backgrounds and how we would overcome them. When Dave wanted me to go to Buffalo with him to meet his parents, I agreed reluctantly and tried to prepare myself for what they would be like. The image I created was one of a small, perhaps slightly ramshackle house that was, in essence, a pretty cottage.

I was unprepared for what I saw that weekend. The house that Dave's parents lived in consisted of a kitchen with a toilet behind a curtain, a tiny living room, and a bedroom closed off only by another curtain which was large enough only for a double bed. Clothes had to be piled on the floor and hung on nails in the wall. Dave and his brother slept in an unheated attic on mattresses on the floor. I was overwhelmed and barely able to talk to his parents, who did not fit my image of a poor, but proud and lovely couple.

I hardly spoke on the way back to school. The discussions that Dave and I had had about our families and how we would deal with our differences seemed very academic. I was repelled, and there was nothing to say. After weeks of turmoil I broke off our relationship. I was disappointed in myself, but I could not be part of Dave's family. I knew that he did not have enough money to go to school the next semester and was relieved when he said that he was taking a semester off to work.

With Dave gone, I no longer had anyone to measure myself against, and I relaxed a bit. But I did not completely give up the vision that had so attracted me. I took the second semester of Dr. Klitzke's art history course and was even more engaged by the material than I had been the first semester. But I also started to date fraternity men again. My new "steady" was an athlete whose main interest besides basketball was me. I was initially attracted to Chris Holmes by his long, lanky body and good looks but soon found his easygoing personality a relief after the intensity of my relationship with Dave. Although Chris was in one of the "jock" fraternities, some of the brothers of Delta Sig were veterans who were going to school on the G.I. bill. I enjoyed meeting these older men, some of whom were serious about learning but didn't feel the need to cut themselves off from the life of the campus as Dave's friends had.

As I approached the end of my sophomore year, the polarity between being a serious, inner-directed person, on the one hand,

and a silly college kid, on the other, had begun to break down. Even so, I was often confused and wanted help, but I had no idea where to get it. I had heard about psychoanalysis in one of the psychology courses I had taken, and I was secretly attracted to the idea of therapy, but whenever I thought about seeing a therapist I was filled with fear. Psychiatrists were for crazy people, and I vaguely wondered if I were crazy because sometimes I wanted to see one. Even if I had not been terrified at the prospect of analysis, I would not have known how to find it. There was no counseling offered at my college in the 1950s, and telling my parents I wanted to see a psychiatrist was out of the question. The teacher I had for the introductory psychology course fit my mental picture of an ideal therapist: a quiet, middle-aged, tall, and good-looking man. When I wrote the psychological autobiography he required, I expressed an occasional desire to "talk with someone" about my problems, with the hope that he would ask to see me. Disappointingly, I received an A on my paper instead of the help I had obliquely sought.

I knew what I didn't want to be. I was no longer content to merely have a good social life. I felt I ought to be more mature, but I didn't really know what that meant. I certainly did not want to be like my mother, although my relationship with her had improved since I left home. Of course, I wanted to get married and have a family, but her life and those of my aunts and older cousins seemed so dull. I wanted more than cooking, cleaning, and caring for a husband and children. In some ways I was clear that my life would be different. I would have friends, and they would not be Armenian. My husband would love me and show his affection, and he would also be interested in my ideas. I would have interests other than husband and family, but I could not imagine what they would be.

When I thought about these things I sometimes felt overwhelmed with doubts that I would ever know what I wanted, but, despite my confusion about my life and its direction, I began my junior year in the fall of 1958 optimistically. I had had an uneventful summer. Chris lived near my parents' house, and we saw each other regularly. He had graduated that spring but was waiting for his army commission to come through. It was nice to be with Chris, though sometimes I was a little bored. When September came I was anxious to get back to school, even though it meant leaving Chris.

My parents were not pleased when we drove up to the sorority house where I would be living that year. When my father saw the old frame house on the top of a steep hill, he commented that it looked like a firetrap to him. When we got to my room they were even more concerned because they saw there were no beds in it. Instead of sharing a room with one other woman as I had for the last two years, my bed was now on the sleeping porch along with about ten others. I shared a smaller room, which had one closet and an odd assortment of desks and dressers, with three women. My parents could not understand why I had chosen to move out of the nice modern dorm for this old and run-down house, although I had explained that sorority life meant living in the house with your sisters. They agreed that the food in the house would probably be better than in the dorm, and it would be nice to have access to the kitchen for snacks, but they were not convinced I had made the right choice. I was grateful that they had not insisted that I live in the dorm, although I was also glad that they had not seen the house before I moved in. They helped me unpack and left, taking their doubts with them.

Hoping to gain some insight into who I really was and what I really wanted, I had decided to major in psychology, and the choice of courses was relatively easy. Though I was disappointed that Dr. Klitzke was not offering anything I could take, I began the semester with a determination to learn. My initial optimism began to fade shortly after the semester began. My courses, instead of helping me to understand myself and others, seemed to have very little to do with real life and real people.

The disappointment on the academic side of school that semester was disturbing, but what was beginning to happen socially was alarming. After the first few weeks of being happy to see my friends again, I began to feel critical of many of them for not talking about much more than dates and boyfriends. While I was still unclear about what Dave and his friends had represented to me, I was disturbed that so many of the women I lived with seemed so frivolous. I wanted them to be more like the men I knew—to talk about life and its meaning.

There was group of women in the house whom I admired greatly, however, because they seemed to have a real sense of dedication to something important. They were ceramic design majors who had found an old wood kiln on the hill behind our house and decided to restore it. They interested other designers and the Ceramic School eventually gave them a grant to pay for materials. For weeks I woke up on Saturday and Sunday mornings to see them on the hill working on the kiln. I was almost as excited as they were when the kiln was ready to fire. I learned that the process would last long into the night and happily offered to stay up and make coffee and sandwiches for them. In order to bake the clay and melt the glazes properly the kiln had to reach a temperature that was so high it could only be measured by cones of clay that melted at different temperatures. I joined the cheers as each cone melted, but in the end the last cones did not melt. Despite the fact that the project had been a failure, I envied those students for their sense of purpose and the feelings they developed for each other through their work. But watching them work together for months restoring the kiln made me even more discontented with my situation.

I wanted to be serious about something, but I had no idea what it might be. I began to analyze the various personalities in the house, something that did not enhance my popularity. I was particularly focused on two women whose relationship disturbed me. I had known Jean and Amy since we were freshmen together. Their friendship, which had been close since the first few weeks of school, had never seemed more than that of "best friends." Being with them in the close quarters of the sorority house, however, I was uncomfortable with the way they related to each other. Jean seemed to hang on Amy's every word, and sometimes I found her sitting next to Amy's bed, which was one of the few that was not on a sleeping porch. Jean watched Amy as she slept. I had no idea what was going on between them, but, whatever it was, it seemed wrong to me. I wanted to do something about it. I began to talk about it, and most people let me know that I was wrong to bring it up. I couldn't understand why they did not see that it was our obligation to try to correct a situation that was, to my mind, just not right. When I suggested that we talk to the dean of women, I was told directly that I was ridiculous. I thought they were all being foolish and just didn't have the insight I did.

My criticisms of people in the sorority didn't affect my social life with men. I had many offers for dates every weekend, and during the week I spent a good deal of time with Tom O'Brien, one of Chris's friends. Tom, one of the vets in Chris's fraternity, seemed very wise to me. I tentatively discussed my situation at the sorority house with him, and, despite the fact that he was president of his fraternity, he supported my feeling that sororities were silly and that I was probably too thoughtful for most of those women.

Toward the middle of the semester I ran into Dr. Klitzke who invited me to his home for dinner the next night. I was overwhelmed. Dr. Klitzke was the smartest person I had ever met, and now he had befriended me. As I walked the short distance to his house, I thought about his courses and how excited I had been by the connections he made between the art and the spirit of the times in which it was created. Nothing that semester had interested me as his class had. I was anxious to meet Mrs. Klitzke, who was filling in as acting dean of women.

The evening passed like a dream. The Klitzkes seemed to me a perfect couple. She was intelligent and very outspoken. She shocked me by saying that many of the rules for women at Alfred were ridiculous. Not only was she disturbed by the way women students were treated but also other aspects of the school. It was generally too conservative for her tastes. I was flattered that she was so frank with me—a mere student.

After dinner Dr. Klitzke showed me some of the prints he had been collecting, most of them by Käthe Kollwitz, a German artist he had discussed in his course. Hearing him talk about these powerful lithographs that cried out against war and poverty, I thought again about how boring and irrelevant my courses that semester were. When I looked at the clock I realized that I had only ten minutes before curfew and got ready to leave. Dean Klitzke said I should stay if I felt like it, and if there were any trouble about getting in after curfew I should tell my housemother to get in touch with her. Because I was afraid of what might happen if I stayed out past curfew, I said I was tired and accepted Dr. Klitzke's offer of a ride back to the house.

Over the next few days I thought about my excitement when Dr. Klitzke talked about Kollwitz and Dean Klitzke about Alfred. Maybe I had outgrown the place. I had certainly needed what I had gotten from the school for the first two years, but maybe it was time to move on. I made an appointment to talk with Dr. Klitzke about majoring in art history. He was very encouraging. He thought I would make a fine art historian and agreed that it might be time for me to leave Alfred. Like his wife, he thought the school was very provincial, and they had decided to leave at the end of that school year. I told him that I was considering living at home because I was tired of campus social life, and he suggested that I think about going to Columbia University since Meyer Shapiro, a well-known art historian, was on the faculty there. I left his office elated. I had found what I wanted to do with my life. I would leave Alfred, go into art history, and devote myself to learning all there was to know.

I almost ran up the steep hill to the house to share my discovery with Sally, my roommate of the previous year and still a good friend. She had decided to major in music, and we had often talked about styles of music and visual arts in various historical periods. Sally did not disappoint my expectation that she would share my excitement. We talked about my vision for my new life—immersion in intellectual work. I thought about Tom, and I suggested to Sally that we go to the student union where we found him at his usual table. He decided that we should celebrate my news with a few beers, and, as we drove to our regular bar in the next town, I thought about my quick decision to leave Alfred and felt relieved that I would only have to live in the sorority house a little while longer. I didn't even consider what it would be like to live with my parents again.

The next day I wrote to Columbia for an application and to my parents to tell them of my plans. They were worried. I had told them that I would probably not be able to start school until the fall since it was too late to expect to begin in the spring semester, and my father said that if I stayed out of school for nine months that I would probably not return. He had no idea that I had a new sense of purpose—that I was finally going to school to study. I had tried to explain how I felt about art history, but to him it simply seemed impractical. Why didn't I take up something I could teach? Of course, I couldn't think of a thing I could do with my new major, beyond working in the Metropolitan Museum shop, but a job was not my concern. I was going to be a serious student because I would be studying a subject that probed beneath the surface to find the real meaning of art and through art the life of the time. Despite my father's doubts, my parents said that, if I felt as strongly as I did about leaving Alfred, they would accept my decision.

I looked forward to real scholarship at Columbia and to taking full advantage of the museums and galleries in New York City. I had had my fun, and now I was going to be a student.

Chapter 7

Coming home to Glen Rock did not seem difficult at first. I still had my own room. Even though my brother was approaching adolescence, he continued to share his room with my grandmother. Chris had not heard about his commission yet, and I was glad to see him again. I also saw Shirley frequently. She had gotten married to a man she knew before coming to Alfred and had had her first child.

Within a few weeks of my move back home I began to look for a job. All of my work experience had been as a salesgirl in department stores. I wanted to try something else, but I didn't know what. I could not become a waitress since my father had already made it very clear that serving people for money was not proper work for an Avakian girl, and I didn't want to risk a fight with my parents. We were getting along rather well. I went to a few employment agencies in Glen Rock and Ridgewood, hoping that there might be some jobs available I had not thought of, but, as soon as I came through the door, I was told that they had nothing for someone like me. They specialized in domestic help. I wondered why they assumed I would not be interested in such work, but of course I had no intention of being a maid. There seemed to be nothing for me but sales. I got a job at one of the smaller stores at the Garden State Plaza.

My excitement at the beginning of a new life diminished in the drudgery of standing behind a counter for eight hours a day. I had intended to use my time out of school to try to learn what I had missed in my two and a half years at Alfred, but I lacked the discipline to read on my own. Living with my family also proved to be more difficult than I had imagined. My mother assumed that I would attend every family event and always seemed to be telling me what to do. My relationship with my brother, which had been better while I was away at college, deteriorated daily. My mother and grandmother hovered over him still, and I resented their expectations that I would help with the housework while he had no responsibilities.

Being with Chris, outside the environment of Alfred, was even less satisfying than it had been the previous summer. Then I had been merely bored. Now, increasingly, he seemed unsuited to my new dedication to the life of the mind. When his commission finally came through in April I wondered what it would be like not to have him around, but I also felt that his departure might be a good way to end our relationship. Shortly after he left, however, I felt terribly lonely.

I decided that I wanted to go back to Alfred for a visit and tried to convince my father to let me take the car. He refused. Although I had been driving for three years, he felt that I did not have enough experience to take a long trip alone. He was sure that if the car, which seemed in mint condition to me, broke down, I would be helpless. I realized it was no use arguing with him. It was true that I did not know how to diagnose and fix a broken fan belt or change a flat tire, but I wondered if it was really necessary to have the skills of a mechanic to take a trip. I was frustrated with my father's "what ifs?" but stopped arguing and took the train. On the long trip I began to think about Tom. I had written to say that I was coming and had asked him to pick me up at the station. As we approached the western part of the state, the conductor asked me if I was going to see someone special. I thought of Tom and said I guessed I was.

When the train pulled into the station and I caught sight of Tom's old brown car, it became clear then that he was the reason I had wanted to visit Alfred. But when I saw him he was not alone. Teddy Saltzman, one of my sisters at Theta, was with him. I was surprised both by her presence and my jealousy. After a rather quiet ride into Alfred they dropped me off at the sorority house, and Tom said they would see me later. Since I had no desire to see "them," I was equally vague about my plans.

Strangely enough, it felt good to be back in the house. In some ways it felt more like home than my parents' house in Glen Rock. People seemed surprised to see me, but most were very nice, and when Sally came into the room I wondered for a moment why I had left. After a while I casually asked her about Tom and Teddy, and she told me that they had been dating fairly steadily for a few months. I didn't hear from Tom that afternoon, and after dinner Sally and I went to the bar with some friends.

When we got there I was delighted to see that Tom was there without Teddy. We talked and danced for most of the evening, and I became more and more tense as the time to leave approached. I accepted his offer of a ride back to Alfred, and, as we walked to the car, I heard myself tell Tom that I loved him. I was as shocked by what I had said as he was, and we decided that it was impossible for me to go back to the house. Curfew was only a half an hour off, and we would need more time than that.

We drove to a secluded spot and spent the rest of the night in the car. Tom told me that he had fallen in love with me the previous year, but since I was Chris's girlfriend he had tried to put me out of his mind. He had thought he was over his feelings for me when he began to date Teddy, but that night I had brought them back. I was ecstatic. Tom was the kind of man I wanted. He was someone I could look up to. He was six years older than I, and his plans for the future were much more advanced than mine. I was planning to be a serious undergraduate student, but Tom had already decided to be a college professor. We spent the next two days together, and when he took me to the train it was with the promise that he would write often.

On the train ride back to Glen Rock I felt like a new person. I was happy, and I felt secure. I had so much to learn from Tom. I worried a little that I was not smart enough to keep him, but I also knew that I had some power over Tom because he was a man. I felt much more vulnerable with women who, I thought, could see right through me. Men, on the other hand, could be easily fooled by flirtatious and sexually suggestive behavior. One had to be careful, of course, not to endanger one's reputation by crossing the thin line between acceptable flirtation and acting like a ''bad'' woman, but I thought I was rather skilled at walking that particular tightrope.

Shortly after I got home from my trip to Alfred I heard from Columbia. I had been accepted, but, because of my less than exceptional record at Alfred and my low grade on the writing section of the entrance exam, I would be on probation for a year, and I was required to take an advanced composition class. I had been so anxious the day of that exam that my mother had offered me one of her pills. I hadn't known before then that she had been taking tranquilizers, though I had noticed that she had been more nervous and volatile the past year. I gladly accepted both her pill and her concern.

As the summer approached, I decided to apply for my old job at Bambergers, and I looked forward to Tom coming home. Instead of shopping for bargains during my lunch hour, as I had other summers, I spent most of my time at Sam Goody's, a large record store in the plaza. Because of my frequent visits I became friendly with some of the salespeople, and one young man in particular.

Richard Brooks was a college student and, like me, a real jazz fan. We spent as much time as we could talking about our favorite artists. One day, when we were particularly frustrated because our conversation was constantly being interrupted by customers, he suggested that we go out for lunch sometime. While I was delighted that he had asked me, I was also somewhat taken aback because Richard was a Negro. I said sure, let's do that sometime, hoping that he would not suggest a date right away. But he asked how about tomorrow, and I answered fine.

When I did have time to think about having lunch with Richard, I decided that there was nothing wrong with it. He was a college man, very well mannered and very good looking. During the rest of the day I kept thinking about Madeline, my friend at the pool at George Washington, and about how my feelings about Negroes had changed because of her. Before our friendship all Negroes were alien and to be avoided as much as possible, but Madeline was not one of "them." She was my friend, at least at school. At Alfred I met Warren Sutton, the star of the basketball team. One night when Chris and I were at a fraternity party I saw Warren standing alone—he was the only Negro at the party. I was concerned that he might be feeling strange and went over to talk to him. What I wanted to show him was that for me he was just like anyone else. It was just like that with Richard, I thought. Why should it matter that his skin is dark?

By lunchtime the next day I had convinced myself that there was nothing extraordinary about spending an hour with my friend from Sam Goody's. The restaurant we chose because of its good hamburgers and deli-style pickles was crowded with shoppers, mostly women. By the time we got a table and had ordered, it was clear that by having lunch with Richard I had done something wrong. Many of the women as well as the few men at the other tables were staring at us. As we struggled to make conversation, which had always been so easy in the record store, I heard one women say, "She looks like such a nice girl. Isn't it a shame." We ate as quickly as we could and left. As we walked back toward Bambergers, I was aware that more heads turned to stare at us. I was furious and a little frightened. Perfect strangers felt they had the right to comment on my choice of friends.

This wasn't the South, I thought, but Richard patiently explained that attitudes in the North were not as liberal as most people believed. My hatred for New Jersey, which was generally just below the surface, erupted. I was sure, I told Richard, that people in New York City would not have reacted the way these suburban idiots had. He said he wasn't so sure. We decided tha we would have lunch together the next day but that we would bring sandwiches and eat outside.

I didn't mention Richard to my mother until he asked me for a date. I had stopped asking her whether I could go out, but I knew I had to tell her about Richard being a Negro. Unlike the time in high school when I had asked her if I could go to Madeline's house, this time I really hoped she would not have any objections. My parents were conservative in most areas and gave no indication that their views on race relations were liberal, but we had virtually no contact with Negroes, and I was able to delude myself that my mother would welcome Richard into our home. I began by talking about how intelligent Richard was, that he went to Fairleigh Dickinson University, and that he wanted to take me out. Finally, I said that he was a Negro. My mother looked at me as if I had lost my mind. It was out of the question. I could not go out with a Negro. Even if she didn't mind, which she decidedly did, she had to think of her neighbors. She owed it to them not to allow any Negro into the neighborhood. I said he wasn't moving in, only coming to the door to pick me up. She turned her back and walked out of my room, saying that I had gone too far. I quickly realized that this was one argument that I could not win and decided to quit before my mother got hysterical. But I did tell her that she had disappointed me because I had thought she was above such foolish prejudice.

Nevertheless, I was going to go out with Richard. I really enjoyed my time with him, and we shared many interests. Richard also met one of my main criteria in a man: He had something to teach me. He wrote poetry, and I looked forward to learning about a form of writing that had always been mysterious to me. When I told Richard what had happened and that I still wanted to go out with him, we arranged for one of his white friends to pick me up. That night was only the first of many "dates" with Richard's friend. One week when we both had the same day off we decided to go to the beach. This time, since we wanted to be alone, I told my mother I was going to the beach with friends from work and drove to Richard's house in Teaneck. I had been anxious to see where he lived. When I came to his street the split-levels didn't look any different from those on any other street, but all the people I saw on the block were Negro. It seemed wonderful to me, more evidence that we were really all the same except for skin color. The weather was clear and hot, and I looked forward to a whole day with Richard.

When we got to the beach I was flooded with childhood memories of wonderful days playing in the surf. After we had unpacked our towels and lunch and settled down on our blanket, I began to notice that people were staring at us. This wasn't New Jersey, and I knew that many people from New York City went to Jones Beach, but the looks on people's faces were the same as they had been at the Garden State Plaza. Richard had been right after all. I forced myself to ignore the looks, but the day was tainted.

I felt lucky that summer to be dating two men who had so much to offer me. Tom and I often went to Greenwich Village and sat for hours, talking over cups of expresso. Tom had overcome so much and I knew he was really intelligent. His parents had no interest in education, although they had sent him to a Catholic high school. Like most of his high school friends, he had joined the army when he graduated and only thought about going to college because he had the G.I. bill. Despite the disadvantages of his upbringing, Tom was becoming an intellectual. He was a political science major and really understood what was happening in the world. I felt so good— so intelligent myself—when I was with him. Tom listened closely to what I had to say, and, although he seemed so much more mature than I, I felt completely at ease with him. We shared good memories of Alfred and were able to laugh at the same things.

Richard was also someone I had fun with and could look up to. But I was afraid of how much I liked being with Richard and wondered what would happen if our relationship became really serious. Would my family disown me? Did I have the strength to face a disapproving world? I had already paid for my friendship with Richard. After being chosen for two years to be on the Bambergers' College Board—a group of salesgirls who specialized in advising college-bound customers about clothes—I had been passed over that summer. My boss intimated that the company I had been keeping during my lunch hour had conflicted with the image the store wanted to project.

I had not had the courage to deal with the differences between Dave and me, but Richard and I did not have those kinds of problems. His parents obviously had enough money to buy a new house in Teaneck, and, from what he said about them, Richard's parents were more like mine than they were like Dave's or even Tom's. Tom's father worked for the gas company as a meter reader, and his mother also worked to supplement the family income. They lived in a three-room apartment in the Bronx which did not contain one book. They had accepted Tom's desire to go to college but now could not understand why he wanted to go to graduate school. But Richard was a Negro and I was white, and even strangers felt they had the right to let us know that they disapproved of our relationship. Despite the fact that Tom had decided to go to Syracuse University for his master's degree, I told Richard that I was involved in another relationship that had become serious. While it was true that my relationship with Tom had deepened, it was also true that I wanted to stop seeing Richard because I was afraid that I might grow to love him.

Although I had ended my relationship with Richard, and Tom was away at Syracuse, I was happy that September and was eager to start school. When registration day came, however, I felt like a freshman again. The lines at Columbia were endless, and I was so confused that I spent more than an hour waiting in the wrong line. The advisors hardly seemed to have time to fill in the students' schedules, and, as I waited my turn, I realized that the long talk with my new advisor that I had dreamt about was not part of what Columbia had to offer. I knew that I had to take advanced composition and that Columbia required three years of a foreign language. I had barely passed the two required years of German at Alfred by sitting in the back, not looking at Dr. Buchanan, and learning only enough to pass tests. I convinced my advisor to allow me to repeat the second year of German. Since I had gotten a D in one of my semesters of science, the course would not fulfill Columbia's requirement, and I had to take a year of science. I also needed a year of math. I had never done much studying and, as my entrance exam showed, my writing skills weren't very good. I had confidence only in my ability in art history. But, despite my fears, I was eager to begin as a serious student for the first semester of my life.

By the middle of the semester it was clear that I had enough discipline to study, and I realized with a shock that math was my best subject. The real disappointment was my art history courses.

They were very large lectures with no discussion. I was disturbed too by the professors' approach to the art. Instead of placing it within its historical and cultural context as Dr. Klitzke had done, they explored only its structure. Dr. Klitzke had recommended Columbia because Meyer Shapiro was on the faculty, but he taught only graduate students; his classes were also in such demand that only students who reserved their place a year in advance were admitted. I hoped that the next semester I would have a professor whose perspective was like Dr. Klitzke's, even if I had no hopes of getting into Professor Shapiro's classes. In the meantime I was able to do well but had no particular interest in the "beauty of the line" or the elements that distinguished the various periods of painting from each other.

For the first time in my college career I ended the semester with better than average grades, and also for the first time I was proud, not embarrassed, by my achievement. I did even better the next semester, but was more disappointed than before by my art history classes. I began to wonder if there were something wrong with me. Why wasn't I satisfied with appreciating the aesthetic qualities of the works? None of the other students seemed to think that the professors' approach to works of art was limited. A few of the readings for my courses did make connections that interested me, particularly Erwin Panofsky's *Early Netherlandish Painting*, which I treasured. At the end of the Northern Renaissance painting course the professor said that it was, of course, impossible to understand the work we had been studying all semester without a knowledge of the philosophy current at the time when the paintings had been created. I felt cheated. If he really did believe what he said, why hadn't he incorporated that material into the course?

Despite all my difficulties with art history, I was glad to be at Columbia, but I missed Tom. He visited only a few weekends each semester. Although my confidence was buoyed by my ability to do well in school and get along with the few friends I had made at Columbia, I felt whole only when I was with Tom.

One night, a few days after Tom left, I was feeling particularly lonely for him when my grandmother came into my room. She asked me why I was so sad. I was surprised both by her visit to my room, which was, as far as I could remember, the first, and by her interest in my feelings—unusual not only for her but for the whole family. I told her that I missed Tom. She responded with an empathy uncharacteristic of our rather strained relationship. It didn't seem to matter to her that Tom was not Armenian. He was going to be a college professor, and he was my man. She didn't say much, but I understood that she knew more than I would ever know about what it was to long for your man. It was a moment when I felt that we were two women together, not grandmother and grandaughter. I had a man and was, in my grandmother's eyes, no longer a child.

As the end of the spring semester approached, I began to think about what I would do for the summer. I was determined not to go back to Bambergers after they had penalized me for being seen with Richard. I was also no longer interested in selling clothes. I wanted to be in New York City. After a year at Columbia, New York felt like home again. I decided to talk to my father about working at Avakian Brothers. Many of my cousins had worked there for a summer or two, and I thought it was probably my turn. My father seemed pleased by my decision and agreed to talk to Uncle Alex about it. The next time we saw my uncle he told me he would be delighted to have me in the office for the summer.

The first morning I walked through the double doors I was overwhelmed with nostalgia for Aunty Lucy's lap and hot tea in a glass. I had loved going to Avakian Brothers as a child. The huge room with high ceilings was filled with stacks of Oriental rugs, some well over my head but others that I could easily climb. My cousins Rita and Susan and I had played on those stacks as long as our parents would allow. Almost everyone in Avakian Brothers was either related to us or was a family friend. Even the few people I did not know seemed familiar, since everyone spoke Armenian. Uncle Alex greeted me, introduced me to the secretary and the bookkeeper, and showed me my desk.

The hierarchy that was so obvious in family gatherings was even more pronounced at Avakian Brothers. Uncle Mesrop, the oldest member of the firm, was clearly at the top of the structure. He had a large private office away from the secretary and bookkeeper, and everyone deferred to him. Uncle Alex was next in line, also with a private office but one that opened out onto where the secretary and bookkeeper sat. Hemeyak and Amis, the youngest members of the business, didn't have an office. There was one salesman, who was not a relative but who was Armenian. He had the lowest status among the men who worked in the front of the large room. The men who worked in the back, the shipping clerk, and the men who moved the rugs around and opened them for customers were non-

Armenian. The only Armenian who worked in the back was the rug weaver. And all of those men were "boys." I was introduced to them by the secretaries only when they came to the front room. I never did meet the old man who repaired rugs.

The phone began to ring, and a customer came through the double doors signaling the beginning of the workday. The secretary had me type consignment orders and bills, and, hearing the bell ring all morning as customers came and went, I felt I had made the right decision. It felt good to be working at Avakian Brothers.

After the first few weeks, however, my nostalgia was gone, and I realized why I had thought of Aunty Lucy when I came through the doors that first morning. Being at Avakian Brothers was like being at her house; it was a little piece of Armenia. The area where the secretary and bookkeeper sat and the back of the store seemed like islands of America to me, although the women in the front were both Jewish, and most of the "boys" were Puerto Rican. All the customers were short, dark men who, like my uncles and cousins, spoke English only when necessary. And everything seemed so old-fashioned. As the weather got warmer, for example, and the smell of wool and mothballs became oppressive, it seemed ridiculous to me that the showroom was not air-conditioned. I asked the book-keeper if anyone had thought of air-conditioning. She gave me a look that said that I should know better and asked me if I really thought the Avakians would consider spending money on such an unnecessary luxury. I said I guessed not and asked myself my old question again: Why did my family have to be so old country? Any American business of the size and prominence of Avakian Brothers could surely have made their offices and showrooms more comfortable for their customers, if not for themselves and their workers.

My relatives were, on the other hand, all too American in their attitudes about race relations. One morning Uncle Mesrop came in and walked directly to Uncle Alex who was standing in front of the bookkeeper's desk. I knew something important must have happened because he usually went to his office and waited for Uncle Alex, Amis, and Hemeyak to go to see him. He was holding a *New York Times* in his hand and was obviously disturbed. He pointed to a picture of a leader of one of the newly independent African states and said in Armenian, "Animals in suits." Uncle Alex, Amis, and Hemeyak all shook their heads in dismay, not at their uncle's comment, but at the specter of Negro men in positions of power. I knew nothing about the man whose picture was on the front page of the *Times* or the politics of Africa, but I was furious at the blatant prejudice of my family. I had no idea what to say to them, but at that moment I hated them. I looked at my dark hairy relatives and thought they looked more like gorillas than Richard Brooks did.

That night I told my parents what Uncle Mesrop had said and how angry I was. My father said that there were differences between the races and that science had proven that Negroes were not as well developed as whites. It was a fact that he had learned when he himself was a student at Columbia. There was scientific evidence that Negroes' brains were smaller than whites' and that, while Negro babies might develop faster than white babies, their development stopped at a lower stage. Negroes were, in that way, more like animals, whose rates of development were certainly more rapid, though less advanced, than humans. I was not as shocked as I had been when I first heard the idea that Negroes were closer to animals than whites and now was better able to respond. I couldn't argue with my father, however, who said he had science on his side.

While my time at Avakian Brothers did not live up to its early promise, the summer with Tom was all that I had hoped for. Sometimes he met me at the office, and we walked from Thirty-third Street down to Greenwich Village, which was one of my favorite places in New York City. In the Village, it seemed, people could be what they wanted to be. Sometimes we went to hear jazz, but most of the time we had something to eat and walked and talked for the rest of the evening.

I felt as if I could talk about anything with Tom. He was interested in my frustration with my art history courses and supported my ideas. I was also able to share the problems I was having with my mother. My resolve to try to be nicer to her had not lasted long. We always seemed to be fighting about something—the clothes I wore, the music I listened to, the friends I had. According to my mother, I never did enough with the family. My perception was that the family was like an octopus. If one set of relatives was not making demands one weekend, another set was. My mother and I were polarized just as we had been when I was in high school, and living with her seemed to be a constant struggle.

Earlier that year my cousin Elise, a women in her early thirties, had moved into her own apartment. My mother, who had always liked Elise very much, censured her severely for leaving her mother. I was furious. Elise was a grown woman, I said, even if she wasn't married. Besides her mother was not alone. Her husband was with her as well as her younger daughter. But my mother insisted that it just wasn't right for Elise to have moved away from her parents. I argued that she would not have disapproved had Elise been a man, but my mother reminded me that none of my male cousins had moved out of their parents' home before marriage. I stomped out of the kitchen, screaming that ordinary people—Americans—allowed their children to live in their own apartments when they were in their twenties, and Elise was over thirty years old.

When I had calmed down, I thought again about my male cousins. All but one of them had moved out of their parents' homes only when married. Elise was very brave and I admired her courage, but I was furious that she had to be a hero just to move out of her parents' home.

I did not have the courage—or the means—to move out without my parents' consent. I was still in school and financially dependent on them. Further, I didn't want to live alone, and all my women friends were either engaged or already married. Columbia provided no dorms for general studies students. As far as I could see, there was no way for me to get out of the house, at least not until I graduated and got a job. I had no plans past graduation, and, though it was only a year away, it seemed very far into the future.

Toward the end of the summer, Tom asked me to marry him, and I accepted happily. My vision of our lives together was idyllic. We would live in an apartment in New York City, furnished sparsely with white bookcases, a good FM radio and hi-fi set, and no television or Oriental rugs. Of course, I wanted children eventually, but they were in the future. In 1960 for a woman to consider whether or not she wanted children seemed the height of perversion, but one could put them off. I knew I wasn't ready to be a mother. I had just begun to feel comfortable with who I was, and marriage to Tom, I thought, would only enhance that process.

Once we had set the date we told my parents. They were decidedly not happy with my decision. I was too young. I hadn't graduated from college yet. But they saw that we were determined and did not argue. Only my grandmother was happy: I had my man. She immediately began to treat Tom like a king, cooking special foods for him and praising his intelligence. It made me uncomfortable to see her cater to him, but at least she seemed glad for me.

Telling my father and mother, however, was not the final step in getting approval for my marriage. My father had to tell his older brother, and we arranged to go to Uncle Alex's house. Tom was not invited. After dinner, approaching his brother just as Tom had approached him, my father told Uncle Alex of my decision to marry Tom. Uncle Alex asked my father about Tom's background and future plans. My father began by saying that Tom was an ordinary person, and, when I spoke up to offer some more positive information, I quickly sensed that I had broken one of their rules, and I stopped speaking. My father explained that Tom had a master's degree and intended to enter a Ph.D. program because he wanted to teach at a college. My cousin Emik, who had met Tom, broke in to tell his father how smart he thought Tom was, but he too retreated into silence when neither his father nor mine responded.

Uncle Alex, who was much more exacting then my father, thought it would be wiser if we waited until Tom got his degree and would be better able to provide for me. I hated what was going on and decided to speak for myself, rules or no rules. I said I didn't want to wait. We were in love and had decided to marry now. Probably realizing that I was not going to be quiet anymore, Uncle Alex broke the rules, too, and asked me how I would like being poor, the wife of a student. I said that it didn't make any difference to me as long as we could be together, that I didn't need much money. I wasn't interested in having a lot of things but in sharing a good relationship.

Since the rules were already broken, Aunty Goharik told me that she, too, had wanted to marry Uncle Alex before he went into the army, but her parents had decided that she should wait. She had waited, and everything had turned out fine. I quietly responded that it was nice that things had turned out well for her, but this was not the old country, and I was going to get married when I wanted to. I thought about both of my grandmothers, who had been married to men they didn't even know, and was outraged that my family was trying to make me follow rules that applied to another time and place. I was an American, and American couples did not allow their parents or relatives to tell them when to get married.

My uncle finally gave his approval, and then Aunty Goharik congratulated me. Although I felt that getting Uncle Alex's approval was merely going through a ritual, once I had it the marriage seemed very real.

I thought that telling Tom's mother our decision would be comparatively easy. She was shocked by the news, however, and in some ways less willing to accept it than my family had been. He was an only child, and she had lost her husband the previous year.

We hoped that in time she would accept our decision.

I began to think about what kind of wife I wanted to be. I knew for sure that I didn't want to be like the women in my family. Whether their husbands were authoritarian, like Uncle Ashot and Uncle George, or more willing to make decisions with their wives, like my father, the women all devoted themselves to their husbands and families. I wanted a life of my own, not one that would be lived through other people. Though we hadn't discussed the details and had no plan for making it work, Tom and I had agreed in principle that our marriage should be a fifty-fifty partnership. One imperative was clear: Since Tom was planning to earn a doctorate, and I would have to support us, we would not have children immediately.

I had been advised by a friend at Columbia that the safest method of birth control was a diaphragm, and I made an appointment with the gynecologist she had recommended. Since I was ignorant about the procedure for being fitted for the device, I was very nervous on my way to the doctor's office. By the time he came into the examining room my anxiety had made my blood pressure rise alarmingly. Dr. Kerman, a tall man in his thirties, patted my hand and asked me what was wrong. As I floundered for an answer, his nurse said, "You would be nervous too if you were waiting for your first internal." I looked at her gratefully and hoped she felt my thanks, since I was unable to speak. She took my hand, and I relaxed. I left the office with my diaphragm and my first conscious connection with another women through our shared experience. The nurse had been right. Dr. Kerman would never know what it felt like to have an internal examination.

When I got home I tried to talk to my mother about the diaphragm, but, because it was related to sex, the subject was impossible for us. She said she was busy and left the room. I had hoped to share with her some of my feelings about being examined, but I was as inept in my attempt to be "modern" about sexuality as she was closed to the subject.

My parents assumed that Tom and I would be married in the Armenian church in our old neighborhood. Tom had been raised as a Catholic, but he had fallen away from the church after high school and had no objection to complying with my parents' wishes. I was ambivalent about getting married in the Holy Cross Armenian Apostolic Church, though I never seriously considered doing anything else. On the one hand, I liked the continuity of being married in the same church as my parents and where my brother and I and most of my cousins had been christened. On the other hand, my old feelings about the church that had so incontrovertibly defined my difference were still with me. I had long ceased to look to religion to fulfill any of my needs—spiritual or social. When I was a freshman at Alfred I had learned the word *agnostic* and had adopted that label for my own attitude toward God. The next year I crossed the line and became an atheist. Since I had not attended any church other than the one in the city, I had no desire to pick a church out of a phone book and be married by a stranger. I did decide to talk to the priest about shortening the wedding ceremony, however, which I knew could last for more than an hour.

I had not spoken to a priest since I was a little girl, when *Der Hayr* used to occasionally come to our house for dinner after church, and I was not looking forward to the meeting that Tom and I were required to have with him before the wedding. I listened as he told me that I would have to take communion the day before the wedding to insure my purity before taking the holy sacrament of marriage. Since Tom was not a member of our church, he had no such obligation, though *Der Hayr* said he hoped that Tom would see his priest. I was outraged at the assumption that I was impure, but I seemed to have no choice other than going through the ritual. He reminded me that I must not eat before communion, and I nodded my head. When he was finished I asked him if it was possible to keep the ceremony down to a half an hour, and he assured me he would do what he could.

I awoke the day before the wedding excited, nervous, and hungry. My mother and grandmother were busy cooking for the dinner after the rehearsal. The smells in the kitchen whetted my appetite, and I decided to eat. My mother reminded me that I was supposed to fast, but I said I was hungry and didn't believe in any of that stuff anyway. Surprisingly, neither she nor my grandmother seemed to mind as I ate a hearty breakfast. Later that day when I met the priest for communion he asked me if I had eaten, and I heard myself saying "yes." I had meant to lie, but when the time came I realized that I had taken some pleasure in defying *Der Hayr*. I could not have communion. I guessed Tom would have to accept me in an impure state.

That night, when all the guests had left the house, Tom and I sat around the dining room table with my parents and my grandmother having a last cup of coffee. My mother left the room for a moment and came back with a packet of small papers tied with a

pink ribbon. She handed them to Tom. When he looked at the packet in confusion, she informed him that they were all my doctor bills,
from my infancy to the present. She wanted him to know that they
had taken very good care of me and that she expected him to do
the same. I was mortified.

The morning of the wedding was like a dream. My godmother,
an artist with a needle, had made my gown, silk satin with a silk
brocade overskirt. The sleeves were long, tight, and buttoned at the
wrist with eight tiny satin covered buttons. The straight skirt reached
to my ankles in the front and lengthened into a train in the back.
The whole process of making this gown had been pure joy. We had
gone "shopping" for the gown at the best stores in New York, and
when we had found the one I liked Ana carefully studied how it
was constructed while the saleswoman was out of the dressing
room. The next Sunday we went to the Lower East Side to buy
material. As I stood in the gown that hugged my body perfectly,
I felt a flood of warmth for my godmother whose skill had produced
an exact copy of the original we had seen at Bonwit Tellers. For the
first time in my life I was really satisfied with how I looked.

When we reached the church it was crowded, and I took my
father's arm for the walk down the aisle. As we approached the altar and Tom stepped forward to receive me, the image of being
handed from one man to another flashed across my mind. For a split
second I wanted to kick off my shoes, four-inch spiked heels, and
run out of the church. But, as I stepped toward Tom, the feeling
disappeared. The ceremony was as unintelligible to me as the services had been to me as a child. I had decided to get married in this
church, but, as the service dragged on endlessly, I wondered again
why Armenians had to be so old-fashioned. My parents had been
married at this very altar, but I felt nothing. My feet hurt, and I was
so thirsty that when the glass of wine that the wedding party was
to share was handed to me I almost finished it off. Finally it was
over, and Tom and I walked back down the aisle as man and wife.

Chapter 8

It felt wonderful to return from our honeymoon to our little apartment. Because we had been unable to find an affordable apartment in a nice neighborhood in the city, we looked north of my old neighborhood in Riverdale. Our apartment was only a one-room efficiency, but it was large and had lots of windows. We painted the walls off-white and Tom put stripping on one wall to hold the teak shelves we had bought from the Door Store in the Village. We slept on a modern couch we'd found on sale. I varnished the top of the round pine kitchen table we had bought at an unfinished furniture store and painted the legs and the four-ladder back chairs matte black. Our hi-fi, records, and more books were stored in a bookcase in the hall. I was even pleased with the way the large Oriental rug, a gift from the family business, looked in our sparsely furnished apartment. I had one more semester at Columbia to finish my B.A. Tom continued teaching high school and applied to graduate schools for the next year.

Although Tom and I had talked about equality in our relationship before our marriage, it had never occurred to me that such an arrangement would mean that he would do housework. Before my marriage I had been interested neither in cooking nor cleaning. In my mind both activities were identified with the kind of devotion to husband and children that I rejected. Now that I had my own apartment, however, cleaning did not seem so bad, and I was surprised by how much I enjoyed preparing food. My mother and Aunty Ars were delighted by my new interest and taught me the basics of Armenian cooking. As I made each new dish, I was anxious for Tom's reaction but not crushed when he complained, as he often did, that the food was too spicy. I loved to eat, and I liked my own creations.

When the second semester began at Columbia, I changed my last name on my records. It sounded so strange to me—Arlene Voski O'Brien—but I guessed I'd get used to it. It was impossible, however, to accept "Mrs. O'Brien." I was glad no one had occasion to call me that. It always made me think of Tom's mother. But since I did have an Irish last name, I wanted to know something about Irish culture beyond the stereotypes I had learned as a child. I needed something more substantial than *Father Flannigan's Boy's Town* and *The Bells of St. Mary's*. I decided to do my senior seminar paper on the tracery in Irish illuminated manuscripts of the seventh and eighth centuries. My work on this paper was the extent of my interest in Irish culture at the time. Studying the art and learning that Irish monks of that period had been highly respected throughout Europe had been enough to counteract the image of dirty, drinking Irish who had too many children.

While my new life as a married woman did not exactly fit my idyllic image, after the first month of marriage I was reasonably satisfied. I would have preferred it if Tom's mother had not called every night at seven. I tried to remember not to answer the phone when it rang at that hour because she always asked for Tom without making even the slightest pretense of saying a few words to me. I was also bothered that he talked to her for what seemed like forever and never mentioned anything about me. I wanted him to tell her not to be so rude to me, but I didn't feel that I had the right to complain to either of them. Nevertheless, I was absolutely delighted to have my own home.

At the beginning of February I thought I was getting the flu. I was tired all the time and woke up nauseated. When I told the doctor my symptoms, he replied that I could be pregnant. I thought that was the most ridiculous thing I had ever heard. I had used my diaphragm faithfully. I was sure I had a stomach flu, but, when I didn't get better and I missed a period, I began to worry. I made an appointment with Dr. Kerman, despite the fact that Tom belonged to a health maintenance group where I could see a gynecologist for free. I hated going to that group. It felt like a clinic, a place for poor people. I preferred Dr. Kerman.

After he examined me and took a urine sample, he said it was too early to be sure, but he thought I could very well be pregnant. I made an appointment for the next week—Saint Patrick's Day. This time I wanted Tom to come with me. The news was devastating. I was pregnant. As I held back my tears, Dr. Kerman patted me on the shoulder and said it would work out fine. Even though we had not planned a baby so soon, he was sure that once we got used to the idea we would be very happy. Tom was shocked but said he also felt proud and, like Dr. Kerman, was also sure everything would be fine.

For the next few weeks I battled nausea and exhaustion and tried to finish my courses. Once school was over and I had graduated, however, I felt worse. It seemed to me that this pregnancy was the worst thing that could have happened to me. I felt as if my life were over and in a way I knew that the life I had envisioned for myself indeeed was gone. Now I would not be a scholar but a mother. I had heard of abortions but had no idea how to go about getting one. Abortion was for poor women and Negro women. They probably knew how to get one, but it was not something anyone like me did. I wished I would fall down a flight of stairs. Women in the movies always lost their babies after such a fall. Not having the courage to throw myself down the stairs, I tried another method. For some reason I thought hot baths might bring on early labor, and for the rest of my pregnancy I scalded myself in the hottest water I could stand.

I knew that I should get a job. We needed the money, particularly with the baby coming, but I had neither energy nor motivation to look for work. Tom had a summer job at a detention center for delinquents and worked twelve-hour shifts. While he was gone I spent most of the time sitting in the apartment and staring at the walls. I didn't even turn on the radio or play a record. I didn't want to see anyone, and I couldn't read. I just sat and waited for the baby that had already changed my life.

Tom's life, on the other hand, seemed not to have changed very much at all. Before my pregnancy we had decided that he would go to graduate school as soon as possible. Now that I was going to have a baby in late October or early November, he would have to wait to start in the spring instead of the fall. His plans were delayed but not changed. I wanted to move to get away from his mother. Mrs. O'Brien's refusal to accept my existence and her nightly phone calls were driving me crazy. I was also having my usual trouble with my family's demands. With regard to my responsibilities to the extended family, it seemed as if I hadn't left home at all. Every weekend there was some family event I was expected to attend. If it wasn't a cousin's birthday or an aunt's and uncle's anniversary, it was a relative visiting from another state or just someone who, my mother said, wanted to see me. As always, my mother could not understand how I could think of disappointing my relatives. The only difference now that I was married was that I now had the acceptable excuse of having to visit Tom's mother and aunt, but that was not a better prospect than being with my own family.

Tom was offered a scholarship at the University of Massachusetts, and, when we visited the quaint New England town where it was located, I fell in love. Amherst was the kind of American town I had pictured as being the "real thing." Tom liked it too and was pleased with the faculty in the political science department. He accepted their offer, and we were put on the waiting list for married student housing.

By September, with our plans for moving settled and Tom working regular hours and at home more, I began to come out of my depression. I thought about the baby a little and realized that I knew nothing about taking care of an infant and even less about the birth process. My doctor offered no information, and I was too ignorant to formulate any decent questions. I guessed I would learn about it all when the time came.

My parents had been surprised that I had gotten pregnant so soon, but my mother seemed happy to be having a grandchild. My father treated me as an invalid, not allowing me to carry anything heavier than my pocketbook. While great attention was paid to my physical being, no one seemed to notice how I felt, and I was relieved. To admit that this pregnancy had sent me into a deep depression would be to admit to decidedly unnatural feelings. Indeed, I was suspicious that there was something wrong with me because I was not elated. I worked very hard to convince myself that I really wanted the baby after all, and, by the time I had reached the end of my pregnancy, I was looking forward to its birth.

Tom and I began to discuss names. The thought of giving my baby an Armenian name had never crossed my mind, but I thought it would be nice to honor tradition in some way. We decided that the baby's middle name would be Christopher, a translation of Khrosrov, my father's father's name. His first name would be Neal.

On the morning of October 31, 1961, I was awakened by a flood of water gushing out from between my legs. I ran to the bathtub and wondered if my hot baths had worked. Tom was talking to the doctor who said that there was nothing to worry about. My "water had broken," and I would probably go into labor soon. He would meet us at the hospital. Labor didn't seem very bad at first. The contractions were mild, and I could read the Russian novel by Turgenev that I had brought with me, *Fathers and Sons*. The nurses were surprised by what I was reading. They said I was the only woman in maternity who had come without Dr. Spock's *Baby and Child Care*. Well, I thought, I guess I'm a different kind of mother.

Eight hours later I was in what the nurses called "hard labor." I had been given something for the pain, but the drug affected my ability to speak more than the agony in my abdomen. I was wheeled into the labor room, which looked like a dungeon from the adult-sized crib they had put me into. As the pain wracked my body, I felt the hand of the nurse on my abdomen, and I heard her tell the other nurse that she didn't know why I was making such a fuss. I wasn't having a contraction. I wanted to scream that it wasn't her body, but I had lost all power of speech and managed to utter only an incomprehensible murmur.

An eternity later my son was born. The nurses handed me a swaddled bundle with large dark eyes, but I wanted only to go to sleep. I waited for them to take him away.

I stayed in the hospital for the usual six days and learned how to feed and burp Neal. I had not considered nursing. I thought it was old-fashioned, and my doctor agreed. With a bottle, he said, you always knew exactly what and how much the baby was getting—a decided improvement over the breast.

We had decided to go to my parents' house so my mother could help with Neal until I felt strong enough to care for him myself. The first few days we were there many of my relatives came to see the baby. He was a beautiful baby, I thought, and I was proud to show him off. One night after we ate and all the women were in the kitchen cleaning up, Aunty Ars looked at me and said, "So, now you know what we all went through for you. Now you are a woman." I didn't really know what she meant. But I did know that no matter how I, as an individual, felt about my experience I was now part of a group that thought it knew my feelings. I didn't ask her whether she meant the pregnancy, the birth, the caretaking that babies required, or all of those things. My ambivalence about being part of the group was so great that I had no desire to talk about it. If she knew that pregnancy had touched off a depression, would she still include me in the group, or could it be that experiencing that depression might be part of what it meant to be a woman? I felt sure, however, that my feelings at the moment were not normal. Having babies and caring for them was natural for a woman. I had not only not wanted this baby, but now that he was born I hadn't the faintest idea of how to care for him. Maybe, I thought, I should read Dr. Spock. I resolved to get the book as soon as I got home.

My mother, on the other hand, handled Neal with authority. She seemed totally calm giving him his first bath and cutting his tiny nails. I wondered whether I would ever feel such confidence. After two weeks I decided that it was time to go home. I could no longer bear the humiliation of being terrified of caring for my own child.

The first morning we were home I felt Tom's reluctance to go to work. I asked him if he was scared to leave Neal with me. He admitted he was. So was I, although twenty-four hours later I felt like an old hand; it was exciting to be learning so much so fast. Within a few days I was so exhausted, however, that I felt as if I were walking under water. No matter what we did, Neal cried all night, his surprisingly loud voice resounding through the small apartment. Within a few weeks he did sleep for a few hours a night, and I began to pack for our move. Had I not been so tired, I would have felt more—both excitement and fear. As it was, I barely managed to get our belongings into boxes.

Chapter 9

We arrived in Amherst in January, 1962, and moved into the university's married student housing, a sprawling two-story complex. Our two-room apartment offered a little more space than our New York efficiency, but here there was the added advantage of a yard where I could set out Neal's carriage in nice weather, and in the spring I would be able to cook on a grill. While it had not been easy to leave the familiarity of New York City, I was glad to be a four-hour drive from my family and Tom's mother.

I had gotten a part-time job at the library shelving books. It was important to me that I had a job. Not only did my salary help to support us, but I had a place to go regularly where I did some work I thought was useful. While shelving and checking out books was not what I would have considered a "real" job, it did help me to keep at least a small part of my identity from being subsumed in motherhood.

Tom and I had arranged our schedules so that he could be at home with Neal when I was at work. I felt slightly guilty because I looked forward to those days when I worked, but I reasoned with myself that I hadn't left Neal with strangers. Tom was, after all, Neal's father. What could be wrong with him spending a few hours a week with his son? Besides, we really did need the money.

After a few months, however, my job in the library felt no different from cleaning and taking care of Neal. The books, like Neal's clothes and toys and Tom's papers and books, were taken off the shelves and had to be put away, and there was always someone at the desk wanting attention.

The rest of my life was also not living up to my hopes. When we moved into married student housing, I had looked forward to meeting other young mothers who might become my friends. I was anxious to know if any other women had ambivalent feelings about motherhood, although I never expected to tell anyone the depth of my pain during my pregnancy or that even now I still often wished I had not had a baby. I had met some mothers of young children—the wives of other students—in the common yard behind our apartments and gladly accepted an invitation to one of their weekly "coffee klatches." But the talk consisted of their children's development, and I was quickly bored with details of how Johnny had begun to crawl and Sarah had started to feed herself. I was upset, too, that Neal's development did not seem as rapid as the descriptions of infants his age. I was relieved when they seemed to be running out of toddler achievements for the week, but the next topic of conversation, the various tactics they used to get husbands to help with housework, was not much better. Worse yet, most of the evening was devoted to an animated discussion of what had happened on the soap operas that week. As I listened to the arguments about their favorite characters, I thought about my grandmother. When our family finally got a television in the early 1950s (because my mother said she didn't want me going to someone else's house to watch it), I always knew where my grandmother would be when I came home for lunch—watching "The Guiding Light" and "Search for Tomorrow." I didn't have any problems with my grandmother's devotion to her programs. She was old and, as far as I could see, didn't have any kind of life of her own. These women, on the other hand, were my age or younger and had families and a future ahead of them. It was clear to me that I would find no friends among this group of women, and I vowed that I would never become like them.

To my great surprise, I was also lonely for my family sometimes. We were unable to go home that first Easter, and, as the holiday approached, I was surprised at how much I missed our Easter rituals. I decided to color eggs, but it seemed a futile effort. I could not get the proper bread nor fresh dill—absolute necessities for the beginning of an Easter dinner. An egg fight between Tom and me would also be a poor substitute for a table full of people battling with the eggs they had carefully chosen from the large bowl on the table. I thought again of my grandmother, who had lamented that I would be all alone in Massachusetts. I had tried to assure her that I had my husband and child and was sure to make friends quickly, but I knew that my grandmother would not be comforted by any of my associations with people who were not blood relations. I had thought that the fact that I was going away not alone but with my husband would reassure her, but it seemed that being with one's man was not always enough.

On the morning of Good Friday I was sitting at the kitchen table wondering whether my grandmother had made stuffed mussels or artichokes when the doorbell rang. I went to the door to find the mailman, who was holding a large box at arm's length. I took the box, which had a strong odor and was surrounded by little flying insects, and went into the yard to open it. It was from my grandmother—a box of very rancid stuffed mussels. As I threw the box into the garbage, I thought that maybe my grandmother had been right. We were, in a very real sense, alone. Yet I was touched that she had sent the *media* even if they had gone bad.

Most disturbing of all, my relationship with Tom was alarmingly distant. He was often preoccupied and sometimes admitted to being depressed, although he never knew what was bothering him. I ached for the closeness we had had before we were married. Then we had often talked into the night. Now we barely talked at all about little things, and I had not ventured to say anything to him about my concern that Neal's development seemed slower than it ought to be.

I tried to tell myself that real life was not like the movies, that no one's love could remain as it was before marriage. But the vision I had had of our lives together was so different from the reality I was living that, toward the end of our first spring in Amherst, I, too, felt depressed. Some mornings I woke up feeling so awful that I spent the first hour of my day crying. I began to wonder if I really had needed the psychiatrist I had wanted to see when I was in college.

Tom did little to reassure me that he cared or that things would get better. One night I tried to articulate how badly I was feeling, that I felt invisible to him and terribly alone. He said little until he calmly suggested that we might consider a divorce. I was terrified. I knew that the only recourse I would have without Tom would be to live with my parents. That prospect was unacceptable. I responded, not so calmly, that we had a baby in the next room and that we had to think of him. Tom said he guessed I was right.

After that night I focused primarily on changing what I could about our lives. Tom did not raise the subject of a separation again, and I suppressed my pain.

Just as I began to think about looking for another job, I got a call from the art department, where I had applied for a job before we moved to Amherst. They were now looking for a departmental assistant. In June I took the job and began to mount and file slides. I would also help to grade papers from the large introductory course when classes began in September. The job also meant a small raise and half an office.

While I was able to perform my duties adequately, working in the art department brought back many of the feelings of inadequacy I had had at Columbia. Something was definitely lacking in my response to art. Like the faculty at Columbia, the professors I worked for seemed to have no interest in the cultural context of the work. The excitement I had experienced over Dr. Klitzke's lectures seemed a fantasy. I guessed that I had made another mistake. Art history was not really my field. It didn't seem to matter much now anyway. Tom would be the scholar, and I would do what I could to help him.

I thought I might feel better if we moved. I was anxious to get away from my neighbors. Although I never attended another "coffee klatch," still I met those women in the yard, and their reports about the growth of their infants and toddlers became more upsetting as Neal, who would be seven months old by the end of the semester, seemed to lag further and further behind. Our pediatrician assured me that Neal was fine, but I was worried by the comparisons to other children his age.

I also thought it would be important to move for Tom's sake. I hoped he would be less distant if our living space were more comfortable. Because our apartment had only two rooms it was hard for Tom to work at home when he had to be there. I suggested that we look for a bigger place to live, and Tom agreed that it would be a good idea to move. We decided to look for a place in the towns around Amherst where the rents were cheaper, and we soon found a lovely light-filled, four-room apartment in an old house in Leverett. We were only fifteen minutes from Amherst, but it seemed to me that we had moved to the country. The first night in our new home I looked out of the window and was startled by the darkness. Yet I loved our new apartment. Neal had his own room, Tom had room for a study in the large entrance hall, and I had a huge kitchen. Although Tom and I had never talked about his work before, I now hoped he would tell me a little about school. What were his courses about? Were the professors like any of the ones we knew at Alfred?

But Tom never talked about graduate school, and I still had no idea what political science was, since, as far as I knew, there were neither women on the faculty nor any female graduate students in the Ph.D. program. The way I thought I could help Tom with his work was to insure that he had as much time as possible to focus on his studies. I had never really expected him to do any house-work, shopping, or cooking, but he did stay home with Neal while I was at work. I arranged with the art department to bring home as much work as possible so that Tom only had to stay with Neal a few hours a week.

I hoped, too, that Tom would bring home some of the friends he had made in the department now that we had a larger apart-ment. Though both of us liked one of the couples we had met in the apartments, and I knew some people I liked from the library and the art department, our real friends, I thought, should be Tom's colleagues. I urged him to invite people over, but our social life over the next year was not very satisfying. The men Tom befriended were, for the most part, uninteresting to me. They talked to each other mainly about courses they were taking and books they were reading. Sometimes the women listened to the men, and other times we talked among ourselves. Both alternatives were difficult. If we listened to the men I usually had no idea what they were talking about, and I assumed the other women were equally ignorant since none participated. Trying to make conversation among ourselves, however, was not much better. Although we were around the same age, mid- to late twenties, and we all had college degrees, we found we had no shared interests. Even discussions of babies were not possible, since I was the only mother in the group. A few of the women complained bitterly about the scarcity of professional jobs in Amherst and their anger at having to do clerical work. I won-dered what kind of work they would have done if they didn't have to be in Amherst but never asked about that because I thought I ought to know. As for myself, I had no idea what I would have been doing had I not had Neal. One night, at someone's else's house, one of the women articulated what I had begun to sense. She resent-ed being forced into a social situation with the wives. We had noth-ing in common besides being married to the men in the political sci-ence department. On the one hand, I was outraged by her rudeness and assumed that her marriage was on the rocks. But I also knew that she was right. Not only did we not have anything in common, we didn't seem to like each other very much. When I told Tom what had happened, however, I expressed only my anger at her and compassion for her husband, who obviously had a bitch for a wife. Although I was not happy with our social life, I continued to want to have our "friends" over for dinner. Nothing seemed to satisfy me as much as cooking a beautiful meal, and I used all my skills to produce meals that were delicious and cheap. I tried to talk to some of the women about cooking, but they were not interested. For them cooking was only another of the household duties they had to perform.

I wondered if their attitudes toward food had something to do with their backgrounds. All of the people we knew in Amherst were either Irish or "American." I missed our friends from the city and I longed for people who were more like me. To my surprise, the people I missed most were Jews. They would certainly appreciate my cooking more than the people we had over for dinner. I thought there must be some people in Tom's department who were Jewish. Why hadn't Tom befriended them? Since we had always liked the same people when we were in college, I guessed that Tom had made the right choices. I sometimes wondered, though, who our friends would be if I had made the choices.

Eventually, I did become friendly with a few women, although I did not feel they were good friends. We went frequently to auctions, a new activity for me. I allowed myself only two dollars for the evening, and it was great fun to see what I could get. In the early 1960s pine was in, and oak was out, so I was able to get a wonderful solid oak lady's desk without going over my limit.

Toward the end of our first year in Amherst we had an invitation to dinner from a couple I had met only briefly. Roger and Elaine were from Boston, and I had heard that Elaine had a professional position in the biology department at Smith College. She was the only wife who was working in her field and enjoying her job, and I was intimidated by that fact alone. When we got to their apartment, however, I felt immediately at ease. Elaine had prepared beautiful appetizers, and I could tell by the smell wafting into the living room from the kitchen that the dinner would probably be equally good. When Elaine told me she was Italian, I felt relieved. Surrounded by Irish and Americans I longed to be with someone who was more like me, someone who at least knew something about good food and came from a home where parents or grandparents had also come from the other side.

Very soon we became friends as couples, and to my delight Elaine and I began to develop our own relationship. I often spent the afternoon with Elaine talking about our childhoods, her job, and cooking.

Yet, although she was my closest friend in Amherst, I did not talk to Elaine about my relationship with Tom or my concerns for Neal, who at a year and a half had not begun to walk and made no sign of speaking. When I asked the pediatrician if he was all right, she responded that I should be patient. He was fine. Still I could not help but worry. He just didn't seem like other children.

I did not talk about Neal to Tom either. Our relationship had greatly improved from what it was during our first few months in Amherst, but it still fell far short of what I wanted. After only two years of marriage I could only vaguely remember what I had felt for him when we were dating. Most of the time I was able to keep from thinking about it. Sometimes, though, when I least expected it—when I was making the bed or folding the laundry—I would feel the loss of how good I had felt about myself when we were together and the vision we had of sharing our lives through intellectual work. I could not afford to give expression to those feelings. There was, after all, nothing I could do to recapture what we had lost. And if I didn't think about it life was not too bad. Tom sometimes seemed to be in another world, and my response to his absence was silent withdrawal. Weeks could go by when we hardly spoke to each other unless we were with people, but usually we were more friendly. I hoped that, when he finished school and was not under financial and academic pressure, he would be more available. I certainly did not want to burden him with my fears about Neal. I was also afraid that talking about my concerns would make them real. After all, the doctor said that Neal was fine.

In the spring of 1963, when Neal was a year and a half, we decided we would try to have another baby. It was unthinkable then to have only one child. It seemed clear to me, and Tom agreed, that parents got too attached to an only child, and when the child became an adult he would be burdened by having to bear responsibility for his parents by himself. It was important, too, for a child to learn to share with a sibling. There was no question that we would have two children, and I was anxious to have the second one soon so that I could be finished with taking care of little children as soon as possible. Tom had the promise of a part-time teaching job the next year, and we thought we could get along on his salary after the baby was born.

It seemed like the right time in other ways as well. I felt that another baby might help Neal, that a brother or sister might spur his growth. For one thing, a baby in the house might help him with his fear of children, which had begun when he was six months old and had intensified over the next year. I also wanted to have the baby before we left Amherst. Tom would be ready to go on the job market at the end of the next academic year, and we would have to move. We decided not to move back to New York City. We agreed that the distance between us and our families had been a good thing.

After a year of living in Massachusetts my relationship with my parents, and even Tom's mother, had improved immeasurably. We went to visit them on most holidays and for long weekends during the summer. They also made occasional trips to see us. Since we had moved Tom's mother rarely called, and I was spared the nightly reminder of her dislike for me. I had also escaped conflict with my mother over my obligations to the family. Now I visited my parents and relatives, not so much out of a sense of duty as from genuine desire.

By July I knew that I was pregnant. The difference from the last time was startling. I had none of the nausea and exhaustion which had plagued me when I was pregnant with Neal, and, instead of being depressed, I was elated. I felt sure that we had made the right decision, and I didn't even mind when my usually slim body grew to accommodate the new baby.

While my life at this time was almost entirely focused on Tom, Neal, and the life we were building, some events in the outside world did catch my attention. I was enchanted by John F. Kennedy, who, it seemed to me, brought a vitality to the White House that made even someone like me interested in politics. The youthfulness of the president and his wife was brought home to me because their son John had been born when Neal had. Tom's initial enthusiasm about Kennedy, on the other hand, had cooled. He said the president was much more conservative than he had seemed when he was first elected, but I didn't know what he was talking about and, as usual, didn't pursue a discussion. I was still fond of the president. He effectively ended the Cuban missile crisis, which had terrified me. I also believed that he was really committed to ending segregation in the South.

I followed reports of the preparations for the March on Washington for Civil Rights and was glad that our public radio station was going to have live coverage. When I woke up on the morning of August 28, 1963, I turned on the radio and began to prepare Neal's breakfast. Tom was going to be in the library all day, and I had planned to catch up on some housework. For most of the morning the radio was a backdrop to my dusting and vacuuming, but by lunchtime I found that I could not leave it. I spent most of the afternoon on the edge of tears, and when Martin Luther King, Jr., made his speech I broke down. Yet that night as Tom and I watched the television coverage of the march, I did not tell Tom how I had felt. I was confused and embarrassed by my response, since he seemed calm but interested. All day long I had thought about the thousands of people who had joined the march. The reports repeatedly pointed out that many of the marchers were white. Who were they, I wondered. How did they get there? Would I have been able to go had I not been married and a mother?

I decided that I had to do something to further the cause, though I had no idea what it could be, and I discussed my feelings with Tom. He also thought that segregation was wrong and that the March on Washington had been a call for justice, but he neither felt compelled to get involved nor did he have any suggestions for me. I finally came up with the idea of finding a local chapter of the National Association for the Advancement of Colored People. The next morning I sat at the phone for a long time with the number of the closest NAACP chapter in Springfield in my hand. I hesitated to dial it. What would I say? What did I have to offer? The only organization I had ever been in was my sorority. The voice that answered my call politely told me that there was nothing I could do at the moment. I should call back in a few weeks; then there might be some way I could help.

I was proud of myself for having made the call and both disappointed and relieved that there was nothing for me to do. Springfield, though it was only a half an hour's drive from Amherst, might as well have been in another state for as much as I knew about it. I had been there only once, to pick up my cousin Emik from the train station, and was not attracted to the old and very run—down city. I also assumed that most of the members of the NAACP would be Negroes, and I was not anxious to be in a group in which I would be one of only a few whites.

Though I did not call the NAACP back in a few weeks as the man had suggested, my interest in civil rights intensified. For the first time in my life I began to read Tom's *New York Times*, and I watched the TV news for reports of sit-ins and other demonstrations. No one around me seemed to share my interest. The March on Washington had not made a dramatic impression on anyone else I knew.

In November, 1963, the world broke in on my life again. We were expecting friends from New York for the weekend, and I was taking a shower while Neal was napping. I was startled by someone screaming at me through the bathroom door. Thinking that something had happened to Neal, I jumped out of the tub, scrambled into my robe, and opened the bathroom door to find my neighbor pacing the living room floor. She told me that the president had been shot in Dallas. Like everyone else, we sat in front of the television for the next four days watching the incredible events. Even Tom seemed visibly moved. As I listened to Lyndon Johnson's drawl, I wondered what would happen to the Negroes' struggle with a Southerner in the White House. By the spring, however, it seemed clear that Johnson would continue in Kennedy's direction on civil rights and that the country was going to be all right.

On the night of March 13, 1964, I heard a lecture that disturbed me even more than the assassination. Tom, who had serious questions about the Warren Commission's verdict that Lee Harvey Oswald had acted alone, wanted to go to hear Mark Lane, a critic of the Commission. Because I was already three days past my due date, I decided to go along just in case I went into labor. As I listened to the facts that Lane had uncovered and heard his allegation that the Warren Commission had not investigated as thoroughly as it might have, I got very interested. I was really alarmed, however, when Lane said that the book he had written on the subject had been published in thirteen countries but that he could not find a publisher in the United States. I had always believed we had freedom of the press, but what if Lane were speaking the truth? After the lecture I asked Tom what he thought, since he seemed to understand much more about the world than I. He also seemed upset. He though Lane had made some good points.

Yet, over the next two days, Mark Lane's allegations were not my main concern. My baby was eight days late. As a distraction, Tom and I decided to go out to dinner, but when we finished eating I felt a slight twinge and told Tom that I might be in labor. By the time we got home the contractions, though slight, had become quite regular, and I knew it was time to go to the hospital. We changed the linen on our bed for our neighbors, who had agreed to stay with Neal, and drove to the hospital in Greenfield, about half an hour away. When we got there Tom seemed so relieved that

I asked him what was going on. He told me that he had been afraid our car (my father had given us his 1950 Oldsmobile when he bought a new one) would break down on the way. Now that we were at the hospital he could relax. During the ride to Greenfield I had begun to think about labor, and when we had walked through the doors I had been overcome with fear about the delivery. Tom's only concern had been getting me there. We really were in different worlds.

I hadn't thought much about the delivery during my pregnancy, but when we got to the hospital, I remembered Dr. Kerman's warning that deliveries would always be hard for me because my pelvis was narrow. The nurse took me to the labor room, where two other women were moaning through their contractions. I knew I would be sharing their agony in a very short while, and when the doctor came I was ready for any painkiller he had to offer, though my contractions were merely a slight discomfort. He said he thought the baby would be born in less than an hour, and I thought to myself that, despite his Harvard degree, he must be a quack. Forty-three minutes later I heard him say, "It's a girl," and I looked up to see my daughter.

We hadn't chosen a name for this baby, so the next day I poured over books of names. Tom suggested Jenny, but I thought it sounded too Irish. My interest in Irish culture and Irish people had been more than fulfilled after living in Amherst for two years, where everyone, it seemed, was Irish. It was enough that my daughter's last name would be O'Brien. I wanted something unusual for her first name. When I came across the name Hannah it seemed to fit my baby, whose hair and eyes were very dark. Hannah was an Old Testament name and a good balance for O'Brien. Tom also seemed to like it well enough.

I felt wonderful. I had wanted a girl. My pregnancy and even the delivery had been remarkably easy. I wondered what had happened to my narrow pelvis. Though I was preoccupied with Hannah, I continued to think about what Mark Lane had said and told my hospital roommates about the lecture. They looked at me in disbelief and changed the subject. The next day I heard that the nurses were gossiping about the woman in room 305 who talked more about a man named Mark Lane than about her baby. I smiled when I heard what was being said about me. Once again, though I did have the book at home this time, I had come to the maternity ward without the requisite Dr. Spock.

The standard stay in this hospital after delivery was three days, and I was anxious to get home. My mother had come to help. It was the first time she had left my father since the polio scare had sent us to Rhode Island for the summers when I was ten and eleven years old. I was glad she was there to take care of Neal and cook for Tom. I laughed when she told me she had insisted that he do something about the doors, which had no locks on them. I tried to reassure her, as he had, that nothing ever happened in Leverett— that no one had locks on their doors, but she was not convinced. Tom had put a lock on the door, and she used it all the time; she said she hoped I would too. I was pleased she was there when I got home from the hospital. She was a great help with Neal and the cooking, and I actually enjoyed being with her. She stayed until the next weekend, when my father came to see us and to take her home. I was glad she had come but also happy when she left. I wanted the four of us to have some time alone. Hannah was a very pleasant, calm baby, and Neal seemed to be taking some interest in her. At least he wasn't afraid of her.

A week after my mother left I developed lower back pain. Recognizing the symptoms of a bladder infection, I called the doctor for an appointment. He listened to my symptoms and said I should try to rest and call him back in a few days. I couldn't understand why he didn't want to see me as soon as possible; my symptoms seemed clear to me. He patiently explained that I was probably experiencing some postpartum depression. I was angry at his assumption about my emotional state. I knew what depression was, and I didn't have it. I had a bladder infection. But he said to call him in a few days. Two days later my symptoms were worse. When I called the office and demanded an appointment the next day, the nurse reluctantly agreed. After examining me, he said that I had a bladder infection but made no reference to his earlier diagnosis. I could only mutter, "I told you so two days ago," but he didn't seem to hear me.

While I was there I thought it would be a good idea to be re-fitted for a diaphragm. The doctor said he would talk about it in his office. As I dressed, I wondered if he were against birth control, but, when I sat down in the chair opposite his huge mahogany desk, he asked if I didn't think that the diaphragm was an awkward method. I agreed that it wasn't the best, but one thing I did not want was another baby. Despite its earlier failure, I still believed the diaphragm was the safest method of birth control, and I was mainly interested in safety. He told me I was wrong. There was a method that was ninety-nine percent effective—the new birth control pill. I questioned him about possible side effects, but he assured me that the pill was fully tested. Women in Puerto Rico had taken it for six years without any complications. Without a thought about the safety of these women, I gladly took the prescription he handed me.

Job prospects in the spring of 1964 were not very promising. Although few of Tom's classmates had found work in academia, a few weeks after Hannah was born, Tom was offered a job by the University of Wisconsin. He would be teaching at two of the university's centers—Manitowoc and Sheboygan. I knew nothing about Wisconsin, but Tom said the state had had a very progressive past. I looked for the two towns on the map and was glad to see that they were both on Lake Michigan. At least we would be near a large body of water, and I heard from some friends that the area around the lake was very beautiful. Since Tom had not received any other offers, we decided to try the Midwest. I was glad that we were a healthy distance from New York and that Roger and Elaine had also decided to take the offer Roger had gotten from the university center in Green Bay, only a short drive up the lake from Manitowoc. Yet I was mainly relieved that Tom had gotten a job and that the pay was decent. At last we would have a little money.

Chapter 10

*T*om and I were both anxious to see what Wisconsin was like, and, as soon as Hannah was old enough to be left with my parents, we planned a trip west to find a place to live. Roger and Elaine decided to go with us. On the long drive through seemingly endless cornfields, Roger and Tom argued about a war in a place called Vietnam, while Elaine and I listened. I knew very little about the war, although Tom had talked before about his anger at our government's involvement. I had little interest in the small country that was somewhere in Indochina. I was preoccupied with what our new home would be like.

Roger and Elaine dropped us off at the one hotel in Manitowoc late that night and went on to Green Bay. The next morning, as Tom and I ate breakfast and looked through the local paper for apartments, I began to worry about what life was going to be like in this little city so far away from the East Coast. Only two apartments were listed in the paper, and neither was very appealing. We tried the few realtors in town, but none carried rentals. We had no choice but to rent one of the two apartments we had seen that morning.

After making arrangements with our new landlord, we drove around Manitowoc to get a better sense of the town. Our first stop was the center, the single building that composed the entire school in which Tom would be teaching. From there we drove downtown again, hoping to improve our negative impressions of the morning. We saw two movie theaters, a few clothing stores, a drugstore, and two very large hardware stores. The most distinctive aspect of downtown was the painting of two huge bottles of Old Milwaukee beer on the grain elevators at the end of the main street. I could hardly believe that I was moving to a town that ended in a brewery.

Though Green Bay was larger than Manitowoc, Roger and Elaine did not have good news either. The center at Green Bay was also one very modern building, and they, too, had found only a few places for rent.

Back home, Leverett looked like Eden compared to Manitowoc, but I didn't have time to be depressed about the move. Tom was finishing the research for his dissertation, and I had a household to pack. Since the children would make the move quite difficult, we decided that Tom would drive to Wisconsin to meet the moving van and that the children and I would fly out a few days later, after he had had a chance to unpack the essentials. My parents and my brother came to help with the last of the packing. Tom left for Wisconsin, my parents left for New Jersey, taking the children with them, and my brother and I waited for the movers.

Those two days were the first I had ever had alone with Paul. Seeing him outside of the family, I realized that my nineteen-year-old brother was a virtual stranger. Of course, I did know some things about him. He was very concerned about his appearance, as I had been at his age. Unlike me, however, he didn't work after school and during the summer but had managed to convince my parents to buy him what he wanted. And he wanted the best—cashmere sweaters and slacks that I had never been able to afford from the exclusive stores in Ridgewood. His greatest interest, cars, was an extension of how he looked. He talked endlessly about whether my father would fulfill his dream by trading in the Oldsmobile for a Cadillac. Paul is really a child of the suburbs, I thought. He had not had the problems I had when we moved, since he had only been nine. As I looked at him that day, I knew his appearance must have helped him in New Jersey. He had light brown hair, the lightest in the family, and his skin was not olive like mine but lighter. His nose, by the standards of my family, was very small. He was well over six feet, tall, slim, and, I realized for the first time, very good looking. While Armenians said that I didn't look Armenian, my friends generally asked me what I was, knowing by my looks that I was something "different." My brother, on the other hand, could very easily be taken for an American.

Paul and I were different in other ways as well. His goal was to make lots of money to buy cars and all the other things he wanted, while I wanted a life that was "meaningful" and felt disdain for mere material possessions. We went out for dinner, and, since neither of us knew what to say to each other, we spent the evening at the movies. The next morning, after the movers had packed the van, we drove to my parents' house in silence.

On the day before my flight to Wisconsin I decided to say a private farewell to New York. I went into the city alone, visited the Metropolitan Museum of Art and the Museum of Modern Art to see those paintings I could still enjoy, went to a matinee, and had dinner at a delicatessen—what I knew would be my last real pastrami sandwich and dill pickle. I took the subway down to the Village and walked until it was time to catch the last bus back to New Jersey.

The next day my parents drove me to Idlewild Airport—which had just been renamed for John Kennedy—and, as I boarded the plane, I felt that this time I was really going off alone into an unknown world. After a few weeks in Manitowoc I realized that I had been right. Even my first trip to the grocery store made it clear that I was in an alien land. I had learned to adjust in Amherst to the lack of what I considered essentials for cooking, but Manitowoc was a real wasteland where food was concerned. In Amherst, for example, I usually couldn't get Italian parsley. The stores carried only the curly kind that was, to my mind, only good for a garnish; it lacked a strong parsley taste. I also never saw fresh dill in Amherst. When we first arrived I asked for it thinking they might have some in the back and hadn't yet put it in the bin. I was sent to the pickle department and almost cried as I looked at the jars of dill pickles. It also wasn't always possible to get olive oil in every store, but the A&P carried it regularly. In Manitowoc even curly parsley wasn't always in the vegetable bins, and none of the stores carried olive oil. They said there was no "call for it." Occasionally they had eggplant, and when I bought one the cashier asked me what it was. Her face showed no recognition when I told her it was an eggplant.

I told myself that one should not judge a town by its grocery stores. Though I was not so sure about my reasoning, I decided to wait until I met some people before I made a final judgment. Soon, I thought, Tom will meet people at work and bring them home. It had taken him a while to do that in Amherst too. I would just have to be patient. But things were different than they had been in Amherst. Tom was now teaching three courses a semester and still working on his dissertation. We interacted even less since there was no room in our apartment for him to work, and he had an office to himself at school. There was also no possibility for me to work now. Even if I were I able to find a sitter, I still had no idea what

I would do in that town. And there was nothing for me at the center, not even courses to take, since they were all at the introductory undergraduate level. My neighbors were much older than I and seemed to want to have nothing to do with the renters in their neighborhood. My only contact those first few months was with Elaine, but she had gotten a job and was busy during the week. I spent most of my time alone with the children. Hannah, who at a year was developing quite normally, to my great relief, was still a sweet and easy baby. But I was deeply bored and more isolated than I had ever been in my life.

I was also very worried about Neal. He was walking quite normally and was even able to ride a tricycle, but as his third birthday approached he had yet to say an intelligible word. He was also so unresponsive that I sometimes wondered whether his hearing was impaired. I knew something was wrong, but Tom didn't want to talk about it. The day before Neal was three I looked through the phone book for some kind of help. I found a listing for the Manitowoc Mental Health Center and made an appointment to take Neal in for an evaluation.

After I had an interview with the psychiatric social worker, Neal was given a series of tests. Weeks later the center called to say that the test results were ready and that the clinical psychologist would like to see me. I asked if it was all right for my husband to come, and the secretary said it would be fine. This time I was determined that Tom would accompany me. It had been painful and frightening to go through the earlier interview alone, and I made an appointment for a time when I knew he was free. Tom agreed to go with me, and I anxiously awaited the time when I would find out what was wrong with my son. But the meeting was inconclusive, since the test results were not clear. We were referred to the director of the center—a psychiatrist.

After several more weeks, I sat in another waiting room terrified. What would he say about Neal? Would he be able to see what a terrible mother I really was, that I had never wanted Neal—that I was unnatural? When the receptionist said we could go into the doctor's office, I walked unsteadily down the narrow hall to the office. Dr. Kowalski was a large, energetic man who rose to greet us when we came through the door. He heartily shook our hands, then sat back down behind his large desk and came right to the point. After reviewing Neal's tests and the report of the interview with me, he felt quite sure that there was nothing physically wrong with Neal. The problem was, in his opinion, psychological and was rooted in Neal's relationship with his mother. He recommended that I begin therapy with him. As I worked out my own problems, Neal's development would proceed normally. His only suggestion for Neal was that we consider enrolling him in the local daycare center for a few hours a week. He would call them to insure Neal's acceptance. I agreed to see Dr. Kowalski and made an appointment for the next week. I didn't seem to have a choice.

As we walked out of the center, I was relieved to learn that whatever was wrong with Neal could be helped. The doctor had been quite clear about that. There was no irreparable brain damage. He had not uttered the word that had plagued me for years. Neal was not "retarded." I was certainly more than willing to do what I could to help my child.

My other feelings, however, were not so sanguine. I felt like a monster. The doctor confirmed my suspicion that my reaction to my pregnancy with Neal had not been natural. My perversion had prevented my innocent baby from being normal. It was my fault. I had not deigned to befriend my neighbors in the married students' apartments yet they were far superior to me: Whatever their problems, they had not destroyed their children.

Clearly I had massive problems. My feelings about pregnancy and my child were not normal. My relationship with Tom had begun with promise but had had almost totally disintegrated. Tom was withdrawn, but I should have been able to bring him out. And why did I feel so alienated from most people? I was committed to trying to change, but I was also terrified of therapy. It was, in my mind, still only for crazy people. I wondered if I was really one of them. I was convinced that therapy would uncover the most horrible aspect of who I really was. I anticipated my first session with Dr. Kowalski both with the hope that my therapy would, in some mysterious way, help Neal and also with dread that my worst fears about myself would be confirmed, but I also had overwhelming guilt over what I had already done to my child.

The next day I enrolled Neal in the daycare center. I anxiously told the woman in charge that he was afraid of other children and that he had a lot of other problems. She told me not to worry; he would do just fine. I guessed he would if he were in the care of a normal woman like her. As I drove away, I wondered if Dr. Kowalski had suggested the daycare center to give Neal an experience with other children or to get him away from me. I decided that his reason must have been the latter.

By the time my first therapy session came I was ready to accept the details of my monstrosity and armed to defend myself against the doctor's attacks. I was angry because he had made me feel terrible, yet he represented the hope that Neal could be like other children. His office seemed much larger than when I had been there with Tom, and the doctor's voice seemed to be coming from a great distance. I was also very cold and huddled in my chair to stop shaking. The only things that I remembered from that first session were Dr. Kowalski's reiteration that Neal would develop into a normal child and that I should see him weekly, though the center allowed only for monthly visits. He could arrange for me to see him monthly at the center and weekly at his private practice. Once again I seemed to have no choice. If Neal were going to get better, I had to get on with working on my problems.

I was surprised that within a few weeks a part of me actually looked forward to my weekly sessions. Although I was so guilt ridden that I was depressed most of the time, at least Dr. Kowalski was someone to talk to. I was actually growing to like him, but much of what he said I didn't understand. What was most confusing to me was his insistence that I lacked "affect." I had no idea what he was talking about until one week some months later when I felt as though I wanted to die. I had begun to cry during the session, and when I went home I cried more. I was miserable for the whole week, and I realized that for the first time I was counting the days until my next session. When I told Dr. Kowalski that I had not been able to stop crying, he rose out of his chair, spread out his arms, and said, "That's wonderful." I hated him at that moment. When he went on to say that I had let myself feel my feelings, however, I felt a deep sense of relief. I did feel better after that painful week, and it seemed to me that Neal was showing some small signs of improvement.

There was some change, too, in my social situation. After months of seeing no one but Roger and Elaine on occasional weekends, we finally had our first invitation from one of Tom's colleagues. Alan Stein taught English at the Sheboygan center, and, though his wife Mary Lee also worked there as a counselor, neither Tom nor I had ever considered her to be Tom's colleague as well. Alan was a real treat for me. He was Jewish and had grown up in Chicago. We often listened to Mort Sahl and Mel Brooks records and sometimes we had kosher salami on "real" rye bread that Alan brought back from Chicago. The four of us grew to be good friends, and we agreed to their suggestion that we should move to Sheboygan. I was willing to try anything. I hated our small and dark apartment, and after almost a year of living in Manitowoc I had found nothing I liked, except Dr. Kowalski, whom I could continue to see.

A few weeks later Mary Lee called to say she had found a beautiful apartment for us. As soon as I could reach Tom and get the car, I drove the twenty-minute ride to Sheboygan. The apartment, half of an old house in the center of town, was more than I expected even from Mary Lee's extravagant description. There was a large kitchen with a butler's pantry, a real dining room, a large living room, a half a bath on the first floor, and four rooms on the second. The children could each have their own room and Tom could have a study as well. As soon as he could, Tom came to see it and we rented it on the spot. This time I packed with optimism. Sheboygan was bigger than Manitowoc. It had one decent department store at least, and was closer to Milwaukee, where we could sometimes see foreign films and I could get olive oil, pine nuts, bulgur, and other necessities at the one Middle Eastern grocery. I expected, too, that through Alan and Mary Lee we would meet some people.

My attitude toward Sheboygan was also influenced by the fact that I was feeling better than ever. The therapy, which had seemed so terrifying, had been responsible for a change in me. It was so vital that I saw my life in 1966 as divided into two sections—before and after therapy. Before therapy I was only minimally aware of my feelings, though I had been the ''screamer'' in the family in my early teens. I had railed against my mother's restrictions, the demands of the extended family and my mother's and grandmother's obvious preferences for my brother. When I got into a rage generally everyone left the room, and my grandmother always said, in Armenian of course, ''The temper has a hold of her.'' Her statement made me angrier. She denied everything that had made me angry and attributed my feelings to a mystical force that had overtaken me.

Except for my outbursts, there was little sign of any kind of feeling in my family. The most lavish expression of love that I ever experienced from the women came through the preparation and serving of food. My grandmother's attempt to make me a part of the family's Easter celebration when I moved to Amherst was by a box of stuffed mussels. I knew I was her favorite female grandchild because she always had given me an extra helping of artichokes. My mother always brought a cooler full of meat, cheeses, breads, dill, and the right kind of parsley when she and my father came to visit us in Massachusetts. When we moved to Wisconsin she could not bring the food with her, so we always went to the grocery store shortly after their arrival where she could buy us at least a week's worth of supplies.

It was not easy to interpret the meaning of these gifts when I saw few signs of physical affection and no one talked about it. I wondered if speaking of love was strictly an American thing to do. While I hadn't seen for myself what happened in American families, affection seemed to be a part of the culture.

Other emotions, it seemed clear to me after therapy, were also being repressed. While my mother often yelled at me in anger and sometimes hit me as well, she usually restrained her emotions with other people. When I was in my teens, however, she did acquire a reputation within the family as being nervous and high strung because of her occasional outbursts of anger at my father, her sister, and her brother. Yet people tried to calm her down rather than deal with what was bothering her. They left her alone emotionally just as they had left the room when I got into a fit of temper as a child.

My father, on the other hand, was known as a man who "takes everything in stride." The closest he ever came to being angry with me or my brother was shaking his head in frustration or raising his voice ever so slightly. I never saw him express even that much emotion with anyone else. It was unthinkable, for example, for my father to be angry with Uncle Alex. There was a lack of emotion among all my father's relatives. The hierarchy determined behavior, and everyone seemed very polite. Grownups endured silently, and I learned to restrain my feelings too. By the time I was eighteen my feelings were so well repressed that I hardly felt them at all.

By some mysterious process, therapy had made me aware of those feelings, and I began to understand how destructive denying emotion had been. Before therapy I sometimes spent weeks, even months, feeling nothing more than a vague depression. I was now trying hard both to be more open to my feelings and to express them. When I felt Tom withdraw, I forced myself to tell him how his behavior affected me rather than retreating into an angry silence. I thought Tom was trying to be more responsive, but still he was distant. I wished he could have a therapist like Dr. Kowalski. I was often unhappy, but now I could also feel some joy.

I felt sure life was going to continue to get better. At least I was not so isolated. Within the first months of our move I had met more people than I had in the nine months in Manitowoc. Shortly after our arrival, Eve Laurence, one of my new friends, asked if I would like to join a group of women who were organizing a chapter of the League of Women Voters. I went to my first meeting and found that the group was preparing for its provisional status, a requirement stipulated by the national organization before a group could become a full-fledged chapter. In order to attain this status the group had to research the city of Sheboygan as well as obtain funds and endorsements from local businessmen. Most of that seemed very boring to me, and I was glad to hear that the group had also decided to study some local and national issues. Each member of the group was to be responsible for a topic of her choice. Most people had chosen their topics, and when I heard the list I offered to do something on race relations. In the silence that followed I heard myself arguing that civil rights was an issue of national importance that I hoped this group would want to know about. Because it was a new topic I was to explain at the next meeting why it should be included.

I was shocked that anyone would question the importance of race relations at a time when reports of demonstrations appeared almost nightly on the evening news. But I told myself that I shouldn't have been. A few months earlier, under orders from local law enforcement officials, Negro college students in the South were sprayed with fire hoses and attacked by German shepherds. When I brought up the brutality in my session with Dr. Kowalski, he wanted to know why I was so upset. I asked him why he wasn't. Had he watched the evening news? Young Americans, who were only trying to obtain the rights that should be theirs by virtue of the Constitution, were being abused and even beaten by people who were supposed to uphold the law and protect the citizens. I refused to discuss why I was upset until he had watched what was happening for himself. The next week he admitted that he had been ignorant about the severity of the situation, and we went on to other topics.

So far as I knew, no Negroes lived in Manitowoc or Sheboygan. I thought that, after studying race relations on a national level, the league could look into the local setting. I presented my arguments, and most of the group agreed that the issue was important, or so they said, but shortly after that meeting Eve asked me why I cared so much about it. The other women in the group had wondered too, she told me. Eve said that they had agreed to take on the subject only because it seemed vital to me. I was stunned. Segregation and race prejudice were *my* issues; no one else cared about them at all. On the night of my presentation someone brought up an issue that had to be dealt with immediately, concerning the responses to the league among the business leaders of Sheboygan. We postponed my discussion until we had more time.

That other time never came for my topic as well as for a few others. Even I had to admit that the league was really in trouble. We could get neither the required financial support from local businesses nor more than one endorsement, and that from the husband of one of our most active members. The women who had spoken to businessmen in Sheboygan reported that most had responded that the league was "pink" and that they wanted to keep it out of their city. We decided to show city leaders that the league was concerned with Sheboygan's welfare. We approached the mayor about speaking at a public meeting, which we would organize, about issues of importance to the city. To our great surprise he agreed, and, as a result, our meeting was fairly well attended.

After a glowing report of Sheboygan's good economic condition, the mayor ended his speech with a discussion of the one problem that had been plaguing the city over the last year, a serious shortage of skilled construction workers. Contractors had traveled as far north as Green Bay and to the western part of the state to try to lure workers to Sheboygan, but their efforts had had only minimal success. I wondered why they had only gone to the north and west. I asked if the contractors looking for workers had gone to Milwaukee. It was a fairly large city, only an hour south of Sheboygan, and I assumed there were some men there who needed work. As soon as I saw that my question had flustered the mayor, I knew the real reason. His response, however, came in the form of questions: "Where would *they* sleep? Where could *they* eat?" The mayor ended his response to my question with only one statement: "*They* would not come here." *They*, I knew, were Negroes.

The next day I asked my friend, whose husband was a contractor, about what the mayor had said. She corroborated that there was a shortage of skilled artisans and said that her husband, in desperation, had once hired three Negro bricklayers, who drove up from Milwaukee in the morning and returned after work. Probably knowing about the "hospitality" of the local restaurants, they had brought their lunch with them. Her husband was told by most of the prominent men in town that, if he ever did such a thing again, they would make sure he would not get any more work himself.

I had already learned from a Pakistani graduate student that some restaurants in Sheboygan refused to serve dark skinned people. Mr. Devi was in Sheboygan for the summer and had moved into a small apartment in the house in which we lived. After he caught the smells coming from my kitchen at dinnertime, we had long conversations about food, and we exchanged recipes. When we had become friends, he told me that one night shortly after his arrival in town he was too tired to bother with cooking dinner and had decided to go out for something to eat. His order was taken but was brought to his table in a paper bag. He had tried a few other places in the city with similar results. Indeed, it would be difficult for *them* to find a place to eat. Sheboygan, it seemed, was no different from the South, except that there were no Negroes. Tom had learned, in fact, that the high school offered exchange programs for seniors only with schools in the South in order to insure that the communities were white and to prevent the possibility of having Sheboygan students go to school with Negroes or having Negro students in their high school.

I was grateful that we had moved out of Manitowoc, but still Sheboygan was a small Wisconsin city, and I felt more and more that it was alien territory. I had made some good friends, it was true, but there were things about me that no one could understand. My interest in race relations was clearly something that made me unique, but it was not the only thing. My atheism also marked me as a dangerous woman. Eve had asked whether Tom and I belonged to a church, and I had told her that neither of us believed in God. She seemed to be tolerant of my nonbelief, although she said she had never met an atheist before. Shortly thereafter people began to ask me about my being an atheist, some with genuine interest and others with hostility.

Tom was also beginning to feel uncomfortable in Wisconsin. His political views were far to the left of most of the faculty at the university centers, and the conservatism of his colleagues was matched by the students. When he came to the McCarthy period in his American Politics course, for example, one of his students asked permission to bring a visitor into the class. Tom agreed, pleased to support any special interests of his students. As Tom began his lecture, the visitor raised his hand. Having been acknowledged, he stood and spoke on the greatness of Joseph McCarthy, ending with an invitation to the class to join the annual motorcade from Milwaukee to Appleton on the anniversary of the senator's death. After that day Tom received anonymous letters warning him not to disparage McCarthy again.

A short while after this incident Tom came home with the news that the John Birch Society had a chapter in Sheboygan and that they were sponsoring a public lecture on a topic that would surely interest me, "Communists in the Civil Rights Movement." The small group of liberal faculty at the center planned to attend, and he thought I would like to come too. It was not unusual for me to go along to some meetings with Tom. There had been so little to do in Manitowoc that I always looked forward to the occasional center system meeting, which were often held at the main campus of the state university in Madison. I loved the large lively campus, and we were always able to have dinner in one of Madison's good restaurants.

I was pleased that Tom had considered my interests and seemed to really want me to join him. Although I was still dissatisfied with our relationship, I was beginning to feel closer to Tom. My growing political awareness gave us more to talk about, and I had developed friends and interests of my own instead of devoting myself to his colleagues and his career. We were also able to talk a little about Neal, who was making good progress.

Going to the lecture I told Tom I felt a little as if we were in alien territory; when it was over I was sure of it. When we got to the hall I was disturbed to see it so crowded that we were lucky to get seats. The league might not think that race relations was an important topic, but it was a hot one for the Birchers. To my great surprise, the speaker was an old Negro man. As I listened to him reiterate the Birch line that all the leaders of the movement, whom I admired, were proven communists and that the organizations they headed were merely Commie fronts, I wondered where he would sleep that night. After the speech some of the men in our group raised their hands to ask questions, but the moderator did not call on one of them.

We had the distinct impression that some of the men in our group, Tom included, were well known not only to the moderator but also to some of the members of the audience, who frequently turned to stare at us. I left the meeting feeling more than uncomfortable. I was frightened. Over the next few weeks Tom and I often talked about the meeting and our growing feeling of being part of a tiny embattled group of liberals.

I had had enough. In the two years we lived in Wisconsin I had felt better than I had in years. I had begun to develop my own interests and had more friends than I ever had, and I was respected for my ideas—I had just been elected president of the League. I had a wonderful therapist who I would hate to leave, but I felt as though I could not bear living in Wisconsin any longer. One night when Tom and I were talking about the conservatism of the area and feeling particularly good together, I asked him what he thought about trying to find a job in the East. He said that he had wanted to finish his dissertation before he looked for another job, but that I might be right about leaving Wisconsin. He thought he might have a chance for a decent job in the East since he had made good progress on his dissertation, especially over the last year. I was elated and gladly typed his letters of application.

But I was worried about leaving Dr. Kowalski. Therapy with him had very possibly been the most important thing in my life. What would happen to me without our weekly sessions? He assured me that I would be fine. Evidence of how much I had changed was clear, he said, in Neal's enormous progress. Neal was quite a different child than when we moved to Wisconsin. It was hard to remember that only a year earlier we had thought he might have been deaf. His fear of other children had diminished, though he still did not play with his peers. The most encouraging thing of all was that he had begun to say some words and had recently even begun to create simple sentences. Although we could not always decipher what he was trying to say, he was attempting to communicate.

Dr. Kowalski thought that Neal might be reaching the point where he could benefit from some therapy himself. He had originally diagnosed Neal as having a form of childhood schizophrenia but had recently changed his mind. Neal's behavior seemed to him to fit more clearly into the category of autism. He suggested that we try to find Neal a therapist as well as some kind of setting where he could be with other children.

As he spoke, I looked lovingly at this man who was responsible for the possibility that my son might someday develop normally. On the ride back to Sheboygan I remembered I had not always felt so good about Dr. Kowalski. Sometimes he had made me furious. After I had been seeing him for about a year, for example, he

suggested that having another baby might make me feel more secure about my femininity. When I responded that the last thing I
wanted was another baby, that I had just about as much as I could
handle at the moment, he suggested that some of my creative needs
might be fulfilled by a baby. I shouted back that I was not a cow;
I was a human being who had more options for creative outlets than
a uterus. Creating a baby was something my body did, not my mind,
and it would not fulfill anything for me. I had already had that experience twice. He finally agreed that he might be wrong. For me,
at least, pregnancy might not be a creative experience.

What he had said *was* awful, but he probably had saved my life.
He had been my therapist, and I also thought of him as my best
friend. I would hate to leave him, but, after even this initial discussion about leaving, I was beginning to feel ready.

The week I was installed as president of the provisional League
of Women Voters in Sheboygan, Wisconsin, Tom got a call from
Ithaca College. They were very interested in his application and
wanted him to come for an interview. I had hoped that I would live
up to the expectations of my friends in my position as league president, but I never got the chance to find out. The next month Tom
accepted the job at the small liberal arts college in New York State,
in the same town as Cornell University and only four hours from
New York City. I felt released from what had seemed a kind of pri-
son. We were going home.

Chapter 11

*I*thaca was as different from Manitowoc and Sheboygan as it could have been. When Tom returned from his interview he said that the city was built up the sides of steep hills. Ithaca College was at the top of one of the hills at the south end of the city, and Cornell University sprawled across the hills to the north. Tom's colleagues told him that housing in Ithaca was difficult to find not because people owned their own homes but because so many people, students as well as faculty, rented apartments and even houses. They said, too, that it was a lively city since both Cornell and Ithaca sponsored many lectures, concerts, plays, and exhibits of all kinds.

Tom had been reluctant to take time away from his dissertation to make the long trip from Sheboygan to Ithaca to look for a place to live, so we rented an apartment through the mail. It was in a new housing complex set on the western hill of the city. The three-bedroom apartment with a galley kitchen pictured in the realtor's brochure looked disturbingly like my parents' house in New Jersey, but I was so happy to be moving out of Wisconsin and to the East that almost anything would have been fine with me.

As we drove into Ithaca on that hot August day in 1966, I was overwhelmed with the beauty of the small city. Tom's description of Ithaca had been both detailed and positive, but I was not prepared for what I saw. The steep hills, a welcome change from the flatness of Wisconsin's terrain, rose from the sides of the long, narrow lake I had seen on the map. Our apartment was as uninteresting as I had expected, but the view of the city and the lake nestled in the hills more than made up for the sterility of our new home.

Within a few days Tom and I met the couple, the Fishers, who lived in the apartment on the floor below us, and to my great delight both of them had been born and raised in New York City and were Jewish. Their move to Ithaca was, in fact, their first. I smiled with recognition as Shelly complained that nothing ever happened in Ithaca; she had spent practically a whole day looking out of her window and hardly saw any people; only grass, trees, and the rare person out for a walk. Since they were as anxious to get out of their apartment as we were, Tom, Neal, Hannah, and I spent our first weekends with Shelly, Martin, and Sandy, their six-year-old daughter. They all accepted Neal's sometimes inappropriate behavior, and Sandy liked playing with Hannah, who was barely two and a half. Very soon Shelly and I and our children were spending part of each day together.

Once we were settled I set myself to the task of finding both a psychologist and a placement for Neal. Manitowoc had had only Dr. Kowalski. Ithaca's phone book, on the other hand, listed many therapists and two who specialized in children. I chose the first one and got an appointment for the next week.

When I met with Dr. Campbell and described Neal, she agreed to see him and suggested that she and I meet regularly. I was glad to comply, relieved to have found someone so quickly, and anxious to have someone to talk to about Neal. She recommended as well that I take Neal to the Special Children's Center for an evaluation and possible placement, so I called the center the next morning for an appointment. I had felt comfortable going to see the psychologist alone, but I wanted Tom with me for the meeting at the center, and I made the appointment for a time when I knew he was available.

When I met Dr. Ann Rizzo, the codirector of the center, I recognized by her spastic movements and the slight difficulty she had forming her words that she had cerebral palsy. Because I was close to my cousin Emik, who also had the disease, I felt at ease and had no trouble understanding her. From our description of Neal she thought he could be helped by the center, but before she made any final decisions he would have to be evaluated by her husband, the codirector. I looked forward to the evaluation. Neal had not had one since I had called the Manitowoc Mental Health Center on his third birthday, and he was now almost five years old.

When we met Dr. Peter Rizzo the next week I was disturbed. He was so severely afflicted by cerebral palsy that even I, who was used to Emik's speech, could barely understand him. How could my son, who had trouble understanding normal speech, be adequately tested by someone whose speech was almost unintelligible to me? I began to wonder how good the center was.

Although Dr. Rizzo's test was inconclusive, both he and his wife agreed that Neal would benefit from their program. I was to take Neal to meet his teacher the next day. The Rizzos had explained that the center was for variously handicapped children, but I didn't really know what that meant. I looked around the room at the children on crutches and in wheelchairs and realized that Neal would be the only child in the class who did not have some kind of physical problem. I tried to listen to what the teacher was saying about the class, but what I really wanted to do was to take Neal and run out of that room. But there seemed to be no choice; this center was the only place for Neal in Ithaca. We went home in silence.

Neal began to attend the center three days a week for a few hours. It was conveniently located at the bottom of our hill. On days when the weather was bad I dropped Hannah off at Shelly's while I walked down the hill with Neal, but usually the three of us went together. For the first few weeks I was consumed with rage and pain at having no alternative for Neal. After we dropped him off I often took Hannah's little hand and squeezed it to help me hold back the tears.

Not only did the center seem wrong for Neal, the building in which it was housed was inappropriate for the children it served. It was a small, two-story building, and the children whose legs were encased in braces struggled to negotiate the steep and narrow stairs. I saw no signs of even the slightest attempt to modify it for wheelchairs. It was dark, old, and run-down—a cast-off building for children, I was beginning to conclude, whom nobody really cared about.

It was beginning to become clear that finding services for Neal would be mostly my responsibility. Though Tom was more willing to talk about Neal's problems than he had been in the past, he focused on the future rather than the present. What would happen to Neal when he was older? What kind of work could he ever find? How would he live? I had no idea what the future would bring. None of the professionals who worked with Neal could give us a diagnosis that fit his behavior. Dr. Kowalski's judgment that Neal was autistic told us very little about his prognosis, and Dr. Peter Rizzo's diagnosis, that he was schizophrenic, if it was to be believed at all, was equally inconclusive about the future. I was impatient with

Tom's inability or unwillingness to focus on Neal in the present and his obsession with Neal's future, which he assumed would be grim. He occasionally talked about institutionalization, but I would not hear of it. Most of Tom's energy, however, was directed to his classes and finishing his dissertation.

Once again he was slow to bring people home, but I was less dependent on him for social contact that I had been either in Amherst or Manitowoc. I had my friendship with Shelly Fisher, and, after my experience of making good friends on my own in Sheboygan, I no longer thought that our *real* friends had to be Tom's colleagues.

Toward the end of the first semester he invited a colleague from the economics department and his wife to dinner at our house. When I first met Carolyn and Richard Vickers I was immediately put off by their thick Southern accents. They were not from the South, they informed me, but from Texas. I had thought that Texas was part of the South, but the Vickers were quite definite that Texas was a very different place from what they considered to be the South. I wondered if it was different where Negroes were concerned, and they assured me that, although most people from their state thought that Negroes were inferior, they were both against segregation. After finding out where they stood on race, I could see that they were very nice people, although I felt very inadequate around Carolyn. She was a real American who was able to get along with everyone and do everything right. She and Richard seemed to have a wonderful relationship, and their three children were equally perfect.

I wanted Carolyn to like me, and I was delighted when she asked me what I thought about marching in the Fifth Avenue Peace Parade. She wanted to go, but with a friend, and she said a group at Cornell had hired buses. We would leave early in the morning, march from the Sheep's Meadow in Central Park to the United Nations and come home the same day. I thought it was great that Carolyn had asked me, and now I wanted to do something about the war in Vietnam. I had learned more about our role in the war and had come to agree with Tom that the United States had no business in another country's civil war. Carolyn said that she thought Sue Ellen Chambers, the dean of women at Ithaca College, and her friend Shirley Foster were also going. I liked Sue Ellen and had met Shirley, whom I was anxious to get to know. My main attraction to Shirley was that she was from New York and she was a Negro.

I had been touched by the Civil Rights Movement but had not had the opportunity to have Negro friends since I had stopped seeing Richard Brooks. I told Carolyn that I would love to join her, and we strategized about how to get Richard and Tom to let us go.

We told them when we were all together. They were both surprised that we wanted to go. We explained that we wanted to stand up for what we believed in, that we would only be gone for a day, and that we would prepare food for them. I heard Richard say to Tom that the real reason we wanted to go was to get next to those "big Negro bucks" who were going to be speaking at the march. I was shocked and furious when Tom agreed with him. I asked Richard to repeat what he had said, but he just smiled and said he guessed it would be all right for us to go. Carolyn and I looked at each other but said nothing. We both understood that if we wanted to go to the march it would be unwise to argue with our husbands at the moment. Later, when Carolyn and I were alone, we wondered about what had happened. Was Richard's comment merely the automatic response of a white Southern—Texan—male to any contact between Negro men and "their women"? Then why had Tom agreed so quickly? Could it be that all white men, regardless of where they are from feared that, given an opportunity, white women would be attracted to Negro men?

We also wondered why Tom and Richard seemed to have no interest in going to the march. Tom had opposed the war when I had no idea what it was about or where Vietnam was; so, apparently, had Richard. Although Carolyn and I had only recently taken an interest in the war, we welcomed the opportunity to take a public stand against it.

We met Shirley and Sue Ellen at the bus and sat together for the trip to New York. As we approached the city, Shirley said she had decided to go to her sister's house for the day. She would meet us at Shea Stadium, where the buses would be parked, for the trip back to Ithaca. I was disappointed that I would not get to spend the day with Shirley. Sue Ellen and Carolyn tried to convince her to come with us. When the bus reached Central Park, Shirley was determined to go to her sister's, and I was embarrassed that Sue Ellen and Carolyn continued to plead with her. I stood apart, wondering if Sue Ellen and Carolyn would have been so insistent if Shirley had been white. I was also impatient to get to the Sheep's Meadow and was glad when Shirley finally left.

We saw that the crowd in the park was already enormous, and, as we waited for the march to begin, more and more people of all ages and backgrounds flooded in. I was glad that we had been able to come. Surely, I thought, this many people could not be dismissed as a gathering of the radical, un-American fringe. Yet when we crowded around another demonstrator's transistor radio we heard that only a few people, mostly college students, had gathered in the park. While I was upset to hear such a blatant distortion, I expected that the report was from one of the smaller, more conservative stations. But at the end of the news broadcast I was dismayed to hear the familiar name of WCBS. All day long the radio reports of the march seemed to describe another scene. We marched sixteen abreast toward the United Nations, and there were so many people that we moved at a snail's pace. The crowds of people on the sidewalks held banners in support of the march, and some applauded as we passed, yet the radio continued to downplay the size of the march as well as the variety of people participating. Before we reached the United Nations Plaza we realized it was time to get the subway to Shea Stadium where our bus was parked.

I boarded the bus physically exhausted and in turmoil. I had gone to the march to take a stand against a policy I considered unwise and morally wrong. I had believed that our leaders would respond to a peaceful protest by serious citizens. I considered my participation in the march to be an act of patriotism just as the civil rights movement had been a cry for America to live up to its ideals. Yet the press not only underestimated the size of the march; it also characterized the participants as idealistic young people at best and unpatriotic fanatics at worst. Carolyn and Sue Ellen were also shaken by our experience. Shirley, who joined us for the ride back to Ithaca, did not seem surprised when we told her about the discrepancy between our experience and the news reports. Although she did not say much, I had the impression that she knew something about our country that we didn't.

I came home from the march with the vague feeling that I had changed in some important ways. Tom listened to my account of the day but didn't seem disturbed by the distortions in the press or excited by the huge numbers of people protesting the war. I wanted to do more, but I didn't know what. At the very least, I knew that I would be skeptical about what I read in the papers or heard on the news.

Later that spring I began to think again about moving. We had not intended to stay in our apartment for very long, and we were approaching the end of our first year in Ithaca. Shelly and Martin were also going to move, but they were looking for a house to buy. Buying a house had not occurred to me before, but now I perused the For Sale column when I read the rental listings. Tom was open to the idea of buying, if we could find a house we could afford. When I saw a listing for a house near Ithaca College for $12,500, I thought we ought to look at it. We first saw the old two-story house at night. The rooms on the first floor were small and badly lit, but the large kitchen with windows on two sides looked as though it were a bright room. There were two large rooms and another small one on the second floor. The owner, an old woman, told us she had lived in the house for forty years. Her husband had recently died, and she said she had to move because she could not meet the tax payments nor keep up the house on her social security benefits.

Though the house looked like it needed work, a friend of Tom's who was a builder found it to be sound. I began to think about living in the house. The downstairs rooms were not as dark as they had looked when we first saw them, but they felt small because the living room and dining room were closed off by a wall in the hallway. If we took that wall down, the resulting space would have a feeling of openness. All the rooms would, of course, be painted white to cover the old-fashioned, flowered wallpaper. Tom even seemed excited by the prospect of having the house, particularly since there was a room on the first floor which would make a nice study for him. I asked him where we would get the down payment since we had no savings. He said he was eligible for a G.I. mortgage, which meant we only needed ten percent of the purchase price for a down payment, and we could borrow that from the bank. We offered twelve thousand dollars for the house, and Mrs. Bailey accepted. She said she hoped that we took good care of it. She had lived in the house for most of her long marriage and had raised her four children there. I tried to reassure her, but it was clear that leaving was very painful for her. After the closing Carolyn and Richard came to help us take down the wall. In the middle of the afternoon the old woman came to get something she had forgotten and was visibly shaken by what she saw. The wall was down, and there was plaster everywhere. In a faltering voice she told me that what we were doing was tearing her apart. I was glad to have the house but miserable that this old woman was forced to leave her house because her social security payments were insufficient to pay her taxes. As I watched her walk down the hill to her apartment, I thought to myself that something was very wrong with a system that put old people out of their homes.

My life took another major change that summer: I was going to start work in the fall. In July I got a call from Stanley Mintz, the chairman of the English department at Ithaca College, whom Tom and I knew socially. He asked me if I would like to be a tutor for the freshman English class. When I said that I had had no experience or training for such a position, he assured me that I would have no problem. The half-time job consisted of attending the large lecture, grading papers, and meeting with a small group of students periodically to discuss their writing. I told him that I would have to think about it and discuss it with Tom.

I put down the phone and was both excited and frightened by the prospect of the job. Writing had been difficult for me when I was in college, and I wondered if I now had the skills to help students. On the other hand, the idea of working at the college was exciting. I could do something besides taking care of children. Tom surprised me by encouraging me to take the job. We could certainly use the money, he said, and he had no question that I would be a good tutor. He could arrange his schedule to be home with Hannah when I was in class if we could not get a sitter. I called Dr. Mintz back that night and told him I would take the job.

I began the semester encouraged by a discussion I had about the course with Henry Townsend, the new director of the freshman writing program, though I was still insecure about my ability to do the job. After some direction from Henry about grading my first set of papers and overcoming my initial nervousness about the first meetings with the students, I became quite comfortable. I was very glad that I had agreed to take the job.

Tom, on the other hand, was not pleased. He had been comfortable with the idea of my working, but the reality of my being on the campus twice a week proved to be difficult. He said he felt that I was invading his territory. It was hard for me to understand that my little job would threaten him. I knew from what he told me, as well as from what I heard from other faculty, that he was a popular teacher and had also earned a reputation as an innovator. He and Sue Ellen Chambers had spearheaded the development of the Economic Opportunity Program (EOP). Combining a package of financial aid and academic support services, the program brought a small number of inner-city students to the college. While final approval of the EOP was still pending, Tom's work on the project had made him a well-known figure on the small campus.

I knew it was my responsibility to try to understand his feelings. He was, after all, my husband, and he was the one who had the *real* job. I tried to be empathetic, but I was annoyed that something that gave me so much pleasure and that I wanted for myself upset him.

Tom's reaction to my job seemed to be another instance of his tendency to be negative. Since the beginning of our marriage I had hoped our relationship would get better when our circumstances improved. While he was in graduate school I thought we would be less distant once he had a job and was making a decent salary. Then I thought he would be more approachable when his dissertation was finished. Though I often felt frustrated with Tom, I also felt that I was primarily responsible for the relationship and that I had obviously messed up. I had had excuses for Tom's preoccupation in the past, but now that he had his degree, a good job, and we had a nice place to live I wondered what else to wait for. Neal, it was true, was still a problem, but he had been progressing very well, and Tom could certainly take some solace in Hannah, who was a delightful child.

My daughter had certainly helped me to gain some confidence in myself as a mother. I was still convinced that Neal's problems were due to my deficiencies, but, because I had begun therapy when Hannah was very young, I had changed enough not to damage her. Hannah had crawled, walked, and talked well within the normal range and was now highly verbal. She interacted with adults and other children and also played by herself. Like many of my friends' children, she liked to draw. By the time she was three some of her creations were quite extraordinary.

Hannah was also beginning to develop a relationship with Neal, who was making more attempts to communicate. While his speech was sometimes unintelligible to me, Hannah understood him and told me what he had said. She was wonderfully "normal"; I only hoped I would be able to keep from hurting her.

By the fall of 1968, at the age of twenty-nine, I was beginning to take myself seriously. I did not try to help Tom with his feelings about me working at the college, although I thought I should. I never considered the possibility of quitting and did not feel guilty about that. By the beginning of the second year I felt confident that I was doing an acceptable job and that I would get better.

Tom had come to accept my invasion of his territory. Yet during that summer he occasionally mentioned that he thought we should have another baby. I was appalled at the idea. I was looking forward to the fall when both children would be away for part of the day. Neal had been progressing so well that the Rizzos thought he was ready for the class for emotionally disturbed children at the public school, where he would stay from nine to three instead of the half day at the Special Children's Center. Hannah was enrolled in the Head Start Program. I was anxious for her to have the opportunity to be with other children, particularly in an economically and racially mixed group. My life would finally be a little less taken up with children. Another baby would change all that. I wondered if Tom was motivated by the desire for another child or if he just wanted to keep me tied down at home.

I usually changed the subject when he brought it up, but one night I told him directly that I didn't want another child. He said that he had hoped to have another son. I had such a good relationship with Hannah, and he wanted to experience that kind of sharing with a son. I was furious and said that Neal might have problems, but he was his son. What was he going to do about Neal if he had another son? And what if the baby were a girl? Would he want me to have another one? I said that I would consider having another baby only if he were prepared to work half-time and share taking care of the child. The subject never came up again.

My relationship to the professionals who saw Neal also changed markedly since I had first seen Dr. Kowalski and had accepted his judgment unquestioningly. All of the specialists who saw Neal tried to fit him into the category of the disorder they knew best and wanted to administer tests to confirm their diagnoses. I was concerned about putting Neal through the ordeal of extensive testing and refused to consider it unless they would help us to develop a treatment that would help. In every case the answer was that the treatment would be no different than it was already.

I found that when I asked the experts questions about their diagnoses and the value of testing they reacted negatively. Sometimes I could almost hear them label me a mother who could not accept her child's limitations. But I was trying to take some control of a very confusing and frustrating situation. Neal had had so many diagnoses—childhood schizophrenia, autism, aphasia, mental retardation—that the label seemed much less important to me than what could be done. Because I was trying to find the best for my child and didn't accept what the experts said without question, I was a rebel.

But there was much I could not control. The Special Children's Center had not been appropriate for Neal, but there had been no alternative. When he went to the class for emotionally disturbed children it was immediately clear that, once again, it was not a good place for Neal. This class was the only one the school system provided for children who could not be in the regular classroom. All the other children were either hyperactive or had acted out in ways that were very disruptive. Neal, who was quiet and passive, needed to be coaxed to speak. He still was not comfortable with other children, and it seemed cruel to place him in a class with children who were aggressive and difficult. Though I liked the teacher and found that she took a great interest in Neal, I didn't doubt that Neal had been placed in this class because it was the only one. I thought the schools had an obligation to provide adequate services for my child. The system, however, was geared to the mainstream—the ''normal'' —and those who didn't fit that description were placed in a back room together, regardless of whether or not they had the same needs.

Questioning the authority of the ''experts'' and seeing major flaws in the way the educational system treated children who had special needs affected my attitude towards authority. During the early 1960s I believed that the protests of the Negro students in the South would make the government aware of a problem it had neglected, and once our leaders recognized the seriousness of segregation they would take decisive action to remedy it. There had been major gains in civil rights since that time, but I was beginning to agree with Black Power advocates (who were decidedly ''black,'' not Negro), who maintained that the system was designed for whites and would move only as long as blacks pushed at it.

The schools, it was becoming clear to me, were designed for normal children and would change only when masses of people forced some accommodation of those who had special needs. Neal's experience with the school system, the services provided by the United Way, and the speech clinic made me less sanguine about people in authority and the systems they created. I was on the outside again, but this time it wasn't because I didn't know how to fit in or was directly excluded, as in high school; rather, I was beginning to see that something was wrong with the way the system operated.

My experience with Neal had opened me up to radical critiques of America, and, to my surprise, they shed light on my past in ways that I had not expected. When I first heard Stokely Carmichael, for example, I was shocked and dismayed by his call for Black Power. Didn't black people want to live in unity with whites? Didn't they want to be like us? Why did they want power over whites? But, as I heard the concept articulated again by students at Ithaca College and Cornell, I realized that the kind of control they were talking about was just what I wanted for Neal. I wanted a system that would be responsive to his needs. It also became clear to me when black students spoke about the very real needs of black children to see themselves in the curriculum that my life might have been very different if I too had had that opportunity. Perhaps being an Armenian might not have been so difficult had I heard about my history and culture in the schools. As it was, even the massacre that had caused my grandfather's death and so much suffering for my family seemed to be unknown to everyone in the world who wasn't Armenian. I saw that Black Power was a very different concept than the struggle to end segregation. While I supported both, Black Power spoke to me in ways that the civil rights movement hadn't. It seemed to me that it was an attempt to change a system to make it serve the needs of the people it had abused.

For the first time I was trying to work through political ideas and coming to some conclusions out of my own experience rather than listening to Tom and his friends' ideas. And I found that I had very strong political convictions. I was suspicious of all kinds of authority and believed that all people in a society should have equal rights. I also felt that it was my responsibility as a politically committed person to speak up for my beliefs. I generally found myself in some kind of debate at most social gatherings we attended, and visits to my family were frequently disrupted by political arguments over "colored people," the war, or student takeovers. My father was outraged that I supported the student strike at Columbia. I had felt avenged for the bad advising, overcrowded classes, and elitism that had barred me from ever seeing Meyer Shapiro, the professor who was the main reason I had chosen the school. The students had a perfect right to participate in decisions about the institution's existence.

The most heated arguments with my parents, however, focused on black people. I tried to explain to my parents that the situation of black people in this country was not unlike that of Armenians in Turkey, but my argument went nowhere, since they were convinced of both the superiority of Armenians and the inferiority of blacks.

Though my mother was always present at these discussions, she was generally quiet. When she did speak it was usually to try to change the subject. I was determined to continue arguing because I really did want to convince my parents that their judgments were based on prejudice and because it felt good to argue with my father. The arguments were the only emotional interchange we had. I was also breaking the rules. Not only was I contradicting my father but, by talking about politics, I had also crossed over into the male world.

In the summer of 1968 I decided to go to the Poor People's March in Washington, D.C. This time I didn't plead with Tom but told him I was going. I had felt so discouraged by what was happening in the struggle for civil rights that I wanted to do something. Medgar Evers had been killed. Three black girls had died in the bombing of a church in Birmingham, Alabama, and no one was indicted. James Meredith had been shot, and Martin Luther King had been assassinated. I no longer expected the media to give an accurate report of the march, and I experienced none of the exhilaration of being with thousands of people who shared my views nor the sense that the government would listen. The struggle for social and economic rights seemed very long and difficult and had to be waged against those in power. I knew that I was marching only to try to make myself feel better.

I was changing so quickly that I hardly knew what was happening. I looked forward to the Democratic convention in August. Surely, I thought, the Democrats could not ignore what had happened over the last few years and nominate Hubert Humphrey. As I watched the party go through its business as usual, as people just like me were being beaten on the streets of Chicago, I began to shake. Despite the oppressive August heat, I watched the television wrapped in a blanket, and I shook for the rest of the night.

Chapter 12

*T*hat fall three of our good friends left Ithaca. Richard, increasingly upset with the conservatism of the sociology department at the college, had been applying for other jobs. Tom and I didn't think he was serious about leaving Ithaca. Carolyn, who had been going to Cornell to work on her B.A., still had two years to complete her degree, and she and I had not even discussed the possibility of a move. But when Richard got an offer from the University of Massachusetts, he accepted it. Although they were both sorry to leave good friends, Carolyn seemed unconcerned about her studies. She could go to the university, she said.

The other surprise was that Jane Latka, who taught history at the college, was also leaving town. Her marriage had broken up, and she had decided to go back to the University of Michigan to finish her dissertation.

The history department at the college found another woman to replace Jane, and she quickly became friendly with Tom and invited us over for dinner. Ruth Berman and her husband, David, were both Jewish; Ruth was from Los Angeles and David from Brooklyn. Ruth's dinner was beautifully prepared and even included a delicious loaf of homemade bread. The conversation at dinner focused on food, and, when I raved about the bread, Ruth offered to teach me how to make it. After dinner the talk turned to politics, and we learned that David was a full-time activist. He was the editor of the local radical newspaper, the *New Day*. At the end of the evening he asked us if we would like to help put the paper out on Sunday mornings. Tom didn't seem interested, but I agreed to go to the office of the Glad Day Press the next day to fold and bundle the paper.

I also decided to take Ruth up on her offer to teach me to make bread, and, while we waited for the dough to rise, we got to know each other a little better. As she talked about the courses she wanted to teach and her dissertation, I was intrigued by her ideas. She was trained as a historian, but Ruth was primarily interested in literature. Although her obvious intelligence and knowledge intimidated me, I was also tremendously excited by her highly animated discussion of the social and political content of works of art. Listening to Ruth, I was reminded of Dr. Klitzke's lectures and wondered what she thought about the visual arts. I gathered my courage and asked her if the kind of analysis she had used for literature could be applied to painting. To my surprise, she said she knew of scholars who had done such interpretations.

After years of not thinking about art because I was ashamed of my inability to see it properly, I wondered again about my experience at Columbia. I told Ruth about what I had encountered, and she told me that there were two schools of criticism—those that looked only at the structure of the works, the "art for art's sake" school, and those who were interested in the relationship between the work and its social context. It seemed clear to her that the faculty at Columbia had been adherents of the school that considered art in isolation. I left Ruth's house with a loaf of freshly baked French bread and some clarity on what had happened to me almost ten years before. I did not need to be ashamed of my perspective on art—I belonged to a "school."

Within the next few months Tom and I saw the Bermans frequently. Though I enjoyed the time we spent together as couples, I always preferred the time that Ruth and I spent together. Among the four of us the conversation seemed to be mainly between the two men, although Ruth and I did participate. After some time I realized that Ruth deferred to David, just as I thought that Tom knew more about politics than I did. Ruth often told me that she considered David to be brilliant, and, though I didn't feel that I was a very good judge of intelligence, I wondered if he were really any smarter than Ruth. I always learned so much more from our conversations when we were alone.

Because we both loved to cook, we often spent Saturdays together creating elaborate meals. While we chopped vegetables for egg rolls, spread melted butter on filo dough for *spanikopita* or peeled peppers for chiles rellenos, we talked about history, literature, teaching, and politics. My conversations with other women friends had focused mainly on our relationships with our husbands and problems with our children. In Ruth's eyes, Dave was practically a saint, and she neither had nor wanted children. Ruth talked about her work. She was planning to incorporate more of her politics into her courses, although she knew her department would react negatively. All courses had a political content, she argued. The only difference between hers and those of her colleagues was that she was conscious and explicit about her perspectives. I heartily agreed since I now knew, from my own experience at Columbia, how destructive it could be to students' sense of self to present material as though it were value free when it was actually only one of many possible perspectives.

One Saturday, while we prepared a Mexican dinner, I told Ruth I was dissatisfied with both the content and the structure of the freshman writing class. The large lectures on writing seemed to be totally useless to the students. They came to class only because we took attendance, and it was obvious most of them did not listen. It didn't seem to me that the way to teach writing was to give lectures on form but to have students discuss the material and write and rewrite short essays about ideas they had talked about with their peers. I had learned from grading papers and my discussions with students that they often had little interest in or knowledge about the assigned topics. They literally had nothing to say and therefore wrote dull and often unintelligible essays. Like Ruth, I agreed with student activists that the classroom should not be divorced from the world but relevant to the lives of the students. If the essay topics were carefully chosen, students would have something to write about. Ruth agreed that the course was destined to fail and made some useful suggestions for readings. She was pessimistic, however, about the possibility of making any changes in the course. From what she knew about the English department, they were as conservative as the rest of the school and afraid of change. She did think that an attempt to do something with this course was worth the effort, since it was a required course for all students.

The next week I talked to one of the other tutors, Kathy Taylor, about my problems with the course and some of my other ideas. Kathy, who had become a good friend, heartily agreed with my assessment of the course. She, too, had been thinking about ways she could bring her political and social concerns into the material we used. We decided to approach Dr. Townsend about incorporating some new material into what was left of the semester, and, though he was generally cool to our suggestion, he did adopt one essay topic that touched on contemporary issues.

Our small success only spurred us to want more change. Kathy and I talked with the other tutors, all of whom agreed that the course was a failure. Students were not learning to write or think. Since we were the only ones who read the students' papers and met with them regularly, we were the ones who really knew what was happening in the course. We all wanted to redesign it and made a proposal to Dr. Townsend that we meet regularly during the summer to work. After much delay he responded that we could do what we wanted over the summer, but he had plans to go away. We could send him our deliberations, and he would respond by mail.

Once our proposal was accepted we were faced with the work required to do what we had suggested. We approached the English department for small stipends for each of us—enough to pay for babysitters—and to our great surprise they agreed to subsidize our work for the month of June.

I had another interesting possibility that summer. Tom and other members of the EOP Steering Committee had gotten funding for a summer program for EOP students who would be entering the college that fall. The students would take some of their freshman requirements in the summer, with tutorial help, and have the added advantage of getting to know each other and acclimate to the campus early. Ruth had agreed to serve as the English tutor and decided to run her tutorial as a class. To my great delight, she asked me to coteach with her. I looked forward to the opportunity of watching Ruth teach, since she had quickly gained the reputation as one of the best teachers at the college.

I was generally pleased with my life in the spring of 1969. I was participating in the struggle for social change by working on *New Day* helping to address and bundle the paper and taking photographs. When Dave heard that I had some skill with a camera and darkroom techniques, he asked if I would take pictures for the paper. I happily agreed. Now, with my two summer jobs, I would be able to bring some of my concerns into the classroom and have the opportunity to help the mostly black and Hispanic EOP students make an easier adjustment to Ithaca College. Neal was still not a "normal" child, but he continued to develop. He and I had been seeing a new therapist since I decided to leave Dr. Campbell the previous September. I had had no idea what went on in her weekly sessions with Neal, but I was not helped in my interactions with him nor in understanding myself. One night she spent half of our session describing a game she played with her highly verbal child, and I decided to call the other therapist in town for an appointment.

From my first meeting with Dr. Loretta Julien I realized that my time with Dr. Campbell had been wasted. Dr. Julien seemed to have empathy for me and to understand Neal. I was able to discuss my deepest feelings about Neal with her as well as the problems in my relationship with Tom. When she encouraged me to be more direct with Tom about my feelings, I realized that I had not been "cured" by my work with Dr. Kowalski. Being aware of what I was feeling and learning to act on that knowledge would be a continuing struggle.

Within a few months Dr. Julien suggested that Tom begin to see her, and, when he agreed, I had high hopes for a change in our relationship. I was encouraged, too, by her assessment that Neal was neither autistic nor schizophrenic. She frankly admitted that she did not have a diagnosis, but she had the ability, unique to my experience, to treat him without putting him into a category.

Hannah continued to be a sweet and easy child. She had done well at the Head Start program and was now in her first year of kindergarten. Sometimes she was reluctant to go to school and did not talk about it, as she had when she came home from Head Start. I was a little concerned, too, that she did not make friends in her class, but she seemed quite content playing in her room or drawing at the kitchen table. When I went to talk with her teacher and observe the class, I was convinced the problem was not Hannah's. The teacher was very conventional and seemed to be interested in keeping the class quiet and orderly. Hannah would be much more comfortable, I knew, at East Hill, the "free" school she would attend in September.

I was thirty years old, but I felt younger than I ever had. The student movement had helped overcome some of my ideas about how a married woman and a mother had to act. I stopped wearing skirts and stockings every day and bought myself some jeans. It was wonderful to be able to wear the kind of clothes I had loved when I was a teenager, and I thought fondly of my cousin Susan when I pulled on my first pair of Landlubber bellbottoms. I let my hair grow long, stopped setting it every night, and didn't always wear makeup.

I also joined the food coop and smiled in delight as I ordered what the natural foods movement thought it had discovered and

I had known all my life. Bulgur and yogurt, it seemed, were vital to a long life. My family did live to be very old, but I ate these foods again because I loved their taste and because they were no longer strange—at least to a small group of people.

Although my growing conviction that those in power were corrupt had put me outside the mainstream, I also felt more comfortable than I had in years. I was part of another group that though small and embattled, was striving for justice and clearly was morally superior to the majority who supported the status quo. Change was sure to come soon, and I would have the pleasure of being on the "right" side.

Encounters with my family, however, were becoming more and more difficult. Earlier visits to New Jersey had been punctuated by arguments with my father, but by 1969 debates predominated. Now they were initiated not only by the comments of my father but by those of my other relatives as well. That Easter I was sitting with my cousins when one of them began to complain about all the problems Negroes were causing (we both used the term *Negro*, since I was afraid to use *black* in front of my cousin). They wanted to be like white people, he said. When I asked him why Negroes shouldn't have the same right to jobs and schools as white people, his wife and another cousin excitedly joined the argument. One said that her parents had worked hard for what they had and that Negroes wanted everything handed to them on a silver platter. When I argued that they had every right to expect everything that her parents had acquired, and that they worked just as hard as anyone, she got very angry. She said they were not like white people in any way. I shouted that a Negro friend of ours had just moved into Larchmont but that he and his wife had to fight the stupidity of people just like her to buy their house. I was becoming frightened by the level of rage at our table. When Melanie said that her husband kept one of his shotguns near the door just in case a "nigger" ever dared to set foot on their property, I left the table terrified.

My relatives, who were usually placid, had turned into monsters. On the way home I talked with Tom about what had happened. He said it was important to understand their perspectives, but I was afraid of their violence. Stokely Carmichael had been right when he said that white people didn't want to go into their own neighborhoods to talk about racism because they knew how dangerous that could be.

The polarization that was evident in my family would overtake

Ithaca that spring. The black students at Cornell had been working with the administration for months to establish a black studies program. It seemed to me that the demand for a concentration of courses that explored the history and lives of black people was not only reasonable but necessary. Black students had every right to see themselves represented in the curriculum of the university they attended. The administration did not refuse the demands outright but seemed to be substituting meeting with the Afro-American Society for any action to establish black studies. Because of the delays, in December, 1968, the Afro-American Society staged a demonstration to protest and publicize the administration's failure to act. Six students who participated in the rather large demonstration were summoned before the Student-Faculty Board on Student Conduct.

Since they felt that they had been arbitrarily singled out for judiciary board action, the six refused to appear before the board. When they were informed that they would face automatic suspension, the six students came to the board meeting with all of the one hundred and fifty members of the Afro-American Society—not to face charges but to present the board with a statement of why they refused to accept its right to sit in judgment. The statement outlined three major points: the board was supposed to be a jury of peers, yet it did not include even one black student; the action for which the students were being tried was political, and since Cornell was a party to the dispute it could not sit in judgment; finally, if those six students were guilty, so were all the others who had participated in the demonstration. The board decided to drop the suspensions, and tension on campus was diminished.

Because the Afro-American Society's dispute with the judiciary board had challenged the university's authority, it was watched closely by people from all parts of the political spectrum. Most of my close friends were convinced of the justice of the society's position, and we were appalled when the judiciary board reversed its earlier decision that spring. The six students were tried in absentia and reprimanded. Tensions increased when a six-foot cross was burned in front of Wari, the black women's housing cooperative, and campus police left the building unguarded for more than an hour after the incident. President Perkins further aggravated the growing atmosphere of fear when he characterized the cross burning as a "prank."

A week after the cross burning, the Afro-American Society occupied Willard Straight Hall, the student union and campus hotel.

There was no question in my mind that the occupation of the Straight was justified, and I hoped that the action would alert Cornell to the seriousness of the black students' situation on campus. That afternoon something happened that exacerbated an already volatile atmosphere. A few white students gained entry into the building and attacked the black students with clubs. They were eventually ejected, but reports that the campus police had once again failed to protect the black students mobilized the Students for a Democratic Society. Members of SDS ringed the building to prevent any other white students from entering the Straight. Meanwhile, I heard from Kathy Taylor, who was a member of the small radical Catholic community, that the Catholic chaplain at Cornell was meeting with two hundred well-armed white students to try to prevent them from storming the building.

The next morning the campus and community were alarmed by the news that the black students had also armed themselves. Large groups of white students and the few faculty who supported the takeover gathered in front of the Straight to show their support and offer whatever protection they could to the students inside. Tom and I decided to join the supporters. It was a balmy Sunday that eerily had the atmosphere of a community festival. Most of our friends were there as well as other people we knew to be radical activists. I was holding Hannah's hand when suddenly I was overcome with fear. I was standing in front of a building with my children, and inside were black men with guns. I quickly found Tom, who was talking to Ruth and David, and whispered that we would have to leave immediately. I must have looked frantic because without hesitating he said good-bye. We walked—I had to force myself not to run—to the car.

In the calm of my living room the fear that had had such a powerful grip on me faded, and I was able to think about what had happened. I realized that the people inside the Straight had ceased to be the students whose activities I had followed and supported. What had scared me was the specter of black men with guns. I realized that, for all of my progressive attitudes, I had not been immune to the racist myth of black men as beasts—the "animals in suits" that Uncle Mesrop had pointed to on the front page of the *Times* so many years ago. I had been shocked and angered by his blatant racism, but that afternoon I learned that I, too, carried the image in my psyche. It was my first understanding of the power of racism to invade my unconscious.

During the next few weeks I had ample opportunity to talk to other whites about racism in all its forms, including my new revelation. Even though the black students had emptied their guns and left the Straight without one shot being fired or any other kind of violence, most people I knew talked only about the fact that the students in the building had guns. *New Day* reported that white students had armed themselves to attack the Straight and that the students inside the building had armed themselves in response to that very real threat, but many of the whites I knew never got past the specter that had so frightened me. Although the white students occupied another building in support of the demands of the black students, the rage of most whites was directed at the Afro-American Society. As a result of President Perkins's courageous refusal to bring in the National Guard to oust the black students, he was forced to resign under pressure brought by a majority of the faculty.

All of my close friends supported the black students, but many people I knew stopped talking to us because of our stand on the Straight takeover. The town was divided, and I held the same position there as I did in my family—the "radical," "fanatic" side. I was truly distressed that most whites seemed to be incapable of seeing the situation from the perspective of the black students.

Although most of my energy was focused on racism, not only within the culture but also in my own psyche, I was also involved in the antiwar movement and became a staunch supporter of the student movement. I had great respect for some of the students I knew. They were so much more aware of the world and their own needs and rights than I had been at their age. I was surprised and inspired by twenty-year-olds who believed they could change the world. I was most impressed with some of the young women who were involved in radical politics and became friendly with Merrill Rubin, one of Tom's students. She told me about the difficulty she and some of the other women were having in getting the men they worked with to take them seriously. Their ideas were not heard, and they were never allowed to speak at public meetings. I sympathized with Merrill and urged her to confront the men directly, although I realized how hard that would be.

My friendship with these young women made me think about my life in terms of women's roles. My initial response to the women's liberation movement had been negative. I was bitter toward a movement that had emerged too late for me. The critique of marriage and family was not helpful, I thought, to someone who had already made that choice. But Tom never ordered me around the way that Martin Fisher told Shelly what to do. He had had problems with my teaching at the college, but he had not asked me to quit.

Other men seemed to think there was something wrong, even dangerous in my behavior. Martin forbade Shelly to see me, but, more amazing to me, rather than confronting her husband, she saw me secretly. My influence on Shelly, as far as I could see, was merely that I encouraged her to use her mind. I knew Martin thought that women's fulfillment came from homemaking. Shortly after we had moved into our house he came over to help paint. I was scrubbing the kitchen floor with steel wool to remove the wax. It was over ninety degrees; I had been working for hours and was only halfway done. When I started to complain about the job I was doing, he said that I should be feeling very good since I was fulfilling my role as a woman. I thought that even Martin Fisher could not be serious and I responded sarcastically, but I realized that he had indeed meant what he said. I was furious and told him he was crazy. I was banished from his house a few weeks later.

I was also anathema to Jane Latka's husband, John. Although he hardly knew me, he thought I had contributed to their separation. One Saturday night when Jane was at a party at our house he called to tell me that I was a dangerous woman—a homebreaker. I could not imagine what I had done and asked him what he meant. He could only answer that I was a witch. I understood Martin's problem with me but was completely mystified by John. Jane thought that my influence had been to befriend her and support any signs of independence that she showed, yet another friend, Bill Johnson, said that Jane was wrong: John Latka thought I was a "dyke." I had never heard that word and asked Bill what he meant. Thinking I hadn't heard him, he repeated, "John Latka thinks you are a dyke." When he finally understood that I really didn't know what the word meant, he told me that it meant that he thought I was in love with Jane—that I was a lesbian. I was speechless. As I looked back on that night spent talking to Merrill, I began to wonder if men were so threatened by close friendships between women that they sexualized the relationships both to stigmatize and dismiss women who cared about each other.

I thought, too, about some of my experiences at the office where *New Day* was published and where I worked in the darkroom. I was often intimidated by the male SDS students, who spent a good deal of time at the office. It seemed impossible to have any kind of decent conversation with them. They had all the right answers to questions I had just begun to formulate. I had not thought then that their behavior had anything to do with the fact that they were male, but now I wondered; I had never encountered such dogmatism from the women radicals I knew. I had also been very disturbed when I came across a set of contact sheets that belonged to Rob Stevens, one of the other photographers. Among the prints of various demonstrations and meetings were four or five sheets of nude women. I had not been able to articulate what had upset me about those pictures, which looked like they might have been taken for a men's magazine, but I was less willing after that to believe in Rob's complete dedication to the cause of freedom for everyone. When I thought about those pictures again and wondered why I had not talked to anyone about them, I knew that most people in the movement wouldn't think there was anything wrong with using women's bodies as sexual objects. I would have been considered a prude, something anyone over twenty-five had to be very careful about.

None of the women my own age seemed interested in the problems of women, so I discussed the subject only with the women students. They had decided to form a new organization, The Ithaca College Women's Liberation Front, and when they asked me to join I immediately agreed. Tom was generally supportive of my participation in the group, but Ruth seemed quite upset. I explained that I thought the role women were expected to play in society had affected my life in very serious ways. She said she could understand how I felt since I had had children at a very young age. She, on the other hand, had not married until she was in graduate school and had decided not to have children. The women's movement really had nothing to say to her. While she could see that I might need it, she hoped that I wouldn't get too carried away and forget about the real struggles.

I was confused by what Ruth said. Though I felt she was wrong, it certainly looked as if she had not been affected much by being a woman. She seemed to do what she wanted. David never complained about her working, but I also know that she supported them so that he could be a full-time activist. She did all the housework, laundry, shopping, and cooking on top of working full-time, but it seemed to be no problem for her. She was not able to work on her dissertation, which sat permanently on a table in the living room. But Ruth seemed perfectly happy with her life with David. Maybe I would feel as she did if I had a career too, but I didn't, and I knew that I couldn't devote myself to any full-time pursuit until the children were older. I didn't know why Ruth had been different from most of the women I knew in college. Few of them had any plans past graduation, but all the men had had something in mind. For most of the women I knew, marriage and children were their major goals in life. If they worked after college, it was only until they had found "Mr. Right." Maybe Ruth had been like the women in the group of bohemian students at Alfred who didn't mind being "brains."

I got support for my growing interest in the women's movement from Carolyn Vickers. She called late that spring to say that she and Richard were going to California in the summer and planned to stop in Ithaca. Richard was doing some research on a new book and Carolyn was going to visit something I had not even heard of—women's centers. I looked forward to seeing her and talking more about women's issues.

When Carolyn came I experienced the relief of talking to someone who shared my interest. Many women our age in Northampton and Amherst were meeting weekly to talk together about their lives as women, she told me. They were also working together to establish a center where other women could come to talk, get information on women's resources in the Connecticut Valley and elsewhere, and generally find support. She had a reading list that a group of women had compiled, which I copied and promised myself I would work my way through when I had some time.

That summer, however, there was very little time. Shortly after school was over the meeting to redesign the freshman English course began. We all agreed that the course should be restructured to allow for a least two small discussion groups a week and that the large lecture should be limited as much as possible. Kathy and I had talked about building each semester around a theme, and she suggested using the conflict between responsibility to one's own beliefs and duty to those in authority as the theme for the first semester. The other tutors agreed, and we began to work on the syllabus.

The design of the first semester went fairly well, and we were anxious to begin our work on the second term but were unable to think of a theme that would allow for as many possibilities as our choice for the first semester had. I was anxious to expand on the struggle against racism that we had introduced in the beginning of the first semester. I also thought it would be interesting to do something about women. I suggested that we use the theme of stereotyping and everyone liked it. The stereotyping of students and black people was an obvious choice and we had ample material on both subjects. Kathy was anxious to include a section on the clergy and the difficulties encountered by the few priests who wanted to break out of their roles to relate to their parishioners as people. She suggested bringing in Father David Connor, the priest who had worked so hard to keep the white students from storming the Straight. Her idea was enthusiastically supported.

It seemed obvious to me that women had at least as many stereotypes to face as priests, and I suggested that the course include a week on women's roles. My colleagues, all of whom were women, balked. Stereotyping was not an issue for women, they informed me. The roles for the sexes were based on nature. Women gave birth to children and therefore should stay home and take care of them. These arguments were presented by women whose children were, at that very moment, being cared for by sitters. Only Kathy Taylor agreed with me. We fought over the issue for days, and I knew that I should give in—that the majority should decide the content of the course—but something in me refused to capitulate. What had begun as an interesting idea had been transformed into a crusade for the recognition that women had very specific problems in our society.

Finally, I said that I could not allow a course that focused on stereotyping to omit women and that if the rest of the group did not want a discussion of women in the course they would have to find another theme. Since our time was coming to an end and people were exhausted by days of debate, my colleagues agreed that we would do a week on women's issues.

I had argued for the inclusion of women, but I had no suggestions for reading for that section. The list that Carolyn had shared with me included only books, and I had not read any of them. What we needed were a few short and concise articles and perhaps a lecture on the issue by a local woman. I took the responsibility of finding two articles and hoped that Carolyn would come back with more references. We sent the final version of the course to Dr. Townsend and ended our work exhausted, a bit embattled, but mostly anxious to teach what we had spent so much energy designing.

Despite feelings of inadequacy because the other women in our group were better read, working on the course had been a wonderful experience for me. I met with peers daily and shared real work with them. I also found that I was good at running a meeting and that, while I could mediate disputes, I could also stand firm for my own beliefs. And I emerged from the argument over the inclusion of women in the course as a firmly committed "women's liberationist."

Although Ruth and I disagreed on the importance of women's liberation, teaching the course with her was just as gratifying as designing the freshman English course had been. The course was a tutorial to help the students with their work in the regular class, and we therefore had no control over the readings. The first assignment, Thoreau's *Walden*, which I had never read before, surprised me by how contemporary it seemed. Tom and I knew students who had formed communes in the country. Their attempts to "get back to nature" seemed like Thoreau's retreat to Walden Pond. I was taken aback when all but one of the students in our class thought that Thoreau had been a fool to give up a good house in town to go and live in a shack.

Ruth's response was not to tell them that they had missed the point of the book, as I might have done, but to encourage them to expand on their ideas. It became clear that for these students, who did not have Thoreau's financial security, the retreat to Walden made no sense. Thoreau had rejected what they were trying to obtain.

I was dismayed at how much I assumed about our students. I knew, of course, that they were poor, but it had not occurred to me that their economic status might have an effect on their response to a book. Our students' views of Thoreau's retreat had exposed my assumptions and made me begin to question how much my responses to the subsequent readings were a function of being middle class and white. Yet, because Ruth and I had taken our students' perceptions of Thoreau seriously, they were able to listen to our understanding of the radical aspects of his philosophy and see him within his historical context. Although the students continued to be critical of the readings for the rest of the course, the class was well attended and the discussions very lively.

The experience of the teacher of the regular class with our students was just the opposite. During a meeting she told us that they cut class often, and when they did come they were usually quiet and sullen, except for one young woman whose voice was so loud and whose bracelets made so much noise that the teacher could hardly conduct the class when this student was present. While we agreed that this student was loud, she was also the only one who had liked *Walden* and was willing to take on the whole class to defend her perception of Thoreau's work. Our students, we found, were much more willing to express their ideas than the other students at the college. I told the teacher that I hoped my class in the fall would be half as stimulating as this one was. She was not convinced, however, of the potential of our students to make her class interesting and lively. As we left the meeting, it seemed clear to me that she had no interest in finding out who our students were and was "freaked out" by a class that was filled with blacks and Hispanics from New York City.

I had no doubt that the woman was a racist, but I thought about her response to our students from another standpoint. It was true that she was from the South, the daughter of a high-ranking military officer, and that the color of our students was certainly a factor in her response. It seemed to me, however, that there was something besides color that elicited such a strong reaction in her, at least with respect to the young women, who seemed to drive her crazy. Ruth and I had often discussed the fact that our students were different from the white students at the College. They were loud and sometimes outspoken. We liked them for that, but the other teacher wanted them to be like her—prim and "proper." She might have been able to accept a class that was half black and Hispanic if they had behaved like her other students. Racism, I was beginning to realize, was very complex.

Just as our course was about to end I finally heard from Henry Townsend. He had basically accepted our syllabus but wanted to discuss it further when he got back to Ithaca. He had arranged for a meeting with those of us who had designed the course and the other tutors, all of whom had been hired during the summer. I wondered why he did not want to meet with us first but was excited that he had accepted the restructuring of the course. I would now have my own discussion group and would meet with it twice a week. I was anxious, too, to hear what the new tutors would think of our work.

Kathy Taylor and I went to the meeting together and listened as Dr. Townsend began the meeting with a rather critical overview of the syllabus. He wasn't sure that the theme made sense, and to him most of the readings did not seem appropriate to the English department. As if on cue, one of the other tutors said he didn't know how he could teach the essays by James Baldwin that we had selected for the section on racism. I had read them just that week and could not see why anyone could not teach what seemed to me to be beautifully constructed and very clear prose. He responded that he knew nothing about the subjects the essays addressed and therefore felt inadequate teaching about them. Kathy said that Baldwin, like any good writer, had provided the necessary information within the piece. One of the other tutors agreed that it was also impossible for her to teach those essays. She had never lived in Harlem and was not a sociologist. I asked her if she felt comfortable teaching the George Orwell story we had assigned for the same week, and she immediately replied that she would have no problems with "Marrakech." That surprised me, I said, since I assumed she had never been to Morocco, the setting of the story. It seemed to me that Harlem was a lot closer to our experiences than Morocco. The tension in the room was mounting, and I seemed to be the one on the spot. The other tutors who had designed the course had become very quiet. I told myself that we had to be open to criticism on the syllabus. It was our baby. We couldn't expect the people who had not been involved in the design to accept it without question. But there was something about the criticisms of Baldwin that made me furious, and, when one women shouted that Orwell was a real writer and that Baldwin was a sociologist, I began to shake with rage. Baldwin was black and wrote about blacks. He was, therefore, not a *real* writer. Just as our students had not acted the way the teacher had wanted them to be and were in her estimation incorrigible, this woman thought that Baldwin was not a writer because he wrote out of his own concerns and experience. Before I knew what I was saying, I shouted back, "That's a racist comment."

A deathly silence descended on the room broken only by a few gasps. It was acceptable for my colleague to deny James Baldwin's skill as a writer because of his subject matter but to name what she had done went far beyond the limits of convention. Henry Townsend broke the silence by asking me to apologize. I refused, saying that James Baldwin was a writer, not a sociologist. If my colleague would only read the essays we had chosen, she could see that they not only fit the theme of the course but were also very well crafted. We had presented them as literature, not sociology. I was silent while I listened to more complaints about the section on women. I wondered why the other women who had designed the syllabus had been so quiet. Did they agree that Baldwin was not a real writer?

When the meeting was finally over I was gratified that no changes had been made, although a group of the new tutors said they were willing to work with Dr. Townsend to see about altering the latter part of the first semester and changing the second semester. As I gathered my things, I was astounded to see that Kathy had gone to the front of the room to speak to Henry Townsend. As I waited for her, I thought about what had happened. It seemed clear to me that he had sabotaged our whole effort. He had not met with us before the large meeting with the new tutors to go over his concerns about the syllabus and had invited criticisms by his very negative overview. I felt betrayed by him and now by Kathy as I watched them engage in what looked like a very pleasant conversation. Maybe I was unfit for any conventional interchange.

Since Kathy had driven me to the meeting, I had to wait for her to give me a ride home. We walked to her car and rode to my house in silence. As I was about to get out of her car, Kathy apologized for not speaking up in the meeting. She agreed that Townsend had wanted all the criticism about the new syllabus that he could get from the new tutors. She even wondered if he had met with them before the large meeting. She had gone to speak to him for the same reason she had not been able to speak up in the meeting. She couldn't stand conflict. I wondered if her problems stemmed from being a Catholic or a woman but was too exhausted to deal with either. I got out of the car and said we could talk more the next day. We never did have that conversation. I was not willing to open myself to any criticism about my behavior at the meeting. I promised myself that I would try to control my emotions at any future meetings and devoted my energy to preparing for my first class.

The first assignment was "The White Race and Its Heroes," from Eldridge Cleaver's *Soul on Ice*. Since many whites seemed to see all blacks as the same, I thought it was important to present Cleaver within the context of the various strands of black politics.

I walked into the room and was surprised to see a black woman dressed in African clothes sitting in the front row: her name was Elaine Jones. I proceeded to describe the political perspectives of contemporary black leaders, and when I was through Elaine raised her hand. "Let me tell you about Brother Malcolm, Brother King, and Brother Carmichael," she said and turned toward the class to give a lecture on racism and the civil rights movement. Despite the differences among black leaders, she said, all of them were fighting the same evil. The attention of the entire class, including me, was riveted on her. When she was finished I asked her some questions, then the students joined in. The discussion lasted past the hour, and, as the next class came into the room, a small crowd of students were still clustered around Elaine.

Over the next few weeks Elaine's participation in class was less dramatic, but the other students were no less attentive to her comments. I had believed that teachers could learn from their students but as I listened to Elaine's highly sophisticated comments, which seemed to be based on extensive political experience, I wondered what she could learn from me. After she handed in her first paper I decided that it was foolish to demand that she attend this freshman English class. The paper was beautifully written. My limited writing skills could not be helpful to someone at her level. When I returned her paper I told her that I thought the class would be a waste of her time, that I would expect her to do all the readings and assignments but that I could not, in good conscience, require her to come to class. If she wanted to attend I would appreciate her participation since her comments had sparked so much meaningful discussion. She seemed surprised but said she would think about attending class. At the next meeting I was delighted to see Elaine sitting in her familiar seat in the first row.

We sometimes talked after class, and slowly toward the middle of the semester Elaine and I became friends. She had, she told me, not spoken to white people for a very long time unless it was absolutely necessary. After dropping out of college she had worked at various jobs and for the last few years had also been part of a black nationalist organization in Chicago, where she was born and raised. Being at a predominantly white college was very hard on her and living in the dorm and encountering the other students' blatant racism there was almost intolerable.

I wondered how she had chosen Ithaca College and was surprised by her response. She had been having problems with the attitude of the men in the Afro-Arts Center toward the role of women. They believed that women's primary duty was to support men and bolstered their position with the argument that women's subordination was going back to an African tradition. Her decision to leave Chicago came on the evening of the opening performance of a pageant produced by the center. Elaine had been responsible for the design and production of the many elaborate costumes, yet on the afternoon before the performance some of the men had told her to remain backstage. They said they were concerned that she would detract attention from the "brothers" who had worked on the production. Elaine refused to do what they asked and decided that night to leave the center and Chicago. She had heard about the new black studies program that had been instituted at Cornell after the occupation of the Straight and called James Turner, the director, to ask if it were possible to enter that fall. She had known Turner from political work in Chicago. He told her that there were no openings for that fall but there was a program at Ithaca College that could help her financially. If she were a student at Ithaca College, she could take courses at Cornell. Ithaca College had one opening in the EOP, so she decided to apply and was accepted. It was too late, however, for the summer orientation program, which was why she had not been in the class that Ruth and I taught.

While Elaine's belief in women's equality was as strong as mine, there was much about the fledgling women's movement that she did not understand. The women she had known when she was a child had always worked whether or not they were married. Most of her friends worked too. Why was the women's movement so anxious to get women into the workplace? The women she knew hoped to have the opportunity to stay home and take care of their children. Her own mother had never had that luxury. She had worked in a factory when Elaine was a child and now worked at the post office. I told her my experience had been very different. The only woman in the family who worked was my aunt, and it seemed to me that there was some shame associated with the fact that the family was dependent on her income to make ends meet.

But there was also much in her description of growing up in Chicago that made me nostalgic for my old neighborhood. I was able to share some things with Elaine that had not seemed appropriate in my conversations with Ruth, whose fondest memory was the day she got her library card. There was a library in my neighborhood, but my friends and I only visited once to see what it was like. Elaine and I, on the other hand, reminisced over dates, clothes, and learning to dance. We listened to records that Elaine had brought with her from Chicago—Aretha Franklin, Stevie Wonder, and someone I had never heard of, James Cleveland. I knew Aretha and Stevie Wonder but had given up that kind of music for the more politically correct Beatles, Judy Collins, and Bob Dylan. As we listened to Elaine's records, particularly James Cleveland, the gospel singer, I felt that I had come back to the kind of music I had loved when I was younger. Although I had not heard much gospel before, the feelings and rhythm of the music reminded me of the Latin music and jazz I hadn't heard for years and only then realized how much I missed it. Elaine told me about the racism she had encountered in the school she attended where the teachers were all white and the students all black. I thought about my school years in New York City. Although my teachers and I were the same race, I felt strangely out of place, perhaps because I had not spoken English until I went to school. When I thought about my high school years in Ridgewood, however, Elaine's descriptions of the assumptions the teachers had made about the black students' lack of aspirations for a higher education and generally low intellectual ability struck a familiar chord. She seemed to understand the pain I had experienced in ways that no one else had.

We frequently discussed politics and the civil rights movement. Elaine's analysis, based on political experience as well as reading, focused on racism and seemed so clear. Similar discussions with Tom or Ruth or David spun out elaborate conspiracies of the ruling class. I thought it would be quite wonderful for them to have a discussion together, but it seemed difficult to arrange. I hoped that when the spring semester began there would be more opportunity for Elaine and Ruth to get to know each other. They were both so important to me that I wanted them to like each other. The few times they had met, however, had not been very promising. I had told Ruth about Elaine from the day of the first class, and, when we began to be friendly, Ruth invited us for coffee. Elaine seemed reluctant to go but finally agreed. When we got to Ruth's apartment Elaine was unusually quiet and Ruth's effusive manner, which put most of the people I knew at ease, seemed to make Elaine even more withdrawn. The afternoon had been very tense, and I hoped that Elaine's reaction had only been her usual reluctance to be open with white people. After they had been together a few more times and the tension eased only slightly, I began to wonder if they would ever get beyond their mutual discomfort. I was dismayed, too, when Ruth began to tell me that Elaine was not a very serious person. She complained that she did not seem interested in talking about racism or any kind of politics. Elaine had to live with racism, and I could understand why she might not feel like discussing it. Ruth, however, was not convinced.

I was concerned that Ruth and Elaine did not seem to like each other, but I felt wonderful as the semester ended. I was beginning to understand, from what I learned from Elaine, that black people had their own culture and did not necessarily want to be like whites. I looked forward to the next semester when I could convey some of my new insights to my students. I realized, too, as Elaine left for the holidays, that I would miss her. Although we were very different in some ways, I felt very relaxed with Elaine, and we generally had fun when we were together. When she returned in February, I would make sure that she and Ruth saw more of each other. I was certain that, in time, Ruth would be able to see Elaine for the person she was.

Chapter 13

*T*hough in January I needed to prepare for the second semester of the class, I had also promised myself that I would continue the reading I had begun that fall. When Carolyn came through Ithaca on her way back from California, she had much to share about the women's movement on the West Coast. She had gathered more lists of readings, including a few articles that I thought might be useful for the course. She had also been very moved by Doris Lessing's *Children of Violence* series and highly recommended it to me.

I began *Martha Quest* and was overwhelmed by how much of what Lessing wrote seemed to describe my life, although the setting was Africa and the heroine had come to adulthood between the wars. I had found it hard to put *Martha Quest* down and often read long into the night. *A Proper Marriage* was even more gripping. Lessing's books seemed to clearly articulate what had been inchoate in my own thinking. Women were not only prevented from participating in certain activities, but, more important, the limitations became so much a part of their psyches that once socialized they did not think beyond those parameters. In my case, no one had told me directly that I could not have a career, but by the time I was a sophomore in high school I had accepted the idea that women should not be as capable as men. I consciously decided not to be a "brain" and directed most of my energies to what would attract boys. From that point on I assumed that I would be taken care of by someone more capable than myself—a man, of course.

As I began to read *A Proper Marriage* I was glad that the series had five volumes, for Martha Quest had become very important to me. She shared my deepest concerns. Like me, she had married

153

young and shortly after the wedding suspected that she was pregnant. Her reaction to the possibility that she was carrying a child was as "a web that was tight around her." [1] Before going to the doctor to confirm her suspicion, she, too, had tried to induce an abortion by scalding herself in a hot bath. I wondered where we had both gotten the idea that hot water would force out the fetus.

The similarities in our feelings and experiences astounded me. She received the news that she was pregnant with dismay, and her doctor had also assured her that she would soon feel differently. Many young women, he told her, were initially upset by an unplanned baby but had come to be delighted with the prospect of being a mother within a very short time. Though Martha Quest did eventually look forward to the birth of her baby, like me, she was mostly anxious to be finished with being pregnant. Neither crying children nor a dinner waiting to made stopped the reading that had become almost a compulsion. Martha Quest's delivery of her baby had been hard. She had also felt that she and her husband were in different worlds, although her feelings came after the birth of the baby and mine when we reached the hospital when Hannah was about to be born. The details didn't matter. What was important was that another woman had had feelings that were identical to mine.

The congruence of experience and feeling with one other woman, even a fictional one, was very powerful. I began to rethink the years since I learned that I was pregnant with Neal. I was not a monster for not wanting a baby. I was not unnatural for feeling, once he was born, that unending drudgery was driving me crazy. It was understandable to feel that caring for an infant could be maddening. It was hard. It occurred to me that what I was experiencing with this book was what Carolyn and the women in Massachusetts got from their support groups. But I did not envy Carolyn and her group. I had Doris Lessing and Martha Quest. I needed nothing more.

For the next few weeks my life centered on Martha Quest. After I had finished *A Proper Marriage,* I went on to *The Golden Notebook.* Although it was not the next volume of the *Children of Violence* series, Carolyn had told me that it was the book Lessing had written after *A Proper Marriage.* I opened the pages of *The Golden Note-*

---

[1] Doris Lessing, *A Proper Marriage* (New York: New American Library, 1964), 99.

book, anticipating another long conversation with Martha and myself. In this book the main character was Anna Wulf, but the change didn't seem to matter. Whether I was actually reading the book or not, Anna/Martha had become a constant companion. I was so engrossed with her that for the first time in many years Tom got angry with me. I was halfway through *The Golden Notebook* when I heard him shouting that I lived with him, not Martha Quest. I looked up, startled as he grabbed the book out of my hands. I realized then that he had been trying to talk to me, but I had not responded. I also realized that I didn't care how he felt. I only wanted the book back. He stormed out of the room, and, as I picked up *The Golden Notebook* from the corner of the floor where he had flung it, I heard the front door slam. He had left the house. I was glad. Now I could read without being disturbed. For a change, I was the one who was preoccupied.

Anna Wulf had done the unthinkable. She had left not only her husband but her child as well and had moved to England alone. Lessing's description of Anna's feelings and the events that led to her departure made the act seem totally understandable. Anna was not a monstrous, unnatural creature but a woman who was unable to cope with the extreme difficulties of being a wife and mother. While I had never seriously considered leaving Tom and the children, reading about Anna Wulf's decision to leave her family made me feel less guilty about the times when I did feel like running away from them.

My guilt was also assuaged by Lessing's description of Anna's marriage and the relationships she formed with men in England. Perhaps, I thought, as I read about Anna's continual attempts and failures to develop emotional intimacy with the men in her life, the limitations of my marriage were not entirely my fault. Like Tom, Anna's husband and lovers had seemed preoccupied with more important things than relating to her. The emotional intimacy that had been so elusive with men seemed, on the other hand, to come as a matter of course with Anna's friend Molly. Although they often argued, because they were able to share their feelings, the two women developed a loving, supportive relationship. Though their intimacy did not include sexuality, it seemed at times that Molly and Anna's relationship was at the core of their lives rather than the difficult, limited relationships they both had with men. I realized that the quality of my friendships with women was often like what Molly and Anna shared.

When I finished the book Lessing stayed with me, although the semester had begun, and I could not begin the next novel in the series. Even if I had had time I wondered if I would be able to read any more. The three novels I had already read had had such a powerful emotional impact that I felt I would probably be unable to take in more. I seemed to be functioning well enough. My class was going well, and Tom and I resumed giving and going to dinner parties when the semester began again. I slowly realized that something had changed in me over the last month. I was deeply sad—not depressed, but sad. I felt as if I were in a kind of mourning, a grief for the self I had given up so long ago. Reading Doris Lessing had opened me up to the pain that I had put away when I was pregnant with Neal. I was grieving for the part of me that had died when I accepted the role that was proper for females. Becoming a mother had only concluded a long process of giving up my self.

Tom and the children became symbolic of the self I had lost. I knew that it wasn't their fault that I had accepted my role. I knew that it had begun long before I knew Tom. He had been more supportive of my interests than most men I knew of their wives' development. He had certainly been as understanding as a man could of my growing interest in the women's movement. It was ridiculous to blame the children. They had not asked to be born. Although my rational self knew all of this, I could not stop myself from recoiling when Tom or the children came near me. I felt sorry for them, but for months physical contact with my husband and children was agony for me.

Doris Lessing had pushed me over the edge. When I came out of mourning some months after finishing *The Golden Notebook*, I was fully committed to working to change my life and the world. Women, I realized, were not free to develop ourselves. To keep one's "proper place" as a woman was to destroy oneself as a human being. I was convinced, too, that any real change in my life and the world could come only through the cooperative efforts of women with each other. Doris Lessing had already changed my life, and it was perfectly clear to me that those books could not have been written by a man. Just as white people could never really know what it was like to be black, men could only have an outsider's perception of the experience of being a woman. Doris Lessing had opened the door. I was going to find the self I had lost and try to change the world so that other women would not have to choose between committing a kind of suicide and being an outcast.

Author's maternal grandparents and children, 1912. From left: Arsenic, Elmas, Berjouhi, Hampartzum, and Ashot Tutuian. Berjouhi is the author's mother.

Author's paternal grandparents and children, circa 1914. From left: Khrosoff and Vaghinak Avakian; unidentified family member; Voski Avakian. Vaghinak is the author's father.

The author and her parents, 1939.

Family members in New York City, 1937. Rear, from left: Howard Donigian, Berjouhi Avakian, Manoush Avakian, Elmas Tutuian, Goharik Avakian. Center: Arsenic Donigian.

The author and her grandmother, Elmas Tutuian, 1941.

The author and her brother, Paul Avakian, 1946.

*The author (center) at her six-
teenth birthday, 1955.*

The author's son, circa 1968.

The author and her daughter, 1967.

Arlene Avakian, circa 1977.

The author in Amherst, Massachusetts, late seventies.

Chapter 14

*M*y new commitment to women's issues felt like a call to the barricades, but the action I was able to take seemed very modest. I worked with the Ithaca College Women's Liberation Front to organize a rally. The other members of the group encouraged me to speak, and, although I was unsure about my ability to address a large crowd, I agreed. The rally was a great success, and, once I had gotten over the initial shock of feeling my voice detach from my throat as it went through the microphone, I found that I was exhilarated by speaking to so many people. The much disputed women's section of the freshman English course came after the rally, and I not only arranged for an outside speaker but also organized a panel of a few of us from the Women's Liberation Front. I hoped to take more substantive action, but that was still unclear. The fall semester of 1969 was coming to an end, and we agreed to wait until the new term to discuss the direction the Women's Liberation Front would take.

The changes in my life with Tom also seemed mild in comparison to what I considered to be a major breakthrough in my consciousness as a woman. We discussed housework. I didn't want any help with the cooking since I enjoyed creating meals, and, despite my new consciousness, I thought it would be too much to ask Tom to clean up after dinner. Cleaning the house, however, was another matter. I had always hated being responsible for everyone else's mess, and, for as long as I could remember, a day of housework had left me depressed. As soon as the despised tasks were over, it was only a matter of hours before most of the rooms needed straightening again. I wanted help from Tom, and as I talked about the frustration of a job that had no end, I began to cry. I was em-

157

barrassed by my tears. Housework seemed insignificant, but I guessed that I resented cleaning even more than I knew. Tom was very understanding. If it meant that much to me, he said, he would certainly help.

Despite his compassion, Tom never saw what needed to be done, nor was he more likely to pick up his books, papers, or even his laundry than he had been before our conversation. My feelings about housework were intense, but I thought it was petty to make an issue over cleaning. It didn't seem worth the trouble to continually remind Tom to dust or vacuum. I either did it myself or let the dust and dirt collect.

While the distribution of work around the house had not changed much, I was much more vocal about my ideas with Tom as well as with our friends. Conversations that included negative comments about "women's lib" or jokes about women ceased to be light social interaction. No one could make a derogatory comment about women or our movement in my presence without a fight from me. I also tried to raise women's issues in all the contacts I had with people and was, therefore, usually arguing with most of the people I knew. I guessed that I had become what David Berman had feared when he heard that I had become a women's liberationist, "a woman with a chip on her shoulder." I felt that I was at war, and, if David and my other friends didn't like it, that was too bad.

I sensed, too, that Ruth thought I had gone too far. The reality of the oppression of women was firmly in my consciousness, and I saw evidence of it everywhere. There was no turning back. I was becoming very angry, mostly at men. It seemed to me that they benefited from a system that oppressed women, and they refused even to acknowledge that the oppression existed. Ruth never brought up women's issues, and she usually changed the subject when I did.

My relationship with Ruth was also affected by Elaine. My attempts to provide an opportunity for them to get to know each other had been disasters. Ruth had continued to complain about Elaine's lack of commitment to politics, while Elaine and I became closer. Unwilling to accept the possibility that these two very important people in my life might not like each other, I kept trying to get them to know each other as I knew them. Perhaps, I thought, if we all ate together everyone might feel more relaxed. I planned a dinner party. I asked Elaine to come and bring Art, the man she had begun to see regularly. She agreed and asked if she could invite Sam, a friend of theirs. I also knew Sam and thought it was fine for him to join us. I was delighted when Ruth, David, and Phil, a friend who worked at *New Day*, also accepted my invitation.

Ruth, David, and Phil came at the appointed hour, and the men quickly got into one of their political conversations, which always bored me, no matter how hard I tried to concentrate on the intricacies of what they were saying. I had known that Elaine would be late. I had learned early in our relationship never to expect her to arrive on time and had told her to come earlier than I had planned dinner, hoping that she would arrive close to the dinner hour. When she, Art, and Sam finally arrived, Elaine announced that she was starved. I laughed and told her that the appetizers would be ready in a few minutes and were not burned only because I had learned to deal with her time.

When I brought out the Chinese-style barbecued spareribs and shrimp toast, the previously stilted conversation turned to food. Everyone seemed to be talking at once about how good everything was, and I was beginning to hope that the evening would prove to be a success. When we moved into the dining room, however, I watched as people began to talk to the people they knew best. David, Phil, and Tom were discussing a new United States tariff on textiles and its ramifications on Japan's relationship with China. Elaine, Art, and Sam were talking about their days in junior high school. Ruth was quiet, and I was watching the scene. The table was clearly divided. After coffee and dessert Elaine asked if anyone wanted to play cards. Art and Sam said that a game of *bid whist* sounded good. When no one else expressed interest in playing, Elaine asked me for cards and they went into the kitchen.

The living room was silent and tense while whoops of laughter came from the kitchen. It was unusual at the least to have a dinner party split into two groups, but it didn't really upset me. I was often bored by the conversations at dinner parties and thought it might make sense to play cards instead of endlessly talking about the progress of the war and the movement against it. As I listened to Elaine and Art yell at each other over a play one of them had made, I wished that I had gone into the kitchen. Ruth, David, and Phil left shortly after the card game began. Elaine, Art, and Sam finished their game, stayed until I cleaned up, and left thanking me for the wonderful food.

The next morning Ruth called to say that she was very upset.

Elaine, she said, was running my life. She had been able to see that very clearly when Elaine came into the house and ordered me to get the food. I was surprised by Ruth's reaction to what I had taken as the ease with which good friends relate to each other. Ruth was bothered by more than Elaine's domination of my life. She and David had, she told me, repeatedly tried to engage Elaine, Art, and Sam in serious conversation, but they had seemed only to want to be frivolous. I wondered what was wrong with having some fun but didn't have a chance to ask Ruth, who said that the final straw had come when they had decided to play cards. Their rudeness had taken her breath away.

I was becoming very angry listening to Ruth criticize my friend so severely. It seemed to me that if Elaine had been white she would never have been so harsh, knowing as she did that we were very close. I was upset, too, that Ruth's judgment was based on Elaine's refusal to follow our conventions for proper dinner party behavior. If politeness required that my friends had to be like me, then I wanted none of it in my house. And Ruth seemed to think that seriousness was defined by talking about politics. I told Ruth that Elaine had been and was very active politically. Did she know that Elaine had been seriously hurt when she marched in Cicero, Illinois, for open housing? I reminded Ruth that Elaine was responsible for the formation of the Afro-American Society at Ithaca College and that both Art and Sam were members of the Black Liberation Front at Cornell. I was glad, I said, that Elaine felt enough at ease in my house to do what she wanted rather than acting like us so we could be more comfortable. It didn't seem to me that it was intrinsically better to have a political discussion than it was to play cards. It was merely what we did. It had seemed to me that the people in the kitchen were having much more fun than we were, but I didn't bring up that point. Having fun, I knew, was irrelevant—frivolous.

When the conversation was finally over, I hung up the phone and sat at the table. Did Ruth really think there was only one proper way to relate to people? Did we always have to be so serious? Did Elaine dominate me? I knew she was a powerful personality, but I enjoyed her. When Tom came into the kitchen I told him what had happened. He, too, had thought the evening had gone fairly well. No one had stopped him from doing what he usually did at dinner parties.

I decided to call Elaine to ask her what she thought. When she heard my voice she said she was glad I had called. It was getting to be lunchtime, and she could not bear dorm food after eating at my house the previous evening. Were there any leftovers? I told her to come over. There was lots to eat, and I had something I needed to talk to her about. When we had finished lunch I asked her what she had thought about the dinner party. She said it was nice. The food had been great. Art and Sam had told her they had felt welcomed, and she had felt very much at home in my house.

When she wanted to know why I had asked, I told her some of what Ruth had said. Elaine was unusually silent. After a few minutes she said she would tell me how she really felt about Ruth Berman if I wanted to know. She said Ruth was one of the most patronizing white people she had ever encountered; she had felt that the first day we had gone to Ruth's house for coffee but had not said anything to me earlier because she knew that Ruth was a friend of mine. Now that I had seen for myself some of Ruth's problems, Elaine said she could share her feelings with me. She said Ruth would only relate to her if she discussed racial issues, and because of that Elaine had never responded to her attempts at "serious" conversation.

I had learned a very important lesson from my infamous dinner party and its aftermath. Ruth's refusal to accept any behavior other than that she deemed appropriate showed me how subtle racism could be. While she had berated the teacher of the freshman English class the previous summer for not being able to recognize that the EOP students' behavior was part of a different cultural orientation, she expected Elaine and her friends to behave like white academics. Any behavior outside those parameters was seen as an attempt to take over: it was inappropriate and insulting. The dinner party did not end my friendship with Ruth but put it under a severe strain. I was upset with Ruth's attitudes, and she was, I am sure, disturbed that I continued to be "dominated" by Elaine.

Despite all of my problems with Ruth I tried very hard to be a good friend to her when the history department informed her that she would not be rehired. The news was devastating. She had worked very hard at her job and loved teaching. It seemed clear to Tom and me, as well as to most of the liberal faculty at the college, that Ruth's dismissal was for political reasons. She and David were well known in Ithaca as radicals, and it was also well known that Ruth brought her politics into the classroom. As soon as the decision became public, a large committee of faculty and students formed to fight it. Ruth had agreed to wage the battle not only because she loved teaching but because she felt obligated to fight a department that had, by this action and others, so clearly aligned itself with the status quo. When the department heard that she was going to challenge their decision all of the men literally stopped talking to her. The one other woman in the department was pleasant to her but told Ruth that she could not jeopardize her own position since she did not yet have tenure. In the end, the history department saw no need to change its decision.

As the end of the semester approached, I worried about the tutorial for EOP students that Ruth and I had agreed to teach. I had learned, finally, to keep my relationship with her separate from my friendship with Elaine. That summer, however, we were all going to be teaching the tutorial together. Though the Afro-American Society had not stated that they had any problems with us teaching the class, they felt that the students would be more comfortable if a black person were a member of the team. They recommended Elaine. The recommendation had come before the dinner party, but even then I felt that Ruth would be reluctant to teach with Elaine. Since raising an objection to the recommendation of the Afro-American Society would have been difficult, there was no question that we would agree to their suggestion.

While I was nervous about the summer tutorial, I looked forward to the fall when I would be teaching the freshman English course again. I had been generally pleased with the students' response to the material but was also anxious to make some changes. In the spring of 1970 there was still not very much material available on women's issues, but I had read whatever I could find and wanted to expand the section on women. I hoped that we could use *Martha Quest* or at least a section from the novel that had had such a profound effect on my life.

I found out soon, however, that I was not going to have the opportunity to teach anything that fall. Henry Townsend informed me by phone that the department had decided my services would no longer be needed. I was truly stunned by the news. When I asked him why I was being fired, Townsend explained that I was not. The position I had was being terminated. The course had been reorganized, and I was not qualified for the new position. I said that I had not known that the course had been redesigned, and, as far as I knew, none of the other tutors knew anything about such a plan either. He replied that it had been done by the department, which had felt that input from the tutors was not necessary. I shouted that the whole thing sounded like a way to fire me without actually doing it. He hung up in the middle of my tirade.

I immediately called Kathy Taylor to tell her what had happened. She had not known of any plans to redesign the course either and was as shocked as I had been. She agreed to arrange for all the tutors to meet to consider taking action. The next day she said that all of the women were anxious to come to the meeting. The one male tutor said that he didn't want the job the next fall and had no interest in what the department had done.

My relationship with the other tutors, which had had such a stormy beginning, had developed quite well. We rarely met as a group—mostly to listen to directives from Henry Townsend—but we did see each other from time to time. We had demanded office space so that we could meet with our students, and the department had allocated a tiny office for our use that was carved out of a hallway. We got to know each other by literally bumping into each other regularly. I was even on rather cordial terms with the woman I had called a racist at that first meeting in the fall.

By the time we met the next week they had all been informed by the department that the course had been redesigned. They were assured that they would be hired for the new positions, which carried the title of instructor, but kept at the same pay that we had had as tutors. They were all outraged, not only that the department had changed the course without our input but that I had been fired. They decided to draft a letter of protest and urged me to write to Henry Townsend, asking him for a formal letter of termination and reasons that I was not qualified to apply for the new position. They seemed unwilling to accept the department's decision about me, and I was delighted.

Toward the end of the meeting Kathy said that she would be unable to apply for the job. She said she could never live with herself if she took a job that had been denied to me when I was equally well qualified. I was very touched. Kathy had five young children, and I knew that her salary was crucial to the family's income. Other women responded that they would also have problems applying for the job for similar reasons. As they discussed their feelings, someone said that she thought we were overlooking the power that we had. The semester was not over, and, if we all resigned, the department would have to deal with final grades for the entire freshman class. We could demand that I be assured a position in the program for the next year. They decided to meet again to discuss the mass resignation in detail.

I left the meeting moved by the support of my colleagues. While a few of the women worked for self-fulfillment, many, like Kathy, also needed the money. For some the income from the job provided the major support for themselves and their graduate student husbands.

I was late for the next meeting, and when I arrived everyone was excitedly discussing the resignation letter Kathy had drafted. I told them that I appreciated their support but would understand if they felt they needed to keep their jobs. I also suggested that I leave to allow them to have a free discussion. Kathy told me to sit down and get to work on the letter. One of the other women said that she had thought very hard about her decision to resign and had decided that if Townsend felt he could arbitrarily fire me he could do it to her, and she wanted to protest.

Kathy's draft praised my work as a teacher and a colleague and stated that the undersigned refused any further connection with the freshman English course unless I was promised a position in the new program. But when we had put the finishing touches on the letter, Hannah Stewart said she was having second thoughts about our strategy and agreed with me that the group could have a more open discussion if I were not present.

I knew that Hannah's reservations were not based on financial need. She was a middle-class housewife whom I had met the previous year through my work with *New Day*. She and her husband, a Cornell professor, had three children, and once they were all in school she volunteered with various organizations. She had told me that she had been thinking about looking for a job. She had never worked and thought it might be good for her to try. I knew that Townsend was looking for one more tutor and told her about the opening. She applied, used me for a reference, and got the job. Now she was threatening the unity of the group, when our success depended on a group resignation. Over the protests of most of the other women, I rose to leave. I did not want to stay. I was afraid I would be unable to control my anger at Hannah for betraying me.

About an hour after I got home Kathy called to say that Hannah had refused to resign. Everyone was really upset with her, but no one could convince her to change her mind. Since we didn't have a solid front, other people began to question whether resigning would have the desired impact. The group agreed to send the original letter of protest to Townsend with a copy to the department chair. It would not include any resignations. Those who wanted to resign could do it individually. Hannah had declined even to sign the letter, for personal reasons, she said.

The letter was sent. No reply came. I received my official letter of termination, and included in the reasons that I could not be considered for the position of instructor was a reference to my calling a colleague a racist. There was nothing more to do. I was grateful to my colleagues for their support. When Dr. Townsend had called to tell me I would not have a job the next year, my initial response was that I was being fired for personal reasons. I had felt good about my first year of teaching. My classes had been responsive. The students were engaged by the material and wrote better papers; many actually improved their skills over the semester. The attempt on the part of the other tutors to have me rehired reinforced my growing sense that I might be a good teacher.

Those new skills would not be helpful in the EOP session that summer. All my worst fears about Ruth and Elaine were fulfilled. The tension among the three of us was intense, and by the end of the session Ruth and Elaine had stopped talking to each other. I had been able to maintain my friendship with both of them by establishing sharp boundaries. Before the course the three of us were never together, and I was careful not to talk about one to the other. But being with them both in class made it impossible not to choose one friend over the other. Early in the course I had attempted to mediate, but my allegiances were clearly with Elaine, and Ruth barely spoke to me.

When the last class was over I knew that my friendship with Ruth had ended. As I drove home that night, I felt a deep sorrow that Ruth was no longer my friend but also grateful that I had known her. From our first discussion about culture and politics over the rising bread dough, I had learned from Ruth. She had believed in me enough to give me the opportunity to teach this very tutorial with her the previous summer, and I had learned so much about listening to and respecting students. Although we had disagreed about women's liberation, Ruth had clearly played an important role in my growing sense of myself as an intelligent and competent woman. I had lost a good friend, and I had been fired, but I felt as if I had grown enormously over the year. Despite the fact that I didn't have a job, I looked forward to what the fall might bring.

Chapter 15

*T*oward the end of the summer I ran into Barbara Hennis, a woman who worked in the administration at Cornell and had been a guest speaker about women's liberation in the writing course. She told me that the group of faculty and staff who had been working on the development of female studies at Cornell had convinced the administration to fund a position for a half-time executive director. She herself would not be involved in the search, since she had just accepted an administrative position at Oberlin, but she urged me to apply.

I was beside myself with excitement. While I was not very clear about what a female studies program might do or what the duties of an executive director might be, I knew that I would welcome the opportunity to devote my full energies to women's issues. I went home to work on my letter of application and resume. My letter stated that I had become a feminist at six years old when the "important" Avakian child, my brother, was born. My nascent sense of the oppression of women had gone underground until the emergence of the women's movement. To my great delight, a member of the group called me for an interview.

The steering committee, I learned, made the decisions for the program, and it would be the responsibility of the executive director to implement them. It was not clear from the interview what the committee proposed beyond a general desire to alter the curriculum to include women, but I was not concerned with their lack of direction. I left the meeting fairly confident, and at the end of the week Joan Parke, a member of the committee, called to offer me the position. They were still working on getting office space but hoped to have something within the next few days.

I put down the phone both elated and terrified. I had what sounded like a dream job. I could work on women's issues and get paid for it. I would also probably meet many other women who believed as strongly in women's liberation as I did. On the other hand, I wondered if I could really do the job. What did an executive director really do? Some days I felt confident and welcomed the challenge. Other days I thought I had been excellent at convincing the committee that I was the person to hire but that they would soon realize their grave error. One thing I was sure about: I would work very hard because I cared deeply about women.

My feelings of inadequacy increased during my first few weeks on the job. Cornell had neither courses nor any other programming on women. When students inquired about female studies, I could tell them only that we hoped to develop courses and refer them to the few faculty who were on the steering committee. I had no idea where to start and looked forward to my first steering committee meeting where I hoped I would get some clear direction. When it came, however, I had no better idea of what people expected from me. As I listened to faculty discuss longitudinal studies they wanted to undertake and the foundations that might support them, I wondered what role I might play in the project. Despite the fact that I chaired the meeting, the committee seemed unaware of my existence. The one person who did seem concerned about me was Joan Parke, and I decided to talk to her about the problem of not knowing what to do with my time. The group, she said, was unclear about specific, short-term goals. Barbara, the one who first told me about the job, had been a very forceful leader, and the task of getting a funded position had been well defined. Now that we had the position, the group did not seem to know what to do. She suggested that I press the committee to be more specific about its goals.

It was clear that on some levels I would have to create my own job. Since my vision of female studies was that it would develop courses on women, I set out to find faculty who might be receptive to such an innovation. Within a few weeks I had had preliminary discussions with a member of the education department who was willing to consider sponsoring a course on women and education, and had found a person who was interested in developing such a course.

I went to the next meeting of the steering committee armed with news about the course and hopeful that with Joan's help I could focus the discussion on specific goals. Before I could begin with my new agenda, however, a member of the faculty presented us with a proposal for the position of academic coordinator, and another member of the committee, Betty Slater, presented her application for the position.

It seemed strange that I had not been consulted about the position and equally odd that a member of the committee was ready with her application for a position not yet approved by the group. I was still unsure about what I was supposed to do, yet the committee was creating another position. I was disturbed, too, that, when the discussion turned to meeting with the deans to discuss funding for the new position, I was not expected to be involved. My heart sank as I was once again ignored. Had some of the members of the steering committee already realized their mistake in hiring me, and were they now trying to save the program by bringing in Betty Slater? I ended the meeting saying that I hoped that if we did get the funding we would have an open hiring process by advertising the position. I could not support a process that did not allow other women to apply for the job. Other members of the committee came to the defense of my point.

Within a month the funding for the academic coordinator was assured, and we held a search over the objections of a sizable group, who felt that Betty was the best candidate. I had also won my point that students be invited to be on the committee. I had argued that the program was for them, and they should have a major role in deciding its direction. Joan and I had also made some headway focusing the group. The others agreed with our suggestion to write a proposal for the funding of a permanent program.

Even in our preliminary discussion about that proposal I had begun to sense that there was a difference in my perspective about what female studies should be and that of most of the vocal members of the committee. My conception was that any program that dealt with women's issues emerged out of and was stimulated by the growing women's movement. Although I was not clear on details, I saw female studies as the academic arm of that struggle to overthrow the system of male power—to change the world from the way men had organized it. We would create a world based on the female qualities of nurturing and cooperation rather than aggression and competition. Many of my colleagues, to my great surprise, seemed anxious to deny any such connection. Even in our meetings they were uncomfortable articulating the potential for a female studies program to make any major changes in attitudes toward and treatment of women outside of the academy. There were also uninterested in equalizing the student-teacher relationship or using student experiences as a legitimate part of the class material. I wanted to overthrow male power at Cornell, but for many members of the committee, including Betty Slater, Cornell was just fine as it was, except for its omission of women.

Though I wasn't sure what female studies should be, I knew intuitively that any real change in the curriculum would mean more than sticking women into what already existed. I was anxious to talk to other women about possibilities for the program but, aside from Joan Parke, few of the faculty on the steering committee seemed open to any discussions with me. I was delighted when Joan told me that women at the University of Pittsburgh had organized a conference on female studies. She and some of the other members of the steering committee, including Barbara, were going, and she urged me to join them. I thought it would be important for me to go to the conference, both to hear what women at other colleges and universities were thinking and to try to get to know some of the members of the steering committee.

I was uncharacteristically quiet on the long drive. I had promised myself I would listen to the conversation, no matter how hard it might be, to find out what these women thought about female studies and the movement. I had felt more and more strongly after each steering committee meeting that my political perspective was very different from that of most of the faculty. If I used this trip carefully, I could learn the specifics of that difference. I was particularly alert to Barbara Hennis's opinions, since it was clear that everyone thought she was exceptionally astute. I was heartened when I heard her say she thought it was important to include students in the planning of female studies, but I was appalled when she told us why. Their support, she said, was vital, and we could count on it only if they were included. The ensuing discussion of student power inevitably raised the issue of how the program would relate to Afro-American Studies, since black students had initiated much of the activism on campus. Black support, everyone agreed, was not important. Since the Straight takeover, their political strength on campus had diminished. Any alignment with blacks might, in fact, be a serious liability at Cornell.

I was relieved when talk turned to relationships with men. All of the women were married, and though most had some help from their husbands with the housework, all did the cooking for their

families. Preparing meals, they all bitterly complained, was drudgery. The talk turned to how they minimized the amount of cooking
they had to do. One woman served her family peanut butter and
jelly sandwiches or TV dinners two or three times a week, and
another made a large casserole on the weekend which they ate for
most of the week. Clearly these women ate only because they had
to. Their discussion of food neither included the pleasures of cooking nor of eating. I wondered if they would understand the joy of
savoring a succulent morsel of lamb that had been marinated for
a day or more in onions, lemon, oil, wine, and herbs then broiled
over a charcoal fire. They seemed like another species to me, and
I wondered if I could ever bridge the gap between us.

As we approached Pittsburgh and followed our directions to
JoAnn Gardner's house, the conversations about food stopped.
Barbara had met JoAnn at another conference, and she had offered
to put us up. When we drove up to her large home I was physically
and emotionally exhausted. The trip that I had hoped would be an
opportunity for me to get to know my colleagues better had already
made me feel more alienated.

The next day, however, I would hear support for my idea that
including women in the curriculum as it existed was not sufficient.
Florence Howe, a woman who described herself as having come to
a political consciousness during the civil rights movement, gave a
stirring lecture on the importance of keeping a strong political perspective in female studies. Her view of the program's goal was not
only to add women to what existed but also to change the way the
academy operated so that it could incorporate women and our concerns at every level. When she was finished I wanted to stand on
my seat and cheer, and I expected the audience would at least rise
to give her a standing ovation. I was dismayed by the polite but
not wholly enthusiastic applause. I turned to Joan, hoping to find
some support. I was relieved when she said the talk raised very vital issues.

My feelings were very mixed when the conference was over.
On the one hand, I had gotten support from Florence Howe, but,
on the other, what I had learned about the women I had to work
with was very disturbing. They seemed content with the way things
were if only women were included, while I wanted a revolution.
On the ride home I hardly spoke, but, when Barbara said she
thought Florence's speech was idealistic, I calmly told her I disagreed. As we drove out of Philadelphia I insisted that we stop at

a roadside stand. They had beautiful eggplants, which would not be in season in Ithaca for weeks.

I returned from the conference determined that the majority of the committee was not going to have its way without a fight. I was going to do what I could to bring my politics to the program. Joan had also come to see that many of the members of the committee were, indeed, quite conservative despite their support of female studies. She felt there were members of the committee who were not very vocal who might share our view of what the program should be.

As I thought about past meetings in light of what Joan said, I realized that it was quite possible that I had overlooked the support that I had. Some of the staff members on the committee had often agreed with me. I decided to meet individually with them to see what they thought about what we ought to be doing. They all felt that their influence on steering committee decisions was severely limited because they were not faculty. It became quite clear from talking with them that my isolation from the more vocal members of the committee had been influenced by the fact that I only had a B.A. and that my previous associations had been with Ithaca College. Cornell, they told me, was a very elitist institution, and the women on the female studies steering committee were no exception to that rule.

The first major battle in the program came over the selection of the academic coordinator. I had initially insisted that we do a search in the interest of fairness, but, as I came to know Betty Slater, I felt she was wrong for the position. While she felt that the curriculum should include more material on women and that there should be more women on the faculty, she was basically uncritical of the university. In fact, she seemed to love Cornell. My dedication to bring the need for larger change to our efforts would be seriously hampered if Betty Slater became the academic coordinator.

In an effort to find a candidate who shared my vision, I asked Carol Dietrich, the chair of the philosophy department at Ithaca College, if she would be interested in applying for the position. Carol was well respected by her colleagues and students and was one of the few tenured women on the faculty at the college. I was sure that Carol would share some of my views, since she had been instrumental in bringing students into the department decision-making process. Students comprised half of the membership of every departmental committee and were full voting members. Within a few days

Carol responded. She had decided to apply.

I had heard about Carol's intellect from faculty and students, but even I was impressed with the breadth and depth of her answers to the committee. She believed the disciplines were male centered and that they needed to be critically reevaluated from a feminist perspective. She outlined the male bias in her own discipline and attacked the myth that philosophy was a value-free inquiry. I could see that the committee was also impressed, though some of the most conservative members were obviously taken aback by her willingness to apply feminism so directly to an academic discipline.

Carol seemed to articulate what I had been unable to express. A basic critique of the disciplines was the real work of female studies. Women's liberation was not content to merely see women enter male arenas but attacked the male system just as Carol had attacked philosophy for being male defined. With Carol as the academic coordinator of female studies, I believed we could move the new discipline to a truly revolutionary position.

Betty's interview, on the other hand, provided no insights. Her response to what she would do in the position was that she would carry out the wishes of the committee. When pressed to articulate her perspective on female studies, she merely said that she would work to convince faculty to include women in their courses. She hoped that the committee would agree that female studies could benefit from a newsletter, which she hoped to edit. After Betty's interview I was convinced that there was no contest, but I had a good deal to learn about my colleagues.

The debate about the two candidates was not very long. Within a few minutes it became clear that the vote would be overwhelmingly in favor of Betty Slater. I was crushed. When I told Tom what had happened he said he thought the committee had made a mistake. I tried to explain that they had gotten just what they wanted, that they were not interested in a strong leader who was committed to changing the status quo. As I complained about the lack of vision and conservatism of the committee, Tom seemed bored. I stopped talking and waited until I could discuss what had happened with Carol.

She agreed that the committee was threatened by her criticism of the disciplines. She thanked me for my support and told me she thought I had been very politically astute at the interview. My face had been, she said, impassive—a look she had rarely seen on white people. Her comment made me feel very strange. I had thought that my support of Carol was only too obvious, yet I was glad to hear that I was able to disguise my feelings. Since the ride to the conference, I had decided to watch my colleagues and express myself only when I had some idea of what impact my opinions would have. I was clearly an outsider to the group, and if I was going to bring any of my concerns to the program I had to be very careful about what I did.

I came home from my meeting with Carol feeling support from her and wondering why I had felt so different when I had talked with Tom. Although he had been in similar political struggles at the college, he didn't seem to grasp either the significance of the choice of Betty over Carol or the difficulty of my position. I had always supported him when he worked against those who opposed change, and I had only heard his side of the story. I had to admit that he hadn't been there, but I decided that I would be more direct when I felt he was not as supportive as I thought he could be.

At the end of the fall semester of 1970 Betty Slater was installed in a large office next to mine. We had very little contact with each other. It seemed almost as if we worked for two different programs. She was responsible for writing the drafts of the program's funding proposal. She never conferred with me, and we argued over her drafts in the steering committee meetings. Her conception of the program, which was supported by many of the committee members—most of whom had status—was that female studies would augment what existed at Cornell and would in no way bring anything new. In the proposal she stated explicitly that female studies was in no way connected with the women's movement. I was so appalled by what I saw as a betrayal of the movement that I could not help but attack her position. I also stated that as far as I was concerned, there was much at Cornell that I hoped female studies would work to change. The proposal was also criticized by other members of the committee on some minor points. Betty was asked to write another draft.

My work focused on getting new courses on women introduced into the curriculum. Emily Maillet and I had made great headway with the course she had designed on women and education. With the help of the faculty member in the education department she was going to be offering it that spring. Elaine and I had also begun to talk about a course on black and white women. Joan, whose field was American history, was working on a syllabus with us, and we hoped to teach it directly through the female studies program. We intended that it would be team taught by a black and a white woman. I was, of course, very anxious to teach it with Elaine, but it seemed unwise to present it to the curriculum committee with us as the instructors. We decided to try to get the course approved first and then see about the instructors.

I continued to chair the steering committee meetings and to see students who came into the office looking for courses on women. One day a student came in to tell me that she had just learned from a friend about a woman in her eighties who had been a suffragist and was willing to talk about her experiences. I thought it would be good to have her come and give a lecture, but, as she told me more about Florence Luscomb, I began to think that we could have a celebration of women's achievements and dedicate it to one of the women who had struggled for women's rights before most of us had been born. I prepared a proposal for the steering committee for a women's festival in honor of Florence Luscomb and got preliminary approval.

After I spoke to Florence and she agreed to come, the students on the committee immediately contacted campus groups for funding. I called a meeting of the students I knew at Cornell as well as in the Ithaca College Women's Liberation Front to form a committee to work on the festival. I was anxious to find ways for women from Cornell and Ithaca College to work together to bridge the gap between Cornell, the prestigious school, and Ithaca College, the "other" school in town. The meeting was well attended by women from both institutions, and many small task groups were formed. I was responsible for coordinating all the groups and the budget.

It was clear that the "small" celebration was going far beyond my expectations. It seemed as if the students had been waiting for the opportunity to pour their energies into a women's event. If it was to be a real celebration, they insisted, we needed music, and they arranged for a women's country and western band to play on Friday night and the New Haven and Chicago Women's Liberation rock bands for a women's dance Saturday night. The festival was growing into all that I thought female studies ought to be—serious discussions of women's politics including practical workshops on setting up women's centers, daycare, abortion referral services, and health clinics. The festival would be a celebration of our lives.

As the first day of the festival approached, I was pleased at how well the large group of students and I had worked together. I only hoped that everything would go as smoothly during the festival as it had over the months of planning. The first night of the event I sat in the large room where Florence Luscomb was scheduled to speak, and, as I waited for her, I wondered if the months of work had been worth it. When the eighty-one-year-old woman walked into the room with a sure stride and began to speak in an unfaltering voice about her experiences as a worker for women's suffrage, any doubts I had had were gone.

The next day more than two thousand women and some men filled the many workshops. Everything was going beautifully until that evening at the women's dance. We had not talked about what we would do in the event that men wanted to join the dance, and I worried a bit when three men came through the doors. Naomi Weisstein, the piano player for the Chicago band, announced that men were not welcome. Shouts of approval came from the large crowd of women, and the three men left the room. I was also glad they were leaving but worried if that would be the end of it.

When the bands started to play again and I looked around at the room full of women dancing with each other in couples or large circles or even alone, I forgot about the ramifications of having asked the men to leave. It was a wonderfully freeing experience to see hundreds of women enjoying themselves without the company of men. Kathy Taylor was smiling and dancing her heart out, by herself. I realized that I had never seen her dance before, and I joined her. I noticed that Carol who was dancing with Doris Fox, her housemate. I walked in their direction, and, before I could tell them I had never seen them look better, Carol said that the festival was a wonderful event. Ithaca, she said, would never be the same. Once women realized their strength and power there would be no holding them back.

Just as I was beginning to relax and enjoy myself, I was called out into the hall. The security guard was trying to stop a group of fraternity men from storming the dance. He needed some help and had sent for me. I spent most of the rest of the evening talking to men who could not accept the fact that they were not wanted. The security guard was very calm and helpful until one of the men said he must be a ''fag'' if he supported women being alone—without men, that is. At that point I thought they were going to come to blows, and the guard ordered them out of the building. Men seemed so vulnerable to me. The guard had been fine until someone questioned his sexuality. I thanked him for his help and turned to go back to the dance.

I looked at the women in the dimly lit room, dancing in large groups. It felt like a kind of communal rite, women affirming each other. I joined the circle that Kathy was in, and, as I danced, I felt a connection with every woman there. We were, at least at that point in time, sisters.

At the end of the festival I was exhausted but also more exhilarated than I had ever been in my life. It had proved to me that the struggle by women to change ourselves and the world was possible and the most important thing in my life.

I had also been moved by the support I had gotten from Tom. He had been more than helpful with the children, had not complained when seven members of the New Haven band had slept at our house, and had even thought to buy food and make sandwiches for everyone. He also prepared a radio show with an Ithaca College student on what men could learn about themselves from the women's movement.

For the next week my phone at the office and at home rang constantly. Women I didn't even know called to thank me for the festival. I was grateful to the Cornell *Daily Sun* as well as the Ithaca College student newspaper for not sensationalizing the ejection of the men from the dance and for reporting the festival fairly. When I went to the first steering committee meeting after the event, I truly expected thanks from my colleagues, but, once again I had underestimated their conservatism. While a few people praised the festival, the bulk of the discussion was focused on the dance. At the end of the meeting one of the student members told the committee that the festival, including the women's dance, had profoundly changed her life. As she spoke out about what it had meant to her to hear Florence Luscomb and the other women, to celebrate ourselves, she began to cry. If the female studies steering committee did not recognize the importance of the event, she said, they clearly did not understand what female studies was all about. Although I could not have agreed more with what she said, I forced myself to be silent. The committee did not have the same conception of female studies as we did, and there were other battles to be waged.

Shortly after the festival Betty presented another draft of the proposal. The statement of goals did not include any indication that a feminist analysis of the disciplines was necessary. Also omitted was any reference to changing women's status. In the description of the program's structure, Slater had omitted mention of the steering committee. The new structure consisted of an advisory board comprised of representatives of the board of trustees, the deans, the faculty, and the graduate and undergraduate student body. The paid staff, a director, and an administrator would be responsible to this board. The staff women who had worked so hard to institute the program would have no place in the new structure.

The proposal indicated that the program would be reviewed in 1974. At that time, the proposal stated, the university might choose to terminate female studies. Teaching and research on women could be so thoroughly integrated into the university as to make the program unnecessary. On the other hand, if adequate progress toward the goals of female studies had not been reached, the program might have proved to be an inappropriate mechanism. Not only was she willing to destroy the program before it had an opportunity to make any significant changes, Betty was all too anxious to state explicitly that the program did not intend to make change. In a final section entitled "Some Cautions," the proposal stated that the program "should not be seen as a panacea for all the problems of women in the academic community . . . [and] should not be seen as a political effort."

I had expected the worst from Betty's draft, but she had surprised even me with her absolute refusal to incorporate my suggestions and those of other members of the committee. We wanted the proposal to state that it would not be enough to include women in what already existed, and I had said that any reference to the women's liberation movement as a totally separate entity from female studies was unacceptable. Happily I was not the only member of the committee who was disturbed by Betty's draft. Even those members of the committee who were generally silent spoke out against the proposal. But, as I listened to the faculty defend it, I guessed that the draft was not the work of one person; Betty must have had the support of the committee's more conservative members. The battle lines were drawn. Most of the staff and students found the draft totally unacceptable, while the faculty supported it. We argued about it in and out of committee for months.

Because I was beginning to sense that my tenure in the program might not last past my one-year appointment, I was anxious to move on the course that Joan, Elaine, and I had developed. I also began to think about proposing a course that I could teach the next year. Helen Burke, the only faculty member on the committee who did not support the proposal, suggested that I teach one of the freshman humanities seminars and promised to help me get a class through the College of Arts and Sciences curriculum committee. I began to work on a syllabus, while Joan, Elaine, and I strategized about the course on black and white women.

We decided to try to get preliminary approval for the course, but the program curriculum committee would not consider it until we had named the instructors. Joan and I thought that Elaine's participation was crucial, but we all agreed that naming me as the other instructor would assure that the course would not be approved. Joan contacted a graduate student, Liz Palmer, whose field was American history and who was reputed to have some interest in women's issues. As it turned out, she had a great interest in the course as well as some teaching experience. She was in the process of writing her dissertation and had extensive knowledge of slavery and a real interest in women's history. We all agreed that the course should go before the committee as soon as possible. As the debate over the future direction of the program continued, tensions among committee members and between myself and the more conservative members were increasing.

We called a meeting of the curriculum committee and presented the course, this time with Elaine and Liz in attendance. Liz passed out copies of her vita, and, after her interview seemed to be over, the group turned to a discussion of Elaine's credentials. Because she was still an undergraduate, we thought we could bolster her qualifications by support from faculty from the Africana Studies Center. One of them, James Cunningham said at the meeting that he hoped the committee would seriously consider Miss Jones for the position of coinstructor of the course on black and white women. While he recognized she did not have the qualifications generally required of instructors, he could attest to her ability. The committee was strangely silent.

After Liz, Elaine, and the Africana Studies Center faculty left the room, Joan and I were prepared for an argument, but we were astounded when the committee quickly passed both the course and the instructors. It seemed too easy, but the course had been approved in a duly constituted meeting. The next step, we thought, would be a pro forma approval by the college curriculum committee.

Within the next few weeks we found that the struggle for the course had just begun. Liz learned from a friend on the college curriculum committee that the course had been removed from the agenda after some female studies steering committee members had met with the dean. They had passed the course, they told him, only because they had been coerced and intimidated by a contingent of blacks who had come to the meeting.

I called a meeting of the full steering committee to inform them of what a small group had done. The meeting was very heated. No one would admit she had met with the dean. Finally, the majority of the committee agreed to approve the course and ask the dean to put it on the agenda for approval by the curriculum committee. I had been convinced for months that secret meetings were being held by the conservative bloc on the steering committee, and the incident with the course only confirmed my suspicions. Joan had also heard from Barbara that she had been asked to attend one of the meetings, and, though she had been very uncomfortable, she had agreed. She refused to disclose the substance of the meeting but implied that it focused on the debate over the proposal for the program.

We were deadlocked. Our meetings had become hopelessly polarized, with me at one end of the spectrum and Betty at the other. In a desperate attempt to save the program from self-destruction I approached Betty with a proposal. I would offer my resignation if she would agree to do the same. She refused. I considered resigning, but Joan urged me to talk with Alice Cook, the university ombudsman. Alice thought it would be disastrous for either Betty or me to resign at that point. We should, she said, try to come to some compromise. She would come to a meeting to try to mediate an agreement if I thought it would help.

At the next steering committee meeting I told the group I had been to see Alice Cook because I felt that divisions within the program were threatening its existence. I suggested that we invite her to a meeting. When Betty said she didn't know why we needed an outsider, I decided it was time to tell the group how I really felt. Things could hardly have been worse than they were. I said that I knew that a group within the program was having secret meetings to make decisions about the program. We needed to face what was happening and get some help. The university administration would like nothing better than to use the dissension and disorganization within the group as an excuse to terminate our program. We decided to invite Alice to a meeting over the objections of Betty and a small group of faculty.

As I prepared for the meeting with Joan, I realized how upset I was. I had come to this job unskilled, it was true, but I had also had a real commitment to building a program that would reflect a feminist critique of society. I had found that many of the women on the committee wanted nothing more than getting their own feet in the door. While I recognized that there were serious political differences within the group, I blamed myself for the split that now seemed unbridgeable. Joan was very supportive, as was Elaine, who was convinced that those white women were crazy. Despite their assurances that it had not been my fault, I felt very guilty for what had happened and wondered if I were the kind of person who was unable to work in a group.

I often felt strange when I talked to Tom about my problems with various members of the steering committee. It wasn't anything I could put my finger on, but he seemed to want to be able to see the situation from both sides. After conversations with him about what was happening in the program, I found myself thinking back to the times when I had listened to his struggles for hours and hours. I never had been interested in the whole picture. I only wanted to support him.

I went to the meeting with Alice Cook hoping that she would find a way to mediate, but within the first half hour it was clear to me that there was nothing to discuss. I decided to offer my resignation as soon as the course I had proposed to the freshman humanities committee was approved. I was tired of fighting, particularly since there seemed to be no hope of a positive resolution.

On June 4, 1971, after one academic year as executive director of female studies, I resigned from my position but not from the steering committee. I was assured that I would retain the freshman humanities course I was to teach the next year.

Chapter 16

I was plagued with doubts about myself that summer. I was obsessed with the question of responsibility for the disaster in female studies: what part was mine and what part was the inevitable result of directly conflicting political perspectives? What would have happened if someone like Carolyn Vickers had had my position? Would she have been able to bring the two sides together? In her work at the women's center in Massachusetts she seemed to be having none of the problems I had encountered. She was able to get along with all kinds of people, while I seemed only to antagonize individuals and polarize groups. I didn't know why I couldn't be more like Carolyn, but it seemed impossible for me to keep my mouth shut. Maybe I was still the screamer I had been in my early adolescence

During my year at female studies Tom and I had become friendly with Joan and her husband, Steve. We planned to spend part of the summer with them at a house we rented jointly on Cape Cod. It had been ages since I had been at the ocean, and I hoped that sitting on the beach and watching the waves would help me to recover from the trauma of female studies. The Parkes planned to be there for the entire summer, while Tom and I would go for a month, two weeks at the beginning of the summer and two weeks at the end.

I was also thinking about moving again. The house that had felt so spacious when we had first moved in seemed to have shrunk. Tom agreed that a bigger house would be nice. Just before we left for the Cape we made a bid on a beautiful, nine-room, three-story house with a large yard. It would give us all more space and allow for the possibility of having someone live with us. A number of students had stayed with us for short periods of time, and I found that I enjoyed having another adult in the house. I had considered trying to find a student who would help with the children and housework in exchange for room and board, and the new house would be perfect for such an arrangement.

We gave the realtor our number on the Cape and left Ithaca for our first two weeks of vacation. The house the Parkes had rented was fine, but the beach had none of the rolling waves I had hoped to see and the weather was terrible. Despite the disappointments, Tom and I thought the first two weeks had gone rather smoothly. We had not talked much with Joan and Steve about the mechanics of living together before we actually did it, but we seemed to get along quite well. We left hoping that the weather would be better for the last two weeks.

But the Parkes, particularly Steve, did not share our feelings. A few days after we got home we received a letter from them. Steve had written the letter, and Joan had added a note saying that she agreed with Steve's sense of the situation. Their expectations had been that we would spend more time together. They had been upset that we had taken day trips without them and hoped that we could plan outings together when we returned. Tom and I wrote back saying that we would enjoy spending time with them but that we also felt that we needed time alone. Joan and Steve called to say that they were still disturbed but hoped we could talk when we got there. I was not really looking forward to our last two weeks, but I was gratified that Tom and I were in agreement both about what had happened and how we would spend the last two weeks of the summer. I had had enough conflict, and I was focused on our move. Our offer had been accepted, and we were in the midst of negotiations to sell our house.

There were some initial tensions when we returned to Cape Cod, but within a few days it seemed to us that everything was going rather well. The night before we were to leave Steve told us that he had been very upset, and most of his criticism was directed at me. He had found me very distant, he said, even cold. He had expressed his desires, but I had insisted on doing what I wanted. He thought I was a domineering person. He had clearly expected us to completely change our plans because of his needs. I thought he was unreasonable but decided to wait to see what Tom would say before I expressed my opinion. I was also curious to know what Joan thought about our time together, but both she and Tom remained silent. As Steve went on attacking us with a particular focus on me, I realized I could not wait for Tom to respond. I told Steve that we had not been there merely at his invitation. We had paid for our time. It was our vacation, and we expected to do what we wanted for part of the time. Joan said she could no longer stand what was happening and went upstairs.

Tom finally said something, but not in my defense. He said that I had had a hard year, and he began to discuss my needs. As I listened to the two men talk about me, I became so angry at Steve's arrogance and what I saw as Tom's betrayal that I knew I had to leave or my rage would erupt. I told them I could no longer bear listening to either of them. I rose to leave and noticed that Tom looked surprised. Well, I thought, if he wanted to know what upset me, he could ask. I went into the bedroom.

I started to pack our things so that we could leave first thing in the morning. What I really wanted to do was take the children and leave right then, with or without Tom. Somehow I had managed to mess up another group. Steve's complaints about me indicated that I was an unapproachable person. It seemed to me that many people were afraid to confront me directly. If the women in female studies had told me that I was creating serious problems, I might have been able to change, but no one had said anything to me. Steve, too, had not told me how he felt until we were ready to leave. What was it about me, I wondered, that made me so unapproachable? It seemed that people were frightened by me, but what I, too, felt was fear. I was afraid of the job in female studies but had been perceived, among other things, as a person who could not be dealt with directly. Was Betty Slater afraid of me? It seemed impossible, but were the faculty on the steering committee afraid of me?

I was also very disturbed by what Tom had done that evening. He didn't agree with Steve, but he didn't tell Steve that he, too, had wanted part of our time at the Cape to be a family vacation. I had finished packing, and Tom had not yet come to bed. As I lay down and tried to sleep, I could hear the murmur of the two men's voices. I began to feel that I might go crazy if they didn't stop. I jumped out of bed and told them to go outside if they wanted to continue their conversation. I was very tired and was trying to get some sleep.

Shortly after my outburst Tom came into the room. My confusion had become intense. I asked him why he hadn't said that he had also felt that we had the right to do what we wanted. His answer was vague. It had been a hard situation, he said. I pushed him to explain what he meant when he told Steve that I had a strong personality. He said that he felt that I did. Although I feared his answer, I asked him if he thought all the problems during our time with Joan and Steve were my responsibility. He said that I was a difficult person. I was, he said, often a stranger to him. He just didn't understand me. As he elaborated on the problems I had getting along with people, I felt more and more desperate. I tried to defend myself, saying that there were people who did like me. Tom asked who they were. I responded that Elaine was a good friend, and he smiled and said she had the same problems. I frantically searched for another name of someone who liked me and blurted out that Kathy Taylor was a friend—she liked me. Tom said that she was just a good Catholic who was nice to me out of a desire to do good works. When he reminded me that she didn't call much, I began to feel that he was right. I didn't have any friends because I was such a domineering bitch. I was a monster.

But there was also something in me that said I was all right. By that point it seemed as if the room had begun to spin. I could see only a blur with an occasional glimpse of faces of women in female studies, of Ruth Berman, Martin Fisher, Kathy Taylor. I was terribly frightened that I was going crazy and said that I would have to talk about all of this with Dr. Julien. When I said her name I envisioned her office. She was a very gentle woman, but she had never seemed afraid of me. She seemed to respect me. The spinning stopped, and I began to feel very calm. I might be difficult, but I was not a monster.

I realized at that moment that Tom had been undermining me. He had seemed to be supportive of me and my position in female studies, but had subtly let me know that he did not approve of my behavior. The discussion over the hiring of the academic coordinator had only been one example of his ambivalence. I looked Tom in the eyes and told him that I now knew that he had undermined me all year. Without a moment's hesitation he told me I was right. He began to explain that he had been very threatened by my job at Cornell, but I didn't care to hear his explanations just then. I realized that I had to accept who I was even if some people thought I was a bitch. I was exhausted. I told Tom I needed to go to sleep.

I was very quiet on the ride back to Ithaca, preoccupied with what had happened to me. I had been terrified by my utter confusion and sense of the world spinning around me. The vision of Dr.

Julien had calmed me because she accepted me—as I needed to accept myself. This acceptance had begun to grow the previous night. I was convinced that my insight about Tom had been correct, but didn't know what it would mean for our relationship. He was quiet, too, and although I wondered what he was thinking, I decided to let him tell me. My days of trying to make him talk were over. If he had something to say to me, he could say it.

The next few weeks were completely devoted to moving, and I didn't think much about the night at the Cape. After the move I began to get anxious about teaching the freshman humanities course. Although I was eager to begin, it was the first time I would be teaching a course I had developed myself, and I worried about being able to relate to Cornell students, who were much better prepared academically than students at Ithaca College. I was also not looking forward to participating on the female studies steering committee, but I could not abandon my side of the conflict.

That September both children were going to new schools. For Neal it would be no different than any other year. Every fall the special education classes were moved from school to school. It seemed that none of the principals wanted those classes in their schools, that the schools had no responsibility toward these children. Neal would just get used to being in one school, and it would be time to leave. That year the class was about one and a half miles away from our new house—too far to walk and too close for a bus. Tom agreed to drop Neal off before he went to work, and I would pick him up.

Hannah was going into the first grade that fall, and Tom and I had decided to enroll her in East Hill, a "free" school that was part of the public school system. Based on the Summerhill model of experimental education, teachers at East Hill created learning experiences based on students' interests rather than imposing their own sense of priorities on them. One class, for example, had read *Kon-Tiki* and was fascinated by Heyerdahl's narrative of his journey on a raft. The teacher picked up on their interest and suggested making a model of the raft to the scale of the lake that stretched sixty miles from Ithaca to Seneca Falls. The students responded enthusiastically and worked closely with her and in small groups to design the raft and solicit funds and materials from local businesses. They learned arithmetic by doing the calculations to build the raft to scale and finally launched their "seaworthy" craft on Lake Cayuga. They had attached a note to the mast asking that the school be notified if the raft was found. Within a few weeks the school received a call from someone who saw it beached at the top of the lake in Seneca Falls.

I was convinced that Hannah, a very bright and creative child, could benefit from East Hill. I had been very disturbed by the lack of interest she showed in kindergarten. She didn't complain about going to school, but she didn't talk about what she did there and barely answered my questions about it. I was concerned, too, that she would be damaged by traditional attitudes about female children, and I hoped that the teachers at East Hill would treat boys and girls equally.

Just before school opened Tony Sacco, one of my first students at Ithaca College, came to visit. Tony was not like any other male I knew. He seemed to easily share whatever I was doing. If I was folding laundry when he came over, he would join me in picking the clothes out of the basket and adding them to the folded piles. If I was about to go grocery shopping, he was happy to go along. Tony actually seemed to enjoy "women's work," especially cooking, which we often did together. Both children adored him. He and Hannah had very long and involved conversations, and he was able to relate to Neal as no one else could.

Tony said he had come back to Ithaca early to look for a place to live because the arrangement he had made in the spring had fallen through. I got very excited: We had an extra room on the second floor, and Tony could live with us. I wouldn't even have to tell him his responsibilities. I knew that he would help me in whatever housework I was doing. I asked him if he would like to live with us, and he seemed as excited as I was. I ran upstairs to talk to Tom, who also agreed that Tony would fit into our family very well.

My life seemed not to have changed very much since that night in August: I was anxious for Dr. Julien to return from her vacation because I wanted to talk with her about what had happened and thank her for her acceptance of me. Yet, as the day of my appointment approached, I began to consider stopping therapy. She had been wonderfully helpful, and I wanted to continue to see her periodically to discuss Neal's progress, but it was time to live out the acceptance of myself that I had felt so powerfully, not just talk about it. I wanted to see what it would be like to work things out for myself. When I told her about the spinning and the calm that followed when I thought of her and our therapy, she said she was glad she had been helpful. I had, she thought, really begun to accept myself. I felt very warm toward her but did not reconsider my decision to stop seeing her weekly. We agreeed that I would see her once a month to talk about Neal.

I was feeling more and more comfortable with myself. It was as if a great weight had been lifted from my shoulders. Maybe I was hard to get along with for most people, but that was who I was. There were people I respected, after all, who seemed to like me. If Tom was having problems with me, he would have to tell me.

One afternoon he did just that. He told me again it had been very hard on him to have me work at Cornell and to be so involved in the women's movement. He said he really didn't understand me. His words began to sound familiar. When he said that I was really a stranger to him, I knew that he was going to begin to complain about how difficult I was, and this time I was not going to listen. Without thinking about what I was going to say, I launched into a tirade. I told Tom that I was who I was, and he was going to have to deal with that person, not someone he wanted me to be. If he didn't know who I was, he could find out. As far as I was concerned, it was becoming clearer to me each day that we had no relationship left. If he was interested in building one, I would be open to it but he would have to show me by his behavior that he was really committed to relating to me. I was through, I said, with being responsible for his feelings. If he wanted a relationship, it would have to be with the person who sat before him, not some wife whose image he had in his psyche. I was directly and openly angry with him for the first time in my life.

When I was finished saying what I had to say, I got up to leave the room. Tom walked toward me, put his hands on my shoulders, and said he was in awe of my ability to get angry. He said he hoped that I would help him with his fear of my anger. I was furious but said only that I could not do that; he would have to use his own resources. I turned and left the room.

My reaction to Tom surprised me; the words seemed to have rushed out of me. Yet, I now realized that I was being quite honest when I said that we no longer had a relationship; whatever was between us had ended that night in August when I ceased to trust him. I had no intention of leaving him. I would be open to developing a relationship if he was able to show me that he was really committed to it. Until then, however, I had no intention of continuing my role as sympathetic wife.

There were other things I would no longer do. The housework

became an issue again, but this time I did not think it was petty to expect Tom to do his share. It was important, I thought, for the children, who were nine and seven years old, to begin to do their parts. They would be responsible for keeping their rooms straightened, and one of us would help them dust and vacuum. They could also help to set and clear the dinner table. I presented Tom with my plan. He didn't have much to say about it except to agree to participate.

I was also going to stop giving dinner parties for people who were not my friends. Tom had been chair of his department for two years, and that September Tony and I had prepared a beautiful feast for his colleagues and their wives. We had had a wonderful time cooking, but, as the guests arrived, I wanted to stay in the kitchen. I didn't really know his colleagues very well, but I did know, from years of seeing them at college functions, that I had little in common with most of them and their wives. I emerged from the kitchen to greet the guests, but when the party was over I told Tom that it had been the last one I would host for his colleagues. If he felt that, as department chair, he had to entertain them, he could either hire a caterer or take them out.

Though I seemed to know what I would not do, I was less sure about what I wanted. I enjoyed teaching, but I was beginning to feel that I needed more education, that I was only one step ahead of my students. The thought of going back to school for a master's degree had occurred to me, but I had no idea what I wanted to study. Because I had started teaching in the English department, I had used literature in my courses. I had always enjoyed reading novels, though I had no interest in a serious study of literature.

I also knew that the course I was teaching through female studies would be my last connection with the program. Although I hadn't thought it was possible, the situation in the program had gotten worse. I heard from Emily Maillet's husband, Claude, that a proposal for a female studies program had been placed on the agenda of the academic matters committee of the Arts College. The proposal we were drafting in the steering committee was nearly complete, and we had hoped to present it to the dean and the academic matters committee within the month. This proposal was obviously another one; as a member of the committee, Claude had received a copy and was alarmed that the names of many steering committee members did not appear on the document. Though not a liberal, Claude was also concerned by the proposal's conservatism. He wanted to argue against it, and we agreed to discuss strategy.

Even I was shocked at the duplicity of the people who had drafted the proposal. We had seemed to be making some headway in the committee. Now I knew why. Betty and her supporters had never intended for our proposal to reach the administration. As I read through the proposal presented by the newly constituted female studies committee, I was sure it would be approved. It was just what the Cornell administration would want; it included Betty's statement about the nonpolitical nature of female studies and recommended that the program exist for only three years. All appointments in the program would be in conjunction with already established departments, thereby insuring that female studies would have no autonomy. The steering committee was replaced by the advisory board that Betty had proposed in her original draft, but this time student representation was eliminated. The words *innovative, experimental,* and *interdisciplinary* did not appear in the document.

Joan and other members of the steering committee whose names did not appear on the document urged me to contact the dean before the meeting of the academic matters committee. My suspicion that the dean had full knowledge of the "coup" in female studies was confirmed when he did not return any of my many phone calls. The "junta" presented the proposal, and, just as I thought, it was approved. There would clearly be no place for me or any of my concerns in the female studies program. The fight was over, and we had lost.

Chapter 17

I worried about what I would do the next year. Since I was only teaching one course a semester, I had time not only to think about what my next step would be but also to do some of the reading I had put off. Eleanor Flexner's, *A Century of Struggle* had sat on my shelf for almost a year. I thought it was important to know about women's campaign to win the right to vote, but I had never liked history, and after the 1968 Democratic convention, was less interested than ever in electoral politics. I started to read early one morning after the children went to school and was surprised when Tony came in and asked if I was going to have lunch. I had not noticed that hours had passed since I had opened the first page of Flexner's book. This history was not like any history I had ever read.

By the time I finished the book I realized that I was hungry to learn more about the women who had gone before me: we were not the first to complain about women's roles and also not the first to try to do something about it. I also thought more about the kind of history Flexner wrote. Oddly, reading *A Century of Struggle* had reminded me of Dr. Klitzke's lectures. He, too, had talked about what people had thought in earlier times and had focused some on what their daily lives were like. My history courses, on the other hand, had been a recitation of facts, dates, battles, and presidents. Maybe what I had really liked about Dr. Klitzke's lectures was the history not the art.

The more I thought about women's history, the more excited I got. I could work on the questions Elaine and I had talked about so often: What were the historical bases for the similarities and differences between black and white women? What was the relationship between the mistress of the plantation and the female slaves she owned? Did black and white women see any commonality of cause as women? I decided to think about the possibility of graduate work in history with a focus on black and white women.

Going back to school would only be possible if Tom were willing to do more than he was presently doing to help with the children and the running of the house. I also needed to discuss what it would mean to us financially. As usual, he seemed supportive. He thought we could manage with just his salary, and he was willing to take out a loan if we needed it for my tuition. As he told me how to go about applying to graduate school, I realized once again that few men would be so helpful in their wives' attempts to grow. I felt very warm toward him and thought that it might be possible for us to save our relationship.

I needed a place to work, and Tom agreed that I could use part of his study, since he used his office at school for most of his work. I bought a small desk and chair, which fit in a corner of Tom's study, and once my little nook was ready I went to work preparing for the Graduate Record Exam.

I worried about what would happen to my routine when the children were out of school for the summer, but, as things worked out, both of them were occupied. The director of the speech clinic that Neal had been attending for a few years recommended that he attend the clinic's camp. Neal had been making great progress and, the director thought, an unstructured summer would set him back. We had also been pleased with Neal's progress; he was learning to read and to do simple arithmetic. Because he was still not comfortable with other children, we decided to enroll him in the camp's day program. Hannah would be with Tony for the bulk of the day. He had decided to stay in Ithaca for the summer and had come up with the idea of running a day camp out of our house for a group of children Hannah's age. On nice days he would take them to one of the many parks in the area, so they would be in the house only when it rained.

After Neal was at camp for a few days the director suggested that we reconsider our decision to have him attend only during the day. Neal seemed to be quite comfortable, and he assured us that the counselors would monitor him closely. If Neal seemed to be very disturbed, we could certainly return to our original arrangement. I was nervous about leaving Neal at camp, but I thought he would probably be all right. He was still not able to play with his peers but he had developed an ability to relate to adults. The teachers and the students who worked at the clinic repeatedly told us that they loved working with Neal, and we could see for ourselves how he endeared himself to the students who regularly came to our house.

The night before we took him to camp we explained that he would be staying and that we would come to visit on parents' day. I felt that he understood, but when we left him the next morning he looked very sad—a normal reaction to being left at camp, I thought. As Tom drove the car away, I looked back and saw Neal walking up to one of the counselors, smiling. I told Tom to look back. I said Neal would do just fine at camp. Tom, however, was very upset; he was worried about Neal, and I thought I saw tears in his eyes.

I became impatient with what I saw as Tom's inability to see Neal's strengths. He had continued to focus on Neal's bleak future, despite the fact that none of the professionals who worked with him would venture to make a prognosis. His continual progress defied any of the previous diagnoses. He was even beginning to show signs of independence. He wanted to walk the mile and a half to school and was able to save money from his allowance to buy records and books. As I looked at Tom again, I saw that I had been right. He was crying. I repeated that it seemed to me that Neal was fine, but he did not answer me. Tom, not Neal, was the one having the problems with overnight camp.

I told Tom that I was sick of his negative attitude about Neal, that the child had some strengths, and Tom ought to recognize them. Neither of us said more, but I thought to myself that Tom and I really were very different, and I was troubled by his pessimism about Neal and his almost constant depression.

My feeling that Tom was unable to support Neal's strengths was corroborated a few weeks later through an incident with Hannah. It was a very hot weekend, and we had gone to the pool at the college. Hannah came out of the water and sat on the blanket. She looked at Tom and told him she was afraid to put her face in the water. He told her that he knew how she felt. It was okay, he said, to be afraid of the water. I waited for him to say more, but he didn't. I thought to myself that Tom would be content if Hannah never conquered her fear and I was disgusted with him. He didn't seem to want either of the children to develop into strong adults.

When I calmed down I told Hannah that her father was right. There was nothing wrong with being afraid, but it was also possible to learn to do things that were scary. We all had fears about certain things, but they didn't have to stop us. If she wanted to go in the water with me, I would help her put her face in. She said she'd try. Within a few weeks she was swimming.

I had a sense that I might need to protect both children from Tom's influence. It seemed clear to me that he didn't expect or perhaps didn't even want them to be strong and independent. Without being fully conscious of what I was doing, I had tried to counteract Tom's assumption that Neal would always be dependent and to impress Hannah with the knowledge that she was a capable person. For Tom, feeling that one was not adequate to a task was good enough reason not to try it. His weakness, I realized, had forced me to be the parent who pushed the children to do what was difficult for them. Just as he had undermined me, I felt that Tom was subtly manipulating Neal and Hannah.

I had also become very angry at men. I was conscious of sexism everywhere and felt compelled at least to name it. It seemed to me that the world men had created was in their image and for their benefit. I excluded black and working-class men from my anger, but I knew that in individual cases they were often as oppressive to the women in their lives as white men of the middle and upper classes. Tom was working-class, and, though he was not openly authoritarian and often seemed very supportive, he had put me down in ways that were less obvious, though just as damaging.

I began to see the world as divided into male and female, each sex having its own set of values. Though the values of men and women were clearly created by socialization and were not biological, they were powerful and pervasive nonetheless. All the reading I was doing as well as what I saw around me everyday corroborated my analysis. Women were generally interested in relationships—my own endless attempts to "help" Tom relate better were a powerful testament to that. Men depended on relationships with women, but they derived their sense of worth only from the admiration of other men. I even went so far as to think of male homosexuality as the ultimate expression of sexism; most men were totally unable to see women as human beings.

I thought about the pictures of nude women I had found among Rob Stevens's contact prints at the *New Day* office. He had devoted his life to the struggle for justice and at the same time saw women's bodies as objects. Dave Berman was devoted to the cause of freedom for everyone but was upset by my interest in women's liberation. The young people we knew who lived in communes, I now remembered, were trying to change everything about the way they had been raised. They built their own houses, grew their own food, and lived without electricity and running water. None of the men helped with the preparation of food, nor did they lift a finger to assist in the awesome task of cleaning up without running water. I remembered how tired the women in those "idyllic" communities had looked.

Some men, of course, were different, but they were so rare that I assumed men to be male chauvinist pigs until they showed me they were not. Tom was about the best one could expect for a man, but often even he was disappointing. I now understood how Elaine felt about whites. She had told me that, until white people proved to her by the way they acted that they were struggling against the racism in themselves as well as in other whites, she could not trust them. What had seemed to me to be an understandable but somewhat paranoid response now seemed totally appropriate.

Most of the men I knew either ridiculed my arguments about the existence of sexism or quickly changed the subject. Others seemed to delight in harassing me. Howard Clark, a faculty member at the college whom I knew because his daughter Jenny was a good friend of Hannah's, referred to me only as "Hannah's mommy" despite my direct requests that he call me by my name. One day he asked me if I thought there should be men's studies programs at colleges and universities. Before I could respond he told me that it only seemed reasonable that if there were female studies programs there should be something for men. My answer was that we already had men's studies—it was called education. He roared with laughter, and I stopped talking to him from then on unless it was absolutely necessary.

To my great disappointment, most of the women I knew in Ithaca shared neither my concern about sexism nor my anger at men. Friends who were my age seemed to think I had gone off the deep end and acquaintances whom I saw at social gatherings were reluctant to talk to me. Some of their husbands, on the other hand, were only too anxious to argue with me. Going to parties had become a chore, since I was marked as a "women's libber."

Most of my time was spent with Elaine and Tony. Less frequently, I saw some of the young women from the Women's Liberation Front. While I enjoyed my relationship with my young friends, I felt the lack of a friendship with a woman my age who was also married and a mother. I looked forward to the occasional trips Tom and I took to Northampton to visit the Vickers. It was a relief to talk with Carolyn and be able to share my feelings with someone whose circumstances were similar to mine.

I was also corresponding with Jane Latka who, not feeling any more comfortable with her maiden name than she had with her former husband's surname, had taken Smith as her last name. She had finished her degree and was teaching at a black college in Texas. When she visited we talked long into the night. Living in Texas had given Jane a sense of the pervasiveness of racism, and she had turned into as avid a women's liberationist as Carolyn and me. Our new consciousness had changed the quality of our relationships dramatically. I felt a very deep bond with both Jane and Carolyn, and I was grateful for my relationships with them. They helped to keep me from feeling isolated in my preoccupation with women's issues.

It felt strange not to be going back to work at the end of the summer, but I looked forward to preparing for the GRE and taking more courses in history at the college. I had learned as much math as I thought I needed to make a reasonable score on the test and now knew lots of words I had never heard before. I had proved to myself that I was disciplined enough to study on my own. The survey course in American history I had taken at the college had not been inspiring, but I did learn some basics.

The children had both had a good summer. Hannah had enjoyed Tony's "camp" and was anxious to begin her second year at East Hill. At six years of age she had become quite a women's liberationist. One day I overheard her telling her best friend Edward Gooding that girls were just as good as boys. I listened for his response, but when he said nothing I heard Hannah's voice again. This time she demanded an answer by repeating what she had said and adding a fairly threatening "right, Edward?" He agreed and they went on with their game. I hoped she really believed what she was saying. I knew that even with my help she was going to have a difficult time resisting the sexist barrage of the society.

Neal's camp experience seemed to have been positive. He was much easier to understand and was proud of his performance. He had not related much to the other children, but, as I had hoped, he was well liked by the counselors and adored by the few who worked with him most intensely. I was, however, not entirely happy with the camp. Our visit on parents' day had been very disturbing. After the parents met with their childrens' counselors and watched them go through some exercises we were gathered on the main field for what I thought would be a general meeting. The director addressed us, and I began to feel very strange about the way he talked about "these" children. I tried to tell myself that I was too sensitive. They were, after all, children who had serious speech problems. I waited for him to finish so we could spend more time with Neal, but this part of the day was to include a performance. A number of children were led onto the stage, and after their particular problems were described by the director they were urged to go through their exercises so that everyone could see what good work the camp was doing. I was grateful that Neal was not among those chosen for the display.

As I sat through what seemed an interminable variety of speech pathologies, I thought of my family sitting through hours of telethons just to see my cousin Emik, who had cerebral palsy. Recently I had seen part of another telethon. A great deal of money had been pledged during the segment, and the host, Eydie Gorme, was overcome with gratitude. She looked into the camera and with tears in her eyes thanked the viewers, saying that she was so proud to be part of the telethon because only in America could such a wonderful thing happen. I shouted back at the television that only in America do children have to be paraded like specimens before millions of people to raise money for research. I turned off the set and vowed I would never watch a telethon again, even if Emik was going to be on it. Now I sat before the same kind of display and tried to contain my tears of rage.

I was also upset because Tony was moving. He had decided to work in special education and had applied and was admitted to a graduate school in New Haven, Conneticut. He had become so much a part of the fabric of my life that I knew I would miss him terribly. We not only shopped, cooked, cleaned, and did the laundry together but also read some of the same books and shared similar perspectives on many things. He was a good and loving friend, who had been more like family to me than any of my blood kin.

I was anxious to find someone who would at least help me with the children. The plan for dividing the cleaning tasks had gone fairly well, though there were still some problems. Tom did his part only when I told him it needed to be done. What had seemed a petty argument on my part only a year ago was now a serious battle. By cleaning only when I said it was necessary, Tom seemed to reaffirm that housework was primarily my responsibility. There were other ways he underscored this attitude. When he did wash the floor he left the dirty mop in the bathtub. I either had to ask him to wash it and put it away then wait a few days to ask him again or else do it myself. Taking care of the children was still almost totally my job. Tom found it difficult to get home during the day, and I did not feel I could ask him to leave the college to stay with the children.

Just after Tony left my neighbor told me that Nancy Lanni, one of her husband's best students, was looking for a place to live and that she was wonderful with children. After a short interview, I sensed that Lanni, as she preferred to be called, was a very responsible young woman. She accepted my offer of room and board in exchange for help with cleaning and childcare.

Lanni moved in a few days before the college opened. After she had unpacked, I saw her sitting on the porch looking very sad. I went out and asked her if everything was all right. Her room was fine, she said; she was just feeling lonesome for the people she had worked with that summer at a camp near her home in Poughkeepsie, the Metropolitan Baptist camp. I was concerned. Had I invited a fundamentalist into my home? I was greatly relieved when Lanni explained that the camp, while funded and administered by the Baptist church, did not have a religious orientation. The campers and counselors were mostly from New York City, and all but one or two were black. It was a hard transition for her to come back to Ithaca College. She didn't always feel comfortable among the other students, who were generally from wealthy families and almost all of them white. I asked her to come inside, and I put a Motown record on the stereo. She perked up and began to show me the steps she had learned from the kids at camp. Neal and Hannah came in, and Lanni invited them to dance with her. As I looked at the three of them dancing and laughing, I knew we would get along just fine.

I had felt that Lanni would be a good addition to our household, but I had no idea she would become part of our family so quickly. Like Tony, she was Italian, and she loved to cook and eat. We often made dinner together, and, even if we didn't share the actual preparation of the meal, we shared the enjoyment of good food. Tom usually ate without saying much about the food, but Lanni responded to each dish. I found that I often thought of her when planning dinners. Her relationship with Neal and Hannah was excellent. Although she enjoyed being with them and they loved her, she also expected them to respect her solitude when she was busy.

Early in October Tony called to say that he had a three-day weekend and had found a ride to Ithaca. I could hardly wait for the weekend. I had missed him as much as I thought I would. Lanni and I planned the meals. I was sure that they would like each other, and the three of us cooking together would give them a great opportunity to get to know each other. Tony arrived just as Lanni and I had begun the sauce for the lasagna. We greeted each other with great hugs; when Neal and Hannah heard Tony they ran into the kitchen, and there were more hugs and screams. Tom came down from his study, shook hands with Tony, stayed in the kitchen for a short time, and then went back upstairs. Tony, Lanni, and I settled down to stuffing artichokes, tasting and seasoning the sauce, and talking. I felt great waves of warmth and love in my kitchen, which by that time smelled wonderfully of garlic, oregano, and tomatoes.

When we finished assembling the lasagna Tony said that Sue, the woman he had been seeing the summer before he left, was coming over. Did I mind if she stayed for dinner? It was fine with me. Tom had also invited two of his students, Nick Santos and Nelson Bigelow. We weren't too fond of Nick, and Nelson was practically a stranger, but we all felt so good being together that even two political science students could not harm the atmosphere.

Toward the end of the meal I sat back to observe the scene that was giving me so much pleasure. Tom was holding forth on some topic for Nick and Nelson while the people at my end of the table were laughing and talking together. I suddenly realized how far apart Tom and I had grown. My refusal to entertain Tom's friends and colleagues had resulted in each of us developing our own friends, and it was clear to me that our preferences were very different.

The week after Tony left I took the GRE. I felt good. For the first time in my life I had been well prepared, but I was glad to put away my vocabulary flashcards and go back to reading history. I also began to think seriously about where to go to school. Syracuse University was within commuting distance, but I had heard from a graduate student there that it was a difficult place for a woman to be, since very few faculty would even allow that the study of women was a legitimate field of inquiry. She had hoped to focus her dissertation on women but had changed her mind when she realized that she would probably be penalized for her choice of topic. Although I hated the thought of being at Cornell, I got an application and thought I would have to consider it if nothing else looked better.

I had also heard that there were some feminists in the history department at the State University of New York at Binghamton, and I wrote to the department immediately, telling them of my interest in black and white women's history. I received a reply from Mary Ryan, who said she was preparing to teach a course on the history of women the next year and would like to meet me. I drove to Binghamton excited at the possibility of working with someone who was teaching a course on women and I was very encouraged by our conversation. There was no formal female studies program on the campus, but there were a number of women who were interested in developing a graduate program in women's history. She also thought I could find someone to work with in the fairly large black studies department. As I rose to leave she shook my hand and said she would be delighted to have me as her teaching assistant next year.

My new sense of confidence and euphoria made me think about applying for the Danforth fellowship, which was specifically designed for women who were returning to school after an extended absence. As I filled out my application, I thought of how much the women's movement had done for me. I had been a mediocre student with no real aspirations, and now I was applying for a fellowship from a nationally known foundation.

The women's movement had also validated for me the importance of friendships with women, and I sorely missed a friendship in Ithaca with a woman my own age. I was delighted when Jane Smith left her job in Texas for a position at City College in New York City. When she came for a visit shortly after her arrival, she and I stayed up late into the night talking until we could stay awake no longer. She seemed more content than I had ever known her to be, and I went to bed very happy to have such a good friend.

The next morning I noticed that Jane seemed a little nervous. I asked her if anything was wrong, and she told me that she had something very important to tell me and that it was hard for her. I waited for her to continue, wondering if I had said something wrong, but what Jane had to tell me had nothing to do with me. She was in love with a woman, she said. I was shocked that one of my oldest friends had become a lesbian but quickly responded that I was very happy for her. She relaxed and began to tell me about her lover. She had met Pat Clarke in Northampton the previous summer. They had immediately liked each other, and Jane soon realized that she felt more than friendship for Pat. As she told me about her relationship and how supportive it was, I realized that I really was happy for my friend.

When Jane rose to go upstairs to shower and dress she said she was very relieved that I had taken the news that she had "turned queer" so well. She had been worried that I would react badly. I told her that I could see she was happier than I had ever seen her, and it seemed clear that her sense of well-being was the result of her new relationship; any fool could see that, and I could only be glad that she was so happy.

After she left I sat at the table, surprised that I had responded so well. I had known lesbians when I worked in female studies. Two women in particular, Jenny and Christine, had worked very hard on the women's festival and had subsequently joined the steering committee, but I didn't think much about their sexuality. I liked them, and their relationship to each other seemed fine and was really none of my business. As I got to know them better, however, they began to tell me a little about some of the problems they were having. They were upset that they could not be more open about their love for each other. They were not so concerned about negative responses from people when they held hands or hugged each other on the street, but they had also lost some of their closest friends, even though others had been supportive. They worried most about the school discovering their relationship. A lesbian couple Jenny knew had already been expelled. Another major concern were their families, who thought lesbians were sick. It was hard, they said, to hide the wonderful feelings they had for each other. After talking with them, I decided to include something about them in my course. Jenny and Christine, who were both active in the Gay Liberation Front, arranged for speakers to come into the class and suggested that I read *Sappho Was a Right On Woman*. Yet it was one thing to support the rights of gay people and another to have one of your best friends "come out." I guessed I would have to think about it some more, but I really did feel happy for Jane.

Jane came back into the kitchen saying she had had a brilliant thought while she was in the shower. One of the residential colleges at the University of Massachusetts, where she was going to teach a course in women's literature, was devoting a January session to an exploration of racism and sexism. The course I had taught at Cornell was just the kind of thing they were interested in. It was a three-week intensive session, and if I got the job I would have a chance to meet Pat and really get to know her.

I got very excited at the prospect of being away by myself for almost a month. Tom was off for most of the month of January and he was due for a sabbatical in the spring semester. He had not decided what he was going to do, but I thought he would agree to my going to Amherst. That night, when Jane went to see another friend in town, I talked with Tom about her suggestion. He said he'd have to think about it, but it would probably be fine.

Tom really did seem to understand my feelings. I had talked earlier that year about changing my last name to Voski. It had been my grandmother's first name and I liked the idea of following the female line. Tom had agreed that I was not and had never been an "O'Brien," and he said that if I wanted to change my name he would support me. At times like that I wondered what it was I wanted from Tom.

I applied for the January term position at the University of Massachusetts, and just after Thanksgiving I got a call from one of the members of the search committee. They were very interested in my application but felt that an interview with the committee was necessary before any final decisions could be made. I agreed to drive to Amherst if they could meet on a Saturday. Tom suggested that we all go to Massachusetts together; we could use my interview as an opportunity to visit the Vickers.

Not only did the interview go very well but I was also impressed with what I learned about U. Mass. The search committee was composed of the head of residence of one of the dorms, recently renamed the MacKimmie Humanity House, and a group of students who lived in the complex. I learned that the Southwest Residential College had both its own women's center—which would be funding Jane's course and the one I was applying to teach—and a center for racial understanding. It seemed to me that U. Mass was a haven for activists, and I looked forward to being part of such a community, if only for a brief term.

I went back to the Vickers feeling confident. My experience in female studies and my involvement in the women's movement had been invaluable assets. A few days after we got back to Ithaca, Abby Peters, the head of residence, offered me the job, and I happily accepted.

Amherst truly was a feminist paradise, or so it seemed to me in January of 1973. Southwest was sponsoring four courses, all focused on sexism or racism. There were also many related cultural events scheduled for the three-week session.

I had a room in the dorm with a small refrigerator. It felt very strange to be living in one room, and one without a kitchen at that, but Abby and her husband Charles were very hospitable and often invited me for dinner. I was also without transportation, but despite the inconveniences I felt free. For the first time in my adult life I was not responsible for other people.

The three weeks passed by very quickly. I got to know Pat Clarke, who played in a women's rock band, and I met many other women I liked. I realized, too, that my feelings for Jane had become more than friendship. I was attracted to her. I wondered if I, too, had "turned queer," and I was amazed at how calmly I considered the possibility. I guessed that my calm reaction had to do with the fact that she was so obviously in love with Pat and that any sexual involvement with her was out of the question. Jane was unavailable and therefore safe. I supposed that if I had been attracted to a woman who was not involved with someone else I might have been more upset by my feelings.

At the end of the term Tom came with the children to pick me up. It was nice to see them, particularly Neal and Hannah, but I didn't feel ready to go home. My time in Amherst had been a relief. I had met so many women, and even some men, who were feminists. Going back to Ithaca felt like returning to an unnecessary isolation.

The night before we were to go back, Pat's band was playing, and I was very anxious to hear it. Carolyn also wanted to go, and we were glad when Richard and Tom decided to join us. The Rusty Scupper was crowded with women and some men as well, which I was relieved to see. The band started to play. Tom and Richard said they didn't feel like dancing, so Carolyn and I danced together. We tried to lindy and laughed when we realized that neither of us knew how to lead and that we were both unwilling to try to follow. We danced through the whole set. Sometimes Jane or other women we knew joined us. Tom and Richard were still sitting at the table drinking. When the band returned for their second set we asked them again to join us, but they refused. We said that other men were dancing and seemed to be having a good time, but Richard said they were fine. Carolyn and I had no intention of sitting out the set and got up to dance.

After the first song I saw Tom and Richard get up. I thought they were going to join us, but Tom came to say they were leaving. I told him I wanted to stay and could probably find a ride back to the Vickers. Carolyn was talking to Richard. I hoped she wasn't going to leave; we were having such a good time. She came back to the dance floor and started to dance wildly. She leaned over and said that Richard said he was leaving. I said I knew. Carolyn explained that he didn't say he was leaving the bar but that he was leaving. I asked Carolyn what she thought he meant; she wasn't sure. Whatever it was, she had decided to stay.

Within a few minutes I had forgotten about Richard, and it seemed that Carolyn had too. Even though there were a few men on the floor the atmosphere at the Scupper was even better than at the other women's dances I had attended. There were women my age there, and I was dancing with two of my oldest friends. It was like a revival—a celebration of women together.

When the band had finished for the night, Jane suggested that we all go out to get something to eat. Since neither of us seemed ready for the evening to end, we happily accepted her invitation. On the way to the restaurant Carolyn whispered to me that she wondered if Richard would be there when we got home. I said we could go straight home, but she had decided when Richard left the Scupper that she was going to do what she wanted, not what she thought she ought to do.

It was very late when we got back to Carolyn's. All the lights were out, and we fully expected that Tom and Richard would be asleep, but we found them wrapped in blankets, sitting in front of a dying fire. They didn't look up when we came in, but we said hello anyway. They continued to stare at the embers in the fireplace. We went upstairs, and I whispered to Carolyn that we had come from a celebration of life into a room full of death. She agreed. We said goodnight, and I fell asleep before Tom came to bed.

The atmosphere at breakfast was strained, but no one mentioned what had happened the previous evening. Carolyn and I tried to make conversation with Tom and Richard, but they answered only with grunts, so we ended up talking to each other. I was anxious to leave. I had had a wonderful send-off, and now all I wanted to do was to get out of that kitchen. The ride back to Ithaca was more silent than usual, but I refused to ask Tom how he was feeling. I was going to stick to my vow not to help him.

Although I missed being in Amherst, it was nice to be with the children again and, of course, to see Lanni. Shortly after I returned Tom decided he wanted his own room and started to paint the playroom on the third floor. It was beginning to feel more and more as if he were a tenant in my house. On one of my monthly visits to Dr. Julien I asked her how she thought Neal would react if Tom and I separated. She seemed upset and asked if I was considering a divorce. I said no, not at the moment at least, but I was convinced that Tom was not going to change. I would stay as long as he didn't make my life difficult. I knew I wasn't quite ready to be on my own yet, but the possibility that we could rebuild our relationship looked very dim. She said that a decision to leave could often turn into a rededication to the relationship. I didn't feel that way about my marriage. I had told Tom the previous September that our relationship was over in its present form. If he were interested in revitalizing it, he would have to show me that he was willing to take some responsibility for expressing his feelings. While he was outwardly supportive of what I wanted to do, I saw no indication that he was attempting to relate to me honestly. He always seemed preoccupied. Dr. Julien said that, like any child, Neal would be upset by his parents' separation, but she did not think it would trigger a serious regression.

I didn't know what was going to happen in my life. I knew that what I wanted in a relationship was a kind of sharing of which Tom was incapable or unwilling to give me. Although I thought that his influence on the children was not very positive, I also was unsure of my ability to manage them, especially Neal, without him. Because Neal continued to learn it seemed to me that his growth was very much dependent on decisions that we made about schooling and treatment as well as on the quality of our daily interactions with him. I would just have to wait to see what happened.

At the end of February I was in the study when Tom came upstairs with a letter in his hand. It was from the Danforth Foundation. Earlier I had been informed that I was one of the finalists. I opened it and read a very nice rejection letter. I handed it to Tom; he read it, said he was sorry, and turned to leave. He was on sabbatical, and I knew he didn't have any classes or committee meetings. I asked him where he was going. He said he had some things to do in his office. I was amazed by his lack of sensitivity. I'd just learned that I'd been rejected, and all he could do was say he was sorry and leave. I felt that I would have gotten more empathy from a stranger. I was glad that I didn't depend on him for emotional support. I was also very glad that he had moved into his own room.

He had made arrangements to go to the Esalen Institute, a center for Gestalt therapy in California, for a least a month and would be leaving in the middle of March. I wondered how I would feel when he was gone and guessed I would probably miss him somewhat. Despite the distance between us, I had been married to the man for twelve years. Yet, when I dropped him off at the airport, I felt nothing. For the next few days I expected that there would be times when something would make me think of him and wish he were home, but my life went on as usual.

Within a week after Tom left, however, something did happen that was out of the ordinary. Nelson Bigelow, one of the political science students who had been at the house for dinner the night Tony had been back for a visit, came to see me. Like other students of Tom's, Nelson had often dropped in to see him. Over the last few months Nelson and I had gotten to know each other: sometimes, if Tom were not home, he stayed to talk with me. One day that February I was in the kitchen when Nelson knocked on the door. I told him Tom was upstairs watching sports on TV, and I was beginning a tomato sauce; he could have his pick of what to do. Without a moment's hesitation, he had asked for a cutting board and sat opposite me chopping onions. I had particularly enjoyed that afternoon with Nelson. He was interested in my work and plans and also seemed to be able to express his feelings. Now with Tom away I realized that I was attracted to Nelson. I thought that he felt similarly but that I would probably have to make the first move. He was nineteen years old, fifteen years younger than I, and I was the wife of one of his professors. I asked him to come to dinner, and after the children were in bed I took a deep breath and told Nelson I was attracted to him. He responded that he felt the same way. After a few passionate kisses I felt Nelson move away just as I was beginning to have some doubts about what was happening. After an uncomfortable silence, we agreed to think about what we wanted to do.

When Nelson left I tried to think about why I didn't feel guilty. My husband was away trying to "get himself together," and I was contemplating an affair with one of his students. I didn't care if Tom had affairs. In fact, I had urged him to sleep with one of his former students, who had obviously been in love with him for years. When he did finally have a short affair with her, I thought I would have some reaction, but I just didn't care. Why, then, shouldn't I sleep with Nelson if I felt like it? I would have time to think, since Nelson would be going home for spring break in a few days and Tom would be home before Nelson returned to Ithaca.

On the way to the airport to pick up Tom I thought I would

be glad to see him, and I was. He was very excited by what he had experienced in California, and when the children went to bed he told me about it. He had, he said, "gotten in touch with" parts of himself that had been repressed for years. He explained the types of techniques they used at Esalen, and at one point I had the impression that he was trying to use one of them on me. I told him to stop playing shrink, but I was glad that he had gotten so much out of his time at the institute. Later that night he told me that he had had some wonderful sex while he was gone. The women he had met at Esalen were very open about sexuality, and he had had the best orgasms of his life. As I listened to his descriptions of his various sexual encounters, I thought it would probably be a good time to say something about my feelings for Nelson. When he seemed to be finished I quietly said that while he was gone I'd realized that I was attracted to Nelson and would probably sleep with him. Tom was silent for a minute and then said he was glad to see that I was going to work on my sexual problems. An affair with Nelson would probably be good for me. I felt patronized but wondered if he might have felt the same way when I urged him to sleep with his student.

The next day both Lanni and Nelson were due back from spring break. When Lanni came through the door the children ran past me to greet her. I, too, was very happy to have her home. She was hungry, of course, and we went into the kitchen to get something to eat. She told me all about her time in Poughkeepsie, and, just as she asked me about Tom's time in California, he came into the kitchen. He said he was leaving for the rest of the day. He'd probably be back for dinner, but he wasn't sure. I had planned a nice dinner to welcome Lanni home and realized that I didn't care if Tom were there or not.

Lanni went upstairs to unpack, the children followed her, and I wondered if Nelson had returned yet. I would have to be very careful since I wouldn't want the whole town to know that I was having an affair with one of Tom's students. Just before dinner Nelson called to say he was very anxious to see me. He had thought about me all during the break. We made arrangements to meet, and, as I hung up, I smiled to myself. I was actually going to have an affair with a man who was not even twenty years old. It was pretty crazy, but I didn't care. Nelson was a very sweet boy, and I thought it would be fun, at least.

Tom came home for dinner, but he was exceptionally quiet. He went to his room after eating and didn't come downstairs until Neal and Hannah were in bed and Lanni had gone out to the library. He had his hat and coat on. He walked to where I was sitting and said he'd decided he could no longer live with me. I was surprised but said if that was how he felt that was how it would be. He was going out for a while and said we could talk when he got back.

As the door closed behind him, I felt a profound sadness that our relationship had been such a dismal failure. It was finally over. It had actually been over for me since that day over a year ago when I told Tom that he would have to change. I also felt afraid. Could I really manage alone? Could we afford to separate financially? Would I have to give up the house that I had grown to love so much? Could I parent Neal alone? I knew nothing about paying bills. Tom had always done that and taken care of the car as well. I had so much to learn. But, despite my fears, I also felt an enormous sense of relief.

I wondered if when he came home Tom would tell me he had changed his mind. Would he suggest that we try to work something out? Although my emotions wavered between fear and relief, I didn't want to reconsider our separation. I could have lived with Tom longer, perhaps even for a few more years, but, now that I was faced with the probability that we would separate, I was glad.

When Lanni came home I decided to tell her what happened. I knew it was a lot for her to hear, but I also knew that since she lived with us she should know about our decision. As I told her the chain of events, I realized that Tom's reason for being unable to live with me was that I had considered sleeping with Nelson. He hadn't said that. He hadn't given me a reason, and I hadn't asked for one, but clearly what had become intolerable to him was that another man might touch my body. He had not complained when I withdrew emotionally. He had even adjusted to being a virtual tenant in his own house. But the possibility that I might have an affair was too much. It seemed so ridiculous to me that possession of my body meant so much to him while other things that had so much more significance, at least to me, might have caused difficulty but did not seem to warrant his serious attention.

Over the next few weeks I did sleep with Nelson. It was nice to be with him, but I made it quite clear that any relationship that developed between us would have to be on my terms. I had had enough of feeling responsible for someone else's feelings. If he had any problems with anything I did or said, it was up to him to tell me. He had to understand that at that point in my life I was very selfish. Except for the children, I was going to think about what I wanted and needed before I thought about anyone else. Any new relationship I formed would have to be on that basis.

Tom and I were cordial. Sometimes it seemed as if nothing had changed. When we told the children that we were separating, however, our decision became very real. Neal cried, and Hannah was very quiet. We tried to explain to them that we had grown apart, but I knew that what we were saying made no sense to them. We seemed to get along well enough. We never fought. How could children of nine and eleven years of age understand the subtleties of two people growing in different directions? I felt very sorry for them and even wished we had fought more so they might have been more prepared for the separation. But our lack of direct confrontation was part of the problem. I had wanted Tom to fight with me, but he was so detached that it was impossible to get him into a heated debate, let alone an argument.

The separation also took on more reality when I thought about how to tell my parents. I knew it would be hard on them. There had only been one divorce in the family. Uncle Vaghoush had divorced his wife, Vera, when I was about fifteen. I was never clear on the reasons for their separation, but I knew that I was not supposed to mention her name. She was erased from the family memory. Uncle Alex went so far as to go through all of his home movies to splice Vera out of them. She remained only in one sequence, and that was because she was pushing me on a swing. I had loved her and was devastated when I learned I would never see her again. I asked my mother if I could visit her, but she was adamant that I could not. In my family, marriage was eternal.

I decided it would be better to write them a letter than to tell them on the phone. In my letter I tried to reassure them that I would be fine, although I knew it was inconceivable to them that a woman could survive without a man. I also told them that Tom and I had been estranged for some time and that it would be much better for all of us if we separated. They called after receiving my letter, and my mother's first words were "How will you manage?"

After we had told the children, my parents, and Tom's mother, we agreed that we didn't need to keep our separation a secret any longer. I told my friends, and he told his. People we knew in common were as astounded as the children had been. I was sure his colleagues blamed the women's movement, and, in a sense, they were right. Had it not been for women's liberation, I was sure that I would not have had the sense of self which generated so many of the changes that had taken place in my life. I could not imagine making it on my own without the movement. My friends were not surprised. They could see how little Tom and I shared.

The day after I told Elaine about our separation and my affair with Nelson, she called me. Since it was early in the morning, an unusual time for Elaine to call, I asked her what was wrong. She said she had been up all night thinking about me and she had something to say. She asked if I was sitting down and said I had better. When she told me that I should think about moving away from Ithaca, I said that I couldn't do that. Was she crazy? I began to tell her all the reasons why I couldn't leave. She interrupted me, saying I should shut up and listen to her. First of all, she said, never say "can't." She went on to say that she had felt for a long time that Tom was a very bad influence on the children, especially Neal. He didn't really want them to grow up. I had never discussed my feelings about Tom's influence on them with anyone, and I was surprised that Elaine had come to the same conclusion. The time to move them away from Tom was now, she said. I sat on the chair beside the phone and listened hard to what my friend was saying. The older the children got, the harder it would be for them to move. Also, she said, I didn't really have a solid support network in Ithaca. Most of my friends were students, and where would I be when they graduated and left town? I needed to be in a place like Amherst where I knew women my own age who could be there when I needed them, and she would be in Boston, which was only a two-hour drive away. She said I should go someplace where I wouldn't be Tom O'Brien's wife. I needed to start a new life in a new place. And she did not approve of my relationship with Nelson. He was too young for me and sure to leave me soon. She wanted me to get away from him before I was too involved. She ended by saying she was tired. I had kept her up all night, and now she needed to go to sleep. In a few days she and Art were planning to go to Boston, where they were both going to attend graduate school, to look for a place to live and I should go with them. After they were done in Boston we could go to Amherst to see about housing for the children and me and to find out what the schools had to offer Neal.

Elaine was right. No one was home, but I felt I had to get out of the house and think about what she had said. I walked to one of the many little waterfalls near our house and tried to get some clarity. Everything made perfect sense to me except the part about Nelson. If anyone were going to leave, it would be me. What she had said about my other relationships was, however, very true. Becoming a feminist and the debacle at female studies had not been conducive to making or keeping friends my own age. Even Kathy Taylor was in California with her family and had written that they liked it so much they might not return. In Amherst, on the other hand, I would have Carolyn and the friends I'd made last January. There was also a strong possibility that Jane would be there in the fall. Carolyn was trying to create a position for her, and the last I'd heard from Jane was that everything was looking very positive. The women's movement in Amherst was as strong as anywhere in the country outside of a big city, and there was still no real feminist activity in Ithaca. I could even go to school in Amherst. Once I established residency, tuition would not be a problem. I imagined that with all the feminists on campus the history department would certainly be open to work about women. I would hate to give up the opportunity to work on the course with Mary Ryan, but I couldn't have everything.

The more I thought about moving, the more attractive it became. It was certainly worth a trip to Amherst to see what the possibilities were. When Elaine called back later that afternoon I told her I had decided to join them. I told Tom I needed to get away for a few days and was going to Boston with Elaine and Art. He looked surprised but didn't say anything.

Elaine had made arrangements to stay with Merrill Rubin, the young woman who had initiated the Ithaca College Women's Liberation Front and who was now going to law school in Boston. I was happy to see her, but she was very cool to me. I couldn't understand what had happened. I had seen her just a few months earlier and she had been as warm as ever. Elaine told me that Merrill had been very upset that Tom and I were separating. I realized then that we had been a kind of model couple for students, especially young heterosexual women involved in the women's movement. Tom was far more understanding of the movement than most men and seemed so supportive of me that it was difficult for Merrill to imagine that we couldn't make it. I felt that she blamed me for the failure of the marriage. I supposed she thought I expected too much from Tom.

After spending one morning at Merrill's listening to Elaine make phone calls to realtors in her "respectable lady voice," I realized

I couldn't wait for Elaine and Art. It was time for me to see about my own move. I sat in the front seat of the bus to Amherst and made a long list of things to do when I got there. First, I wanted to see what services were available for Neal. He would need a special program in school and a therapist.

I stayed with Kathy Salisbury, an Ithaca College graduate who was in graduate school at U. Mass. She set me up with a phone and some names. By the next day I had talked to the director of special education and one of the teachers, who both explained that they worked toward mainstreaming special children as much as possible. They provided each child with a coordinator who, after consultation with parents and any professionals who had worked with the child, devised an individual plan for six months or a year. The special education director was sure that they would be able to work with Neal.

I decided to find Carolyn at the university. I had told her I was coming and why but had asked her not to tell Richard. She was excited at the prospect that both Jane and I might be in the area. It looked as though Jane's job was going to be funded, and she thought there might be a position for me at the women's center, too. I also went to see Judy Katz, a young woman I had met during the January semester, who was coordinator of the Sylvan Area Women's Center. She also thought there would be a job there. The center was interested in developing women's studies, and she felt sure that I would have a very good chance of getting the position.

By the end of the day I was sure that the move to Amherst would be the best thing for me and the children. I had found more support in one day than I had ever felt in Ithaca. Now that I had decided to move I began to think about finances. I felt that, because I would have both children, I should get half of Tom's salary; the children and I deserved it. I had helped Tom get to where he was by taking care of everything while he was in graduate school and working on his dissertation. Until the last year I had also entertained his colleagues royally, with the best food in town, and had dutifully played the role of faculty wife. I had also worked, taken care of the children, and had major responsibility for the housework and cooking. Now I needed money to support the children and myself while I got an education. Half of Tom's salary and the money from a teaching assistantship would be enough, I thought, for us to live comfortably. I saw no reason that my standard of living should drop dramatically.

Elaine called the next morning to say that she and Art had not found a place to live yet. I told her that I had to get back to Ithaca, since Sunday was Easter. It would be very hard on the children if I were not there. She said Art would stay in Boston and continue to look for a place, and she would get to Amherst as soon as possible.

By the time Elaine came to pick me up I was fully organized. I had Neal's school situation worked out and had met with Judith Tompkins, the therapist whom friends had recommended, and liked her enormously. I felt her empathy for the struggle I had been through to try to get services for Neal and was delighted that she thought she could work with him. I had the application for graduate school and two job possibilities. I planned to come back to look for a house to buy another time. If I were to move we would have to sell our house. It was a large and beautiful house in a good location and I had no doubts that I could, at the very least, get a down payment for a house in Amherst with my share of the profit.

It was later than I had hoped when we set out for Ithaca. I was determined to be home for Easter. We wouldn't have artichokes or even colored eggs, but I wanted to be there. We made it as far as Blanford, Connecticut, when the car started to act very strangely. I pulled into the service area and was told by the mechanic that the clutch was almost gone. I was furious—the car was only a year and a half old—but my rage got me nowhere. I arranged for a Volkswagen dealer in Springfield to pick the car up on Monday and called friends in Amherst to come and get us.

Elaine and I went into Howard Johnson's to wait for our ride. I called Tom to tell him what had happened, and when I came back to the table I noticed that Elaine seemed very nervous. I asked her what was wrong, and she whispered that she hated being in "honky country" alone at night. I realized that what had been merely an inconvenience for me had been much worse for Elaine. Howard Johnson's was a comfortable place for me. It evoked memories of trips with my parents and enjoying the special pleasure of eating at a real American restaurant. I wondered if I would ever stop learning from Elaine about the differences in our lives.

When we got back to Kathy's she was glad to put us up for another night and offered me her car to drive back to Ithaca the next morning. She would get mine when it was ready, and I could come back to exchange cars at my convenience. I was grateful for her generosity and wondered of anyone I knew in Ithaca would be so willing to help me out.

We set out again the next morning as soon as I could get Elaine moving, and made it to Ithaca by early afternoon. I dropped Elaine off at her house, and when I got home Lanni came rushing into the kitchen. She was very glad to have me back. Tom had been very strange while I was gone, she said, and Neal and Hannah were upset. They were in their rooms, looking very sad, but they brightened up a little when they saw me. Lanni had planned a nice dinner. Tom came down from his room, and we salvaged what we could of that Easter celebration.

As soon as the children were in bed and Lanni had gone to her room, I told Tom that I planned to move to Amherst. I explained everything I had learned about schools, housing, and jobs. He was silent for a while and then walked to the kitchen to refill his drink. When he came back into the living room he said that he had known I was planning something. I told him that it had all happened rather suddenly and I hadn't wanted to tell him until I had made a decision. After what seemed to me an eternity of silence, Tom said he thought a move to Amherst might be a good thing for me. He would keep the children with him until I got my life together. I was astounded. I could hardly believe that Tom wanted to keep Neal and Hannah. I shuddered to think of what they would go through with him as their only parent. I told him that it was out of the question: Neal and Hannah would stay with me. If that meant I had to stay in Ithaca, then I wouldn't move. I told him directly that I did not consider him capable of caring for them properly. By the end of the evening he agreed. He also thought that my suggestion of half of his salary was quite fair. As I walked up to my room, I thought that Tom certainly was a decent enough man.

We put the house up for sale, and I made my application to graduate school and sent new resumes to Judy and Carolyn. Tom said he'd like to go with me to Amherst again to look for a house, and we agreed to tell the children that evening that they would be moving sometime during the summer.

I found a small house within walking distance of the university, downtown, and the school that Neal and Hannah would attend. It had been completely modernized, so I wouldn't have to worry about maintenance. I liked it well enough, but it was nothing like the wonderful house I would be leaving. When my offer was accepted, I found that I needed a fairly large sum for a deposit. Tom told me not to worry: I could write a check, and he would cover it.

I also found out that the director of graduate studies in the history department had recommended to the graduate school that I be accepted into the master's program. There was, however, still nothing definite on my job possibilities. The Sylvan Area Women's Center was waiting for funding, and Carolyn said the staff at the U. Mass Women's Center hadn't yet voted on new positions. She had thought I would be best suited to a position as liaison between the center and Third World women on campus and in the community. Like most women's groups, the center was totally white.

After weeks of waiting I finally heard from both places. Carolyn had a tentative approval from the staff for my position, and Judy said that the funding had come through and she was authorized to offer me the job. I felt that I was more qualified for the Sylvan position since it was to develop women's studies. I did not know how to be a liaison with Third World women. I was just coming into the community and had no contacts. I called Carolyn and said I was sorry that I would have to take the other job. I needed a teaching assistantship badly, not only for the money but because it carried a full tuition waiver; I would not have to pay the substantial out-of-state tuition while I waited to establish residency.

The sale of our house did not go smoothly. We accepted an offer from a woman who was moving into town to set up a law practice, but, despite the fact that she had a large down payment, the bank refused to finance the house unless she had a cosigner. She was indignant and refused. We didn't have any other offers, and it soon became clear that we would have to think about renting it for a year. I was frantic about where I would get the down payment for my new house in Amherst, but once again Tom said not to worry. We could take out a home improvement loan using our house as collateral. He would make the payments on the loan, and I could pay him back when our house was finally sold. I was very grateful to him for being so helpful.

We seemed to be getting along better than ever. I wondered if part of the reason for our amicable relations was that, despite my fears about living alone with the children, I was feeling wonderful. Acquaintances offered condolences for the demise of my marriage, and I was quite honest when I told them not to be sorry. I knew it was not appropriate to tell them how I really felt, and I didn't, but I was ecstatic. I was about to live my own life for the first time and was looking forward to it.

Neal and Hannah seemed to be adjusting fairly well to the dramatic changes that had occurred in their lives over the last few months. Neal was going to return to the speech camp, and Hannah was going to the Metropolitan Baptist camp with Lanni for a two-week session. When Lanni suggested that she go, Hannah's immediate reaction was positive. I explained to her that she would have to sleep there and that Lanni would be very busy. I also wanted her to know that she and Lanni might be the only white people at the camp, and Hannah said that as long as Lanni were there she would feel fine. Besides, she said, maybe she could find some other kids at camp who liked the Jackson Five as much as she did. The girls at her school thought she was "weird" because she liked a black group so much. Tom and I told her that we would all think about it and would talk about it again the next day.

After Hannah and Neal went to bed we talked with Lanni about the camp in more detail. I was concerned about its affiliation with a church, but Lanni assured us that the children were not required in any way to attend church services; she felt that the camp would be a wonderful experience for Hannah. We agreed that, if Hannah still wanted to go after she thought about it, we would send her. The next morning Hannah's first words were about camp. She really wanted to go, and, when I told her that Tom and I had decided it would be fine, she beamed at Lanni.

I began to make serious plans for my move. Nelson offered to help me by borrowing his stepfather's truck, and Tom and I divided our possessions without any major problems. I was beginning to think our separation was going to be very easy, but Tom's actual move was traumatic.

I was awakened early one Saturday morning by loud voices that seemed to be coming from the living room. As I got out of bed to see what was happening, Tom came into my room and said I should strip the bed. His friends had arrived to move his things. I was shocked. That moment was the first time I had heard he was moving that day. I screamed that he could have least told me so I could arrange to take the children out of the house.

I dressed as quickly as I could and ran to see where Neal and Hannah were. It was obvious to me that he had also not told them that he was moving that day. They looked very distraught. Tony had come for the weekend, and we had planned a day's outing on a lake near Ithaca with friends. When the children and I got down to the living room Tony was staring at the scene. Tom was carrying furniture out the front door. Hannah began to cry, and Neal ran after Tom telling him to put down the chair he was carrying. Tony got Neal, and we took the children into the kitchen. I could not understand how Tom could be so understanding and helpful on the one hand and so cruel on the other.

I was so angry at Tom that I could hardly speak to him. I only wanted to get away from Ithaca as quickly as possible. Neal was due at camp the day after my move, so Tom and I agreed that Neal would stay with him for the day. Nelson, Tony's friend Sue, and I loaded the truck together, and Nelson left for Amherst while Sue, Hannah, and I went to Poughkeepsie to drop Hannah off at Lanni's. They were leaving for camp in the morning. After a wonderful dinner at Lanni's house and a stop at the Italian grocery store and bakery for bread, cheese, salami, and olives, we made our way to Amherst.

By the time Sue and I got there it was dark, but the house was lit, and I could see people moving back and forth carrying things. As I got out of the car, I was greeted by Jane, Judy, and Kathy. My table and chairs were in place in the kitchen, and Jane took a bottle of champagne out of the refrigerator. I was overwhelmed by the warmth of my friends, old and new. I ran out to the car to get the bag of food. When I put it on the table Jane laughed and said only I would come to a new house with a supply of good food.

Within the next few days all the unpacking was done, and Nelson had gone back to the Adirondacks, where he was working that summer. I walked through my house and reveled in its emptiness. I had loved being greeted by my friends and having Nelson and Sue stay to help, but it was also wonderful, I found, to be alone. I wondered briefly how Neal and Hannah were doing, but I was so delighted with being in my own house in Amherst that I didn't think much about anybody.

The next morning I woke up early and was surprised that I was anxious to start the day. I usually waited until the last possible minute before getting out of bed, but, as I showered, I realized that I didn't want to waste any of my precious time alone. For the first time in my life I had ten days all to myself. After a breakfast of fried eggs and the last of the Italian bread, I walked out into the yard. It was not very big, but I was able to find a spot in the sun for a small garden. I turned the soil and drove to a farm stand I used to go to when Tom and I lived in Leverett. I was delighted that it was still in business and bought some tomato plants, herbs, and zucchini seeds. By evening I had planted my garden. I was exhausted and delighted with myself.

Before I knew it, Hannah's session at camp was over, and so was my time alone. Tom and I had decided it would be important for Neal to see me again and for Hannah to see both him and Neal. He arranged to get Neal out of camp for the weekend, and I was to pick Hannah up and drive to Ithaca. As Hannah and I drove into the town where my life had changed so dramatically, I realized that the only thing I would miss was my house. Elaine had been right. There was nothing for me in Ithaca any longer.

Chapter 18

The summer in Amherst passed quickly. Hannah loved her room, and, though she complained sometimes about being lonely, she seemed to be adjusting to the separation and the move quite well. One of my neighbors ran a ceramics studio at his house, and for a nominal fee he allowed Hannah to work with the clay and fired the hand-built pots she created. She had learned to make pots at East Hill and enjoyed it enormously. She also spent a good deal of time writing. One evening she announced that she needed a new notebook. She had four stories to write, and, she said, had already picked out the titles. I patiently explained that people usually chose their titles when they have finished writing the stories, but she said she already knew what they were about, and I was surprised at her well-developed plots. She spent the next month filling the little notebook she had chosen, encouraging me with her female characters, who had problems with family or friends but had found ways to work through them.

Hannah and I seemed to be coping well that summer, but I knew the real test of how we were going to manage in Amherst, and without Tom, was still before us. When the asparagus fronds began to turn to their beautiful autumn gold and the pumpkins stood large and orange in the fields, I began to feel occasional pangs of fear. Would the Amherst school system, with its emphasis on mainstreaming special children, really be able to meet Neal's needs? He still tended to withdraw, particularly when he was in a stressful situation, and could easily be ignored. I worried, too, about Hannah. She was making a major transition from East Hill to a traditional school. Would she be able to adjust to doing math even if she didn't feel like it? How would she react to the expectation that she be quiet and listen to the teacher or any of the other requirements of a "regular" school?

My greatest fear, however, was how I would do in graduate school. I felt ill prepared for advanced work in history. I tried to tell myself that my performance in the classes I had taken at Ithaca College and the high grade I had achieved on the Graduate Record Exam indicated that I would be able to do the work, but I had also convinced myself that anyone who could read would have done well in those courses and that the GRE must have been particularly easy the year I took it. I had no confidence that I would be up to the task of serious academic work. When school started I would probably find out that I had been fooling myself and that I wasn't really smart after all

The one thing I felt fairly confident about was my job. Jane Smith, whose responsibility at Sylvan was to teach a course at the women's center, asked me if I would like to teach with her, and I happily agreed. We developed a course that focused on women's struggles, called "Climbing the Walls." Using the wall as a metaphor for the sexism in our society, we posed three alternatives for women: getting stuck in the wall, jumping off, or climbing over it. I was very pleased with our syllabus except that we had been unable to think of appropriate books by black women which were in print. We hoped to find money to rent *A Raisin in the Sun*, which we planned to use in the "getting over the wall" section.

Although working on the syllabus with Jane had been stimulating and I had felt that we shared equally, I was less confident about what would happen in the classroom. I looked forward to teaching with Jane more for what I could learn from her than for what I would contribute. Like Ruth Berman, she wanted to create an environment that allowed students and teachers to be equal. Unlike Ruth, however, Jane did not lecture or prepare discussion questions, thereby forcing students to take the responsibility for discussion. In this way, she argued, the students would create the class themselves. I had serious misgivings about such an unstructured situation and tentatively expressed them to Jane. She responded confidently that, if the students did not have anything to say about the readings, we might have to learn to deal with silence. I was not encouraged by her response, but I assumed my fears came from my lack of experience in teaching and my own need for structure. After all, Jane had had real teaching jobs and knew what she was doing.

Despite my fears and apprehensions, I was excited to be starting a life on my own, and Amherst was clearly the best place for me to do it. I had even embarked on a major project with Jane and Carolyn. One night when Pat's band was playing, Jane came to spend some time with me. The previous year she had written and published a book about her experiences as an antiwar activist, and I asked her if she had any thoughts about writing another one. She said she wanted to write about the lives of women like us—women who had gone through major changes as a result of the women's movement. She thought I might be interested in collaborating with her. I was flattered but thought that writing a book was far beyond my abilities. I did, however, have a suggestion. It seemed to me that Carolyn, Jane, and I would be good subjects for such a work. We had met each other when we were faculty wives (although Jane was on the faculty herself at the time, she was identified as a faculty wife since it was her husband who had the "real" job). The women's movement had not come into our lives when we first met, but we had each come to it in our own ways, and it had had profound effects on our lives. Jane was intrigued with the idea but said the project would only be feasible if Carolyn and I worked on it with her. The more we talked about the possibilities of such a book, the more excited we became. It could be a new kind of book—a triple autobiography/biography. We would write about ourselves and each other. We excitedly called Carolyn to say we had something very important to discuss with her and made arrangements to meet early the next week.

Jane left to see Pat's last set, and I went to bed. Although I had felt tired, sleep seemed impossible. I could only think of the book and how good it would be to work with Jane and Carolyn. We were all from different backgrounds: Jane was Norwegian and from a small town in Wisconsin; Carolyn, so American that her ethnicity was not an issue, had been raised in a medium sized city in Texas; and I was an Armenian from New York City. I was fascinated, too, with the prospect of sharing details of our past and learning how I was perceived. I finally fell asleep but woke the next morning with the idea of the book still with me.

Although the thought of writing anything that Jane would read was very frightening to me, I believed anything was possible in my new life. I had done things over the last two years I never imagined I could do. It seemed that once I understood the sources of my feelings of inadequacy—in my family and in the culture—I needed to challenge myself to find out what I could do. Being in Amherst was certainly the result of my new found courage. If I had given in to my doubts and fears, I would still be living with Tom, a horrible thought to me now. The women I knew seemed to share my feelings. We could try anything we wanted to do and support each other for trying.

Carolyn and Richard were building a house, and I was surprised and impressed to hear Carolyn talk knowledgeably about footings, whatever they were, with a group of men. And when I stood in the living room and looked at the beautiful fireplace, I was thrilled for both Carolyn and myself because I knew that she had helped the mason build it.

Not only did we think we could do anything men could do, but we were also convinced that we were better than men. Women were more able to cooperate; we cared about other people's feelings and were certainly more in touch with our own emotions than men. The book would reflect all of these differences. It would not be the work of one person but a collaborative effort that would speak to the experience of women like us. It was also clear that the process of doing the book was as important as the product.

Whatever happened in the fall, I felt that my friendship with Jane and Carolyn would provide me with more real support than I had ever gotten from Tom. Like Elaine, they supported my strengths. They believed in me and wanted to see me succeed.

Neal came home from camp angry at me for moving to Amherst and missing his father, but he also seemed to like some things about his new home. Judy Katz, whom he had met when she came to Ithaca for a visit, took him on a tour of the record stores in town and on campus. Within a few days he began to explore the area on his own. Late in August we had an appointment with the teacher who would coordinate his program. I walked to school with both children to show them the way and to see how long it would take. After twenty minutes of a leisurely walk we arrived, and Neal seemed anxious to explore the large, one-story building. I felt some sense of relief as I looked at the school and realized that Neal would stay at Wildwood until he finished elementary school, rather than moving from school to school as he had done in Ithaca. We met the teacher in a small room. She had received all of Neal's records and wanted some time alone with him. Hannah and I could wait for them in the library. Hannah was very quiet as we entered the large, comfortable room and only shrugged when I said it looked like a nice place to read. We sat on the carpeted steps, and I could feel

Hannah's tension. The summer had come to an end.

I agreed to a plan for Neal that seemed overly cautious. He would begin school by attending for one and a half hours a day, and his coordinator would increase his time as she thought appropriate for his adjustment. The classrooms at Wildwood were organized into large quads of one hundred students with four teachers in each room. The quads could be intimidating, she said, to a child like Neal. My fears about Neal being neglected increased as I thought about a room with one hundred children, but I also wondered how Neal would feel about not going to school all day as he had done for so long. I worried too about what it would mean for me to have Neal home for most of the day. He might have to learn to stay home alone from time to time.

Hannah would, of course, be in school all day. She had made friends with a few of the neighborhood children by the end of the summer, and I was pleased when she said that one of them was in her quad.

The first week of September I also met with my advisor and enrolled in three courses, one of which, to my great delight, was "Comparative Feminism: Britain and the United States." Joyce Berkman, the instructor, had only recently become interested in women's history and was teaching the course for the first time on an experimental basis. My advisor, whose own field was American social and intellectual history, seemed open to my interest in women. As I walked home from our meeting, I felt I might do just as well at the University of Massachusetts as I would have at SUNY-Binghamton.

That week I also met the other staff members at the Sylvan Area Women's Center. It was unclear to me what my duties would be aside from teaching the course with Jane, and after my experience at female studies at Cornell I was determined to clarify my responsibilities. I said that I knew I had been hired because of my expertise in women's studies, but I was not sure how the center wanted to use my skills. I was alarmed when one of my colleagues responded that *she* did women's studies. One of the student staff members suggested that I spend time in the center to see where I would fit in. I replied that I did not have time to hang around the center. I was a single parent and was starting graduate work full time after being out of school for fourteen years. Moreover, I had specific skills to offer. When the meeting was over I knew no more about my job than when I first asked my question.

I taught the course with Jane and attended weekly staff meet ings, which seemed to be more social than productive. Carolyn suggested that I attend the staff meeting at the U. Mass Women's Center, since they had had some of the same problems and had hired a facilitator to help them. I could take what I learned back to the Sylvan Area Women's Center. I made my proposal to the staff, and they agreed that our meetings could be better. Although the result of three weeks at the U. Mass Women's Center was not very illuminating, I was supported in my judgment that the group should designate a rotating chair, that an agenda should be set at the end of one meeting for the next, and that the agenda should be followed. The response to these suggestions was favorable, but after a few weeks of fairly organized meetings we reverted to getting together to catch up on what had happened in our lives over the week. I realized that once again I would have to create my job. What I thought I had been hired to do was being done by someone else, although I didn't know what it was she was doing about women's studies.

Luckily, I had been appointed as the graduate student representative to the women's studies subcommittee of the Faculty Senate Committee on the Status of Women. The work of this group was to write a proposal for a two-year pilot program that would award a B.A. in women's studies. Carolyn was chairwoman of the larger group, and Jane was a member of the subcommittee, as were other faculty who had been teaching women's studies courses in their departments. I was also pleased to see that there was an undergraduate student member of the group. Working on this committee was precisely the kind of thing I had expected to do at the Sylvan Area Women's Center, and I decided to make it my job.

I requested a staff meeting to discuss my duties. I told my colleagues that I had had a month of frustration trying to find work at the center: I had not been doing anything other than teaching the course with Jane and attending staff meetings. I proposed that my work on the women's studies subcommittee be made part of my job description. Since they really had nothing else for me to do, they agreed.

My disappointment with the Sylvan Area Women's Center was matched by my feelings about the progress of the course Jane and I were teaching. Learning to live with the silence in the classroom was as difficult as I had expected, and I was not sure that it was very productive. When we did have discussions I didn't know how much Jane and I should participate. I tried to follow her lead, but

I often felt that I wasn't doing what was required. I wondered if the class would have been better if Jane had been teaching it alone or with someone who was more sensitive to the students. I also wondered if Jane might be giving them too much responsibility. I was not confident enough in my perceptions, however, to discuss them openly with Jane. To raise serious questions about the course might be a challenge to Jane's philosophy; indeed, to question the structure might reveal that I did not fully support the concept of student power. I was reluctant to reveal my latent authoritarianism, particularly when Jane did not seem to be disturbed by the class.

My experience in my own courses was mixed. Women's history was a joy. Joyce Berkman was incredibly thorough and seemed to have a real commitment to women. The other two courses, on the other hand, were very painful. The professors were not only sexist and racist but also constantly talked down to the students. I was also overwhelmed by the amount of work I had to do. My background in history was very thin in spite of all the reading I had done, and there just didn't seemed to be enough time to carefully read all the assignments.

By the middle of the semester Neal was finally in school all day. I didn't know how much attention he was getting but was encouraged by the interest his coordinator had taken in him. He was also seeing his therapist once a week. Her office was not within walking distance from home, and initially I was quite upset that I would have to take the time to drive him there and wait for his session to be over. Time was so precious that it was hard to give up an hour and a half of afternoon time once a week. But I soon found that I looked forward to Thursday afternoons. Judith's office was in her house, and on nice days I sat in her yard and enjoyed the afternoon sun. I had also met Martha Ayres, a therapist who worked with Judith. One rainy Thursday when she had an hour between clients we shared coffee and conversation in Judith's kitchen. She was frequently free during Neal's hour, and I was growing to like her very much.

By the time my first semester came to an end I was so exhausted that I wondered how I would deal with Christmas. All I wanted to do was be alone and sleep, but the holiday would come, and I would have to do something. I knew the children would want to spend the day with Tom and me, and, although I dreaded the thought of another Christmas with him, I felt I should try to give Neal and Hannah a decent day. We decided that the children and I would drive to Ithaca on the day before Christmas, I would spend the night with a friend, and Neal and Hannah would stay with Tom. We would spend Christmas at his apartment. My parents wanted to see the children, and Tom wanted to see his mother. After opening our presents in Ithaca we would all drive to New Jersey, though in separate cars. It was a gray Christmas. Tom's usual depression around the holidays was worse than ever. I was now even less willing to help him out of it and withdrew myself into an angry silence. I had tried my best, but it hadn't worked.

After taking the children to see his mother, Tom left for Ithaca and we stayed with my parents for a few more days. I racked my brains to find a better solution for New Year's Eve. The children seemed as depressed as I was. I remembered Lanni's description of her family's New Year's celebration. It had sounded wonderful. They gathered at her mother's house, played blackjack until midnight and then welcomed in the New Year with sausage and peppers. It would be good to see Lanni and her mother, and I knew Neal and Hannah would be happy to see her again. Lanni was overjoyed when I called to ask if we could come to her house for New Year's.

January 1974 seemed to be filled with less promise than the previous year. Amherst was a good community for feminists but far from the paradise it had seemed to be. My friends were supportive, but I seemed to need more than they could give. I had done well in my courses but had dazzled neither the history department nor myself with my performance. I never seemed to know enough history, and I had also learned that my writing skills were in need of serious improvement. I felt a deep shame when my papers were returned with grammatical and organizational corrections. I was disappointed in myself. Graduate school had been a kind of cause for me. I was going to learn to write women's history not only for myself but for all my sisters. Clearly, I had not, or worse yet, could not live up to the task I had set for myself.

I would get a break from being the only adult in the house that semester. Nelson would be moving in with us at the end of January for a few months. He was going on a student trip to Greece, and since the trip didn't begin until March, he decided to come to Amherst until then. He would stay in the little TV room on the second floor, as I had no intention of sharing my space with anyone. I had grown to love sleeping alone. Our relationship was still remarkably easy; I was able to enjoy him without feeling responsible for his problems.

The first semester of my job at the Sylvan Area Women's Center had been difficult, but because I had taught the course with Jane and had worked on the Women's Studies Committee, I felt I had fulfilled my responsibilities. I could continue my work with the committee, but Jane and I would no longer be teaching a course, and once again I was left with the question of what to do for work. Elaine, who was in Cambridge working on her masters at Harvard, came to visit in January and suggested that we teach the course on black and white women we'd designed and which she'd taught at Cornell. If the center could pay her, she would be willing to come to Amherst once a week. I proposed the course to the women's center staff, and, to my surprise, they not only supported it but also were able to find some money to pay Elaine. I was greatly relieved. Elaine and I had wanted to teach this course together at Cornell; it was certainly needed on this campus, as it had been in Ithaca, and I looked forward to seeing Elaine regularly. There was, however, one problem. Center courses often had low enrollments, and I worried about this one. The topic was difficult. I had not developed much of a reputation among the students, and Elaine was not able to use the network she had had at Cornell to attract students. My fears were well grounded. Two students signed up for the course, and it was cancelled. I decided I had done what I could to find work at the women's center. Since the staff had no suggestions, I continued to work on the women's studies committee and attended weekly staff meetings. I tried not to feel guilty when I picked up my weekly paycheck. I'd tried my best to be flexible, and I hoped I would find another teaching assistantship the next semester.

One place I did not want to work was the history department. I felt alienated from the faculty and the other students. White women and black people were absent from the courses and the consciousnesses of my fellow graduate students. Only Joyce Berkman had an interest in what seemed so vital to me. Other professors, including my advisor, who had seemed so supportive in our initial meetings, couldn't teach me what I felt I needed to know, nor did they consider the study of women to be a valid intellectual enterprise. It also seemed that they put demands on me that were beyond my knowledge and experience. I tried to do my papers on women, but professors indicated that they expected me to not only study women but present a methodology for women's history. I began to seriously question whether I would continue in graduate school beyond the master's level. There were few jobs for historians. My education was giving me more pain than pleasure and very little knowledge that I considered important.

Meetings with the women's studies committee were a vital antidote to my experiences in the history department and the inefficiency at the Sylvan Area Women's Center. While there were some problems in writing the final draft of our proposal, it was the product of all of us and of the consensus we had reached. It called for a major and a minor in women's studies as well as a number of courses taught under the auspices of the program. A policy board of faculty, students, and staff plus a community representative would be the program's decision-making body.

I had heard that a group of socialist feminist faculty and students were disturbed because the proposal was not radical enough, but compared to my experience at Cornell it was amazingly progressive. I didn't know who these women were or what their specific objections were. I was even more ignorant about a rift that was occasionally mentioned between the women on the committee and a group of Third World women. No one I asked seemed to be able to articulate what it was about. I wished I knew some of the women my colleagues referred to, but no one had any regular contact with them.

As the spring of 1974 approached, I began to feel more and more depressed. School was becoming more difficult than ever. I was infuriated because I was continually the only person in my class who seemed to have any interest in white women, black people, or even the daily lives of ordinary working people. In one class I brought the actual lives of factory workers at the turn of the century into a discussion of the industrial system. The professor and the other students in the seminar merely stared at me then went on with the discussion. The conditions under which people worked was obviously not germane to the high academic discourse. Writing papers within this context had become excruciating. Not only did I have to work on my writing skills, but I also felt that each word I wrote had to be documented because what I was interested in was not the concern of ''real'' history. Though I was aware of the political dimension of my professor's criticisms of the work, I often felt very stupid and wondered why I had ever thought I was capable of graduate work.

School was also not going well for Hannah. The creative child who had written four wonderful stories and built beautiful pots during the summer was totally uninterested even in reading and art classes. My general feelings about the school were also negative, but I tried my best not to convey them to Hannah. Despite its "open classroom" structure, the school reminded me of P.S. 189 in 1945. I had noticed on my visits that the teachers' main concern seemed to be control. Children were hurried into long lines only to wait for the order to march to wherever they were going. Hannah seemed so unhappy that I had asked the teacher in her quad for a meeting. While waiting for them I picked up the reader the class was using. It had eight stories. Four of them centered on male characters with females either nonexistent or peripheral, three had male animals as their main characters, and the last story was about a little girl who was a deaf mute. Of course all the characters were white and very middle class. I put down the book and looked at the children's work on the walls. I could see why Hannah was not stimulated. Tacked to the bulletin board were mimeographed copies of snowmen, each with a little paragraph the children had written in response to the picture that was just like the one I remembered from my days in elementary school. Had nothing changed?

By the time the teachers were ready for our conference I was furious. There had been much about East Hill that had disturbed me and I had been genuinely relieved that Hannah was going to attend a "regular" school, but I hadn't expected it to be as rigid and unimaginative as Wildwood seemed to be. The teachers complained that Hannah was very negative, and finally I responded that I could well see why. The meeting was a disaster.

It was also clear that my relationship with Neal's program coordinator was deteriorating. I was beginning to feel that she pitied Neal because he was from a "broken home," and, what was more disturbing, she seemed to underestimate his potential. Dr. Tompkins, like Dr. Julien, believed that, since Neal continued to progress, it was dangerous to his development to make any assumptions about his capabilities. She also agreed with Dr. Julien's assessment that Neal was able to do more than it seemed on the surface and it was crucial that his teachers have high expectations of him. Although this material was in Neal's file and Dr. Tompkins had had a meeting with the coordinator, I had the distinct impression that she thought I was too demanding and was unable to face the reality of Neal's limitations

I was very tired that March. Nelson was gone, but even his presence had not altered my feeling that there was always more to do than I had time or energy for. Sometimes I felt as if I were going to be crushed by the weight of my responsibilities—to the children, to myself, to my friends, to all the women in the world. One day I met a woman on campus whom I had not seen, I suddenly realized, for some time. I asked where she had been, and she said she had collapsed from exhaustion. She had had to stay in bed for a few weeks. While I was sorry to hear what had happened to her, part of me was relieved to hear that another feminist was having some difficulty being and doing everything. The "superwoman syndrome" was beginning to seem almost as dangerous as the sex roles we were trying to overcome.

My relationship with Jane and Carolyn also seemed to be suffering partially because of the demands of appropriate behavior for feminists. The movement had said we had to be strong, and, perhaps because we were so needy and frightened, we were unable to share our real feelings with each other. I knew that Jane's job was very difficult. Her position was split among three divisions of the university: the English department, the U. Mass. Women's Center, and the Sylvan Area Women's Center. Her occasional acerbic and sometimes bitter comments made it clear that she was unhappy, but she was unwilling or unable to talk openly about her difficulties. I did not encourage an honest discussion about it either, because I, too, needed to see Jane as a strong woman. Carolyn's marriage was finally breaking up, and her oldest son was in California in serious psychological trouble. Jane and I tried to do what we could for Carolyn, but she seemed hard to reach. It was also clear to me that what I had to give was limited. My energies were focused on trying to make it myself. We continued to tape sessions together and had them transcribed, but our discussions no longer included ideas on how to organize the material into a book. It seemed to me we were meeting to try to hold each other up without acknowledging that we were faltering.

My Thursday afternoons at Judith Tompkins's house were like an oasis in a desert. Early in April Martha, who was now my close friend, drove up to the house in a very snappy MGB and walked out of the car, smiling and waving hello. As she got closer to me, she immediately asked me what was wrong. Martha was the one person I knew who saw through my facade, perhaps because I didn't keep her out. For some reason, I felt that I could be honest with her. She didn't seem to need to uphold the image of the superwoman. She complained, accepted her own vulnerabilities as a normal part of life, and was able to admit to her fears. I told her I felt awful. I was tired, lonely, and it was my thirty-fourth birthday. No one in Amherst knew it was my birthday because I hadn't told anyone. I looked down to hide the tears that had sprung to my eyes.

I heard Martha tell me to get up. She wanted to take me for a ride in her sports car. We sped off, and I began to feel a little better. If I could have anything I wanted for my birthday, she asked, what would it be? Without thinking for a moment, I said I wanted a garden. The one beside my house was near three large pine trees. It had neither good soil nor enough sun. The seedlings I had so optimistically planted the previous June had produced a very small harvest. Martha was quiet for a few minutes, then she said she thought she could give me my wish. Although she no longer lived there, she was part owner of a house that had a beautiful spot for a garden, and, if I would like, we could plant it together. I was really excited. A garden was just what I needed, and planting and tending it with Martha would only make it better. Digging in the dirt had always helped me relax. I thought only about the soil and the plants and not about all that I had to do. Martha said she would let me know the next Thursday if we could use the land; she felt there would be no problem. I told her that, even if it didn't work out, she had given me one of the best birthday presents I had ever had.

I waited anxiously for the next Thursday and was not disappointed when Martha came into the kitchen and said, "Happy birthday—the garden is yours." Although it was only April I was anxious to start planning. I invited Martha to come to dinner that Saturday to talk about the garden. I wanted to start tomato, eggplant, and pepper seeds. We would have *dolma,* vegetables stuffed with ground lamb and rice. I had made and frozen it in the fall. It would be a celebration of the garden we would share. She agreed to come.

I awoke earlier than usual that morning. Martha was not due until six o'clock, but I could think of little else than her arrival. I decided to clean the house. Cleaning was the lowest of my priorities that year, and the place was filthy. I got Neal and Hannah to do their rooms, too. When the house was done I went out to get graph paper so that Martha and I could make a serious garden plan. I was glad we would have a focus because I was a little nervous about having Martha over. We'd seen each other only one hour a week while Neal was in session with Judith.

Martha arrived on time, and within a few minutes I realized my fears had been groundless. We fell into the easy conversation that had marked our relationship for the past seven months. I was also relieved to see that she was comfortable with Neal and Hannah, and they seemed to like her. The dinner of *dolma*, yogurt, and salad was a huge success, and after the children went to watch television we worked out the garden plan. We agreed that it would be fun to scatter the plants throughout the plot—like a crazy quilt—rather than growing the plants in rows. We laughed as we broke all the traditional rules for gardens while scrupulously following companion planting procedures.

Although it was fairly late when Martha left, I was not ready to see her go, and I saw her often over the next few weeks. I realized that since my birthday, when Martha had given me the garden, I had felt wonderful. School was as difficult as ever, my relationship with Neal's program coordinator had become so bad I wondered if we could work together at all, and my relationship with Jane had deteriorated to the point that we hardly spoke to each other. But I felt better than I had since I had moved to Amherst. Once again everything seemed possible.

Clearly, my feelings for Martha were more than of friendship. When I was not with her I thought about her, and when we were together I longed to be physically close to her. I had assumed from a number of things Martha had said that she was a lesbian, and I tried to convey my feelings in nonverbal ways. After weeks of hinting how I felt with touches on the arm or shoulder and a few very passionate handshakes, I realized she was either not interested in a sexual relationship with me or had seen me as a "straight lady" and was missing all my cues. By the middle of May I had to face the fact that I would have to tell her how I felt—in so many words. I would, however, have to wait until I finished the semester. I couldn't possibly finish my papers and tell Martha my feelings at the same time.

When I thought about what I would say and how Martha might respond I worried most about losing a friendship that had become very important to me. I thought I could accept it if she wasn't interested in a sexual relationship with me, but I would be devastated if I lost her friendship.

We had arranged to meet to buy seeds for the garden, and I decided that I would tell Martha how I felt that day. After our trip to the garden center she asked if I would like to go to her place for coffee. There she noticed that I was unusually quiet and asked me if anything was wrong. I took a deep breath, looked at the floor, and said I had something to tell her. I was very nervous, I said, because I cared very much about our friendship. I went on to say that, if I didn't tell her how I felt, I worried that my feelings would threaten the friendship; they had, in fact, already changed it. I told her I was very attracted to her but I had never been in a relationship with a woman and didn't really know how I would react if it became a reality. I was so intent on what I was saying that I had no idea how Martha was responding. I looked up for the first time since I began speaking and saw that Martha had been completely taken aback by what I'd said. She said nothing for what seemed like hours then asked if I wanted a drink. I nodded and she disappeared into the kitchen. She returned, looking as if she had collected herself somewhat. She was holding a bottle of cooking sherry and two wine glasses. She smiled and apologized for the vintage. It was all she had in the house, but she thought we could both use something.

After a few sips of the awful wine she said she, too, cared for me, but was just coming out of a long-term relationship and was not ready for anything else at that point in her life. As she continued to talk about the complexities of relationships at our particular point in history, I wondered what was really going on. I had just told the woman that I was attracted to her, and she was giving me a sociology lecture on relationships in the 1970s. I waited for her to stop talking, which she eventually did. I looked at her, and she leaned over and kissed me.

I was overjoyed and frightened. I cared for Martha more than I had ever cared for anyone, and her kiss made it very clear that the relationship that might develop between us would be very intense. There would be no clear and distinct boundaries as there had been with Nelson. I looked at my watch. Luckily, it was almost time for the children to get home from school. I rose and told Martha I had to leave but I hoped she would come over later. She said she would give me a call.

I got home just before the children and walked around the house feeling very happy and wondering when Martha would call. I opened the refrigerator to ponder dinner when I heard a car in my driveway. I walked out to the yard and saw Lanni, her cousin Tina, and Tina's daughter, Lisa. I was puzzled for a minute and then remembered we had made plans for them to visit that weekend. My thoughts had been so focused on Martha that I had completely forgotten about Lanni. I quickly collected myself and greeted them, frantically wondering what I would feed six or seven people for dinner.

It turned out to be a wonderful weekend. Martha came over that night, and I was glad that she and Lanni got to meet each other. Both Neal and Hannah were overjoyed to see Lanni, and Hannah and Tina had great fun with each other. When Lanni and I were alone I told her about my feelings for Martha. She looked surprised but said she could see that I was very happy and that Martha seemed like a very warm person. I was delighted that Lanni had so quickly recognized the warmth that had drawn me to Martha so many months ago.

I was deeply in love. Martha and I often talked long into the night, telling each other about our lives. She had been a lesbian since she was an adolescent, and, as she told me about the double life she lived in her small hometown in West Virginia and later in college, I was overcome with guilt for wanting to tell the dean about Amy and Jean when I was at Alfred—because they had made me uncomfortable. Some of the fears that Martha and her lover had to endure when they were in college were certainly the result of people like me. I resolved to tell Martha about this incident so that she would know the worst about me. When I did, I could see that she was shocked but also moved that I had told her. I felt great relief that my secret was out.

My relationship with Martha seemed different from any other. She was there for me when I felt tired and young as well as those times when I felt I could conquer the world. I had never experienced anything like it. Men might protect women from the world in some ways, but I saw that women took care of men emotionally. I had finally refused to take care of Tom and was clear with Nelson from the beginning of our relationship that I had no intention of providing him with emotional support. I realized that I felt I had to protect myself from being used by the men I knew and I had never expected they would give me what I needed. I looked to my women friends for that.

I felt that some of my most significant emotional relationships had been with women, but I did not assume, as did many of the lesbians I knew, that I had always been a lesbian and had only recently acted on my feelings. Women had always been important to me, but so had men. I did not become a lesbian because I hated men; I had not chosen to sleep with women for political reasons. That idea, which was common among many lesbians I knew, did violence to my feelings for Martha. I fell in love with her because of who she was, not because I didn't want to sleep with "the enemy.'' I also realized, however, that if I had not been in Amherst in 1975 where relationships between women were accepted, I might have denied and repressed my feelings for Martha. Despite my disagreements with some of the other lesbians I knew, I felt connected to them in a way I had not before my relationship with Martha. I also had a new feeling of admiration for the courage of women like Martha who had loved women when homosexuality was universally condemned as a perversion.

Clearly, even in Amherst, there were many people who considered lesbians to be sick man-haters, but, with the exception of the faculty in the history department, most of the people I associated with seemed to be very open-minded. Except for Elaine, I had told all my friends about Martha and they all seemed to be very happy for me. I knew that Elaine would not approve, and I decided to wait until we saw each other rather than tell her during one of our regular phone conversations. It never crossed my mind that the healthiest relationship I had ever had in my life might be sick. I worried only about the possibility that Tom might try to take the children away from me if he knew about Martha. I had no intention of telling my parents. I had not told them about Nelson, and they had not asked about the young man who had lived in my house for a few months. They had known so little about my life that my lesbianism was just something else they would not be able to fathom. The children seemed to like Martha, and telling them about my sex life seemed inappropriate. They could only benefit, I thought, from something that gave me so much, and, in any case, they would not be around much that summer. After school was over they were going to Ithaca to visit their father then would both be in camp until August.

I was very excited about a camp I had found for Neal. The speech camp had provided structure and contact with other children, but it did not really suit him. Judith Tompkins had heard about a camp for emotionally disturbed boys that she thought was exceptionally good, and I was impressed with the material I received from Camp Wediko. I filled out the application and waited anxiously to hear whether Neal would be accepted. Late that spring I heard from Harry Parade, one of the directors, that they were interested in Neal but required an interview before they made a final decision.

On the drive to the interview both Neal and I were nervous. Neal had not seemed to like the speech camp, but at least it was a known entity. Now he faced the prospect of a totally new situation. My feelings were familiar: I would be scrutinized by another professional. As we sat in the small waiting room, I tried to think of the therapists who had supported me. When Harry emerged from the inner office, walked right to Neal, and started to talk to him, I was relieved. This interview would clearly be with Neal rather than about his relationship with me. He made it very clear that, while camp was lots of fun, the counselors would expect him to work hard at relating to his peers. He also took what Neal said very seriously, and I was amazed listening to Neal articulate his fears. Harry had engaged Neal in a conversation that was closer to normal than any I had ever heard him participate in.

Toward the end of their talk Harry turned to me and said he thought Neal would fit in well at the camp and they would be happy to have him. I was ecstatic. If the camp was anything like what had just occurred in the last hour, it would be the best thing Neal had had. As we rose to leave, Harry told me he was very impressed with the application I had filled out. It was clear, he said, that I knew Neal very well.

I was grateful for his comments. My contacts with Neal's coordinator at Wildwood had gone from bad to worse. She had written a report in May that stated that I had not set appropriate goals for Neal because I was unwilling to accept his limitations. She also compared my relationship with Neal to the one he had with Tom, characterizing me as cold and even hostile and Tom as warm and affectionate.

It wasn't clear to me what her problem with me was, but I wondered if it might be related to the fact that I had left Tom. Other single mothers I knew had complained that teachers seemed to be very critical of them. Even in Amherst, it seemed, single mothers were by definition bad parents. Clearly, we would have to have it out. I made an appointment to see the coordinator without Neal. While the report played into the great reservoir of guilt that I had about my responsibility for Neal's problems, I was also angry. When we met I told her that she had to understand that I had not set goals for Neal because I was far from sure what they might be. Based on my own knowledge of Neal as well as what I had learned from most of the professionals who worked with him, it was my judgment that it was impossible to know his potential. When he was three years old and had not uttered a word, it might have been "realistic" to consider institutionalization. But at twelve years old he was reading, writing, doing arithmetic, showed an amazing memory for facts, and was able to relate positively to adults. His progress was the result, in some measure, of my struggle to help him develop to his potential, whatever it was. His father, on the other hand, had urged me to consider institutionalizing Neal at various points during his early childhood. She might not like the way I was parenting Neal, I said, but she would have to accept us both.

Hannah had also expressed a desire to go to camp and I found one in Cummington, about an hour from Amherst, that was advertised as a "free" camp. The children and counselors met each morning to plan their activities, and, like at East Hill, the arts were emphasized. The director assured me that the camp was dedicated to providing a nonsexist atmosphere. I thought Hannah needed a break from what I saw as the rigid routine of Wildwood, and, after visiting Shire Village, Hannah decided to give it a try. We were both glad that it was close to home and that I could visit at any time. Hannah's best friend was also going to Shire Village, and I hoped that Hannah would be comfortable enough to make other friends as well.

I wished I could have taken the summer off, but I needed money. Tom and I split the expenses for camp for the children, and my share had wiped out my savings. I hoped to work for the women's studies program, but funding was uncertain. The proposal for the program had been passed by the faculty senate that spring, but, since the senate did not make budgetary decisions, the new program was dependent on the provost for funds. Our requests for money were answered with the suggestion that we administer the program by using faculty members who could get release time from their departments. The committee met to discuss the situation, and I was relieved that many of the faculty were as outraged as I that we were expected to begin the program without funding. With very little discussion we decided to send a memo to the provost stating that the committee was expecting funding, and if we did not receive it we would close the program before it began. The demise of the new program, the memo stated, would be a very public event. Within the week our budget—small, but a beginning—was approved, including money for two summer staff people. I was hired for one of the positions.

It was an enormous relief to me that the committee was willing to take strong action to get what we felt was necessary to the functioning of the program. In the minds of these women there was clearly no distinction between women's studies and the women's

movement. The message we sent to the administration was une-
quivocal. If women's studies was threatened, the committee felt absolutely justified in using the movement, very powerful in the
Amherst area, to protect it. As I began to work in the program, I
was confident that I had something to give and that the committee
would stand behind me.

My co-worker, Marilyn Bogue, was an undergraduate who had
also been on the committee. Since the provost's office had not found
us working space, the U. Mass. Women's Center allocated their hallway for our use and gave us access to its phones and typewriters.
We set up our little office and by early July had more work than
we could handle. We made arrangements for search committees to
hire the coordinator and three other staff members, made a preliminary list of the women's studies courses to be offered in the fall,
and worked with the Five College Women's Studies committee on
a faculty appointment to be shared among the university, Smith,
Mount Holyoke, Amherst, and Hampshire colleges. I had wanted
free time, but I was glad to be working for the program and pleased
when I learned that I would have a teaching assistantship in wom-
en's studies for the next academic year.

Martha and I had a lovely summer, and she suggested that we
take a weekend trip together before the children were due back from
camp. It had been two years since I had gone anywhere for a vacation and that had been at Woods Hole—hardly a fun time. She had
been wanting to go to Nantucket for years, and, since I still loved
the ocean, I happily agreed. I was a little worried, however, about
money. She suggested that we could save a little by packing some
food for the ferry trip. I thought that was a great idea and made
some vichyssoise and roasted chicken. The night before we left we
went to the grocery store to pick up a few more things for our lunch
the next day. Martha didn't say anything as I loaded the shopping
cart with my favorite crackers, pickled tomatoes, and other goodies
but stared at me strangely when I said we would get some French
bread and cheese before we left the next morning. We went back
to my house to pack, and Martha got her empty suitcase out of the
car. I was disturbed. How, I asked her, could we carry the cooler
of food if we had suitcases as well? She looked puzzled but said
she didn't know. I suggested we carry our clothes in backpacks.
That way, I said, our hands would be free to carry the food. She
agreed and took her clothes out of the suitcase that she had begun
to pack, and crammed them into a pack. The meal was complete

when we stopped to get bread and cheese before setting off to catch the ferry to the island.

We got to Falmouth in plenty of time, parked the car, and carried the cooler to the dock. It was quite heavy, since the vichyssoise was in my yellow pot, a favorite, made of cast iron and enamel. By the time we got to the ferry the handle of the cooler had broken, and it was quite awkward to carry. A small price, I thought, to pay for a good lunch. It was a beautiful day, and we sat on the top deck and had a wonderful feast. The vichyssoise, servings for eight, was not finished, of course, but I'd made sure to put enough ice packs in the cooler to keep it and the leftover chicken and cheese from spoiling.

We went to Nantucket without making reservations—something I had never done—but Martha assured me we would find a place to stay. When we got off the ferry we realized we couldn't walk very far with the cooler. And we would have to find a place with a refrigerator; the ice packs would not last for the whole weekend. We hailed a taxi and asked the driver to take us to a guest house he thought might have a vacancy. After a few tries we found one that had a nice room. The proprietors agreed to let us put our food in their refrigerator.

When we finally got settled in our room and put the food away, we went out for a walk. It was a pleasure to be free of the cooler, and I began to think about what I had done. By the time we got back to the guest house I realized that I had packed lunch and dinner for a family. I was mortified and furious at Martha for not stopping me. I asked her how she could let me be so ridiculous. She was used to traveling without children; how could she have let me pack so much food? She reminded me that by the time she had gotten to my house the evening before we left, the vichyssoise and chicken were already made, and I had been so excited in the grocery store she didn't have the heart to stop me. She'd suggested that we had enough bread and didn't really need two boxes of crackers and three kinds of cheese. I would have to learn, I guessed, about packing a light lunch for two. We went out for dinner that night, and when we looked at the prices on the menus displayed in front of the restaurants we laughed and decided we would have leftover vichyssoise and chicken the next night.

Chapter 19

The fall of 1974 held neither the promise nor the fear of the previous year. I had survived. Although at times I had felt desperately alone, I had not felt less so in my relationship with Tom. I missed another adult taking some of the responsibilities, particularly paying bills and dealing with the car. But I felt some pride in having saved some money that year— something Tom and I had never done. I still didn't know much about cars, but I had found a mechanic a few blocks from the house and had learned how to tell him what was wrong with the car and to hear his response; previously, I'd thought I had a rare disease that impaired my brain when I was in the presence of mechanics. Graduate school and my performance had been excruciatingly painful at times, but I had survived that, too, and had confidence that I would at least struggle through another year. I was in a relationship that was giving me real joy, but I had also expected too much of my friends, Amherst, and myself. All three had fallen very short of the mark.

My relationship with Jane Smith had died. It wasn't at all clear to me why we didn't talk to each other, but we didn't. I knew she felt that I didn't support her enough in some of the struggles over the women's studies proposal. I had done what I could at the time, and I didn't think it was a bad proposal. And I knew there were difficulties between Pat Clarke and myself. I felt that she didn't like me, and, was disturbed by what I saw as Jane's dependence on the relationship. I needed Jane to be independent and was threatened by the exclusivity of her relationship with Pat. I knew that Jane's position had not been renewed, and Carolyn had told me that Jane was returning to New York City. Her year had been harder than

243

mine, I guessed. I was very sad that I hadn't been the kind of friend Jane needed, and I mourned the loss of her presence in my life.

That fall my relationship with Carolyn also seemed to be threatened. That summer I had decided my life would be easier if I had another adult in the house, and I had hired Carolyn's new lover, Robert, to finish the room Nelson and I had started to renovate the previous January. It had been a storage shed behind the kitchen and could easily be heated by a wood stove. Nelson and I had laid the floor with beautiful wood from an old silo on his stepfather's farm. Robert would need to build the walls, set in three windows, and construct a simple platform for a loft bed. I didn't know much about construction, but it seemed like a job that could easily be done in a month, or even less. Carolyn's friend came to work sporadically, and by the middle of August it was clear that the room would not be finished by September unless he worked more consistently. I'd found a graduate student who was interested in living with me, and she was understandably anxious to get settled before school began.

I called Robert to say he had better get the room finished, and, when he responded that he would see if he could manage it, I became very angry. Because he had been in need of money I'd advanced him pay for his labor and could not afford to get another carpenter. I told him he was highly irresponsible: he had had more than enough time to get the job done; I had told him when the room was needed; I knew he didn't have any other commitments; I had paid him, and I wanted the work done. He hung up on me. I was upset not only because it looked like the room might never get finished but also because I feared that my difficulties with Robert would endanger my friendship with Carolyn. I vowed to try to keep the situation with Robert as separate from my relationship with Carolyn as possible.

The next night he called to say he wanted to talk to me and asked if he could come over. I agreed and was surprised and upset when he arrived, not alone, but with Carolyn. She had come, she said, because she couldn't stand to see two people she loved upset with each other. As Robert began to tell me that I had no right to talk to him as I had the previous night, I began to wonder if Carolyn had come to protect him from me. I responded that I had every right to be furious and to express my feelings. Nancy was ready to move in, and the room was not ready. He had not come to work for days on end, and when he did come it was only for a few hours. He acted as if the job was a favor he would try to do for me, even though I had already paid him for it.

Carolyn broke in to say that they had worked it all out. She would come over to help him finish the job. They would have it done before school began. I was angrier than ever, and my sense that she had come to protect Robert was confirmed. I said that she could do what she felt she had to but I'd paid Robert to do the work, not her. If he would only work for a few days I was sure he could get the job done. I also told her that I felt betrayed by her. I said her presence there that night was totally inappropriate. My problem was with Robert, and I had been trying my best to keep that situation separate from my relationship with her, which was, I said, very important to me. She had made that separation impossible. If she were going to help Robert, I asked that she let me know so that I could leave the house when she was going to be there. Carolyn was surprised and upset by my reaction. I wanted both of them to leave. Robert sat sullen and quiet, and Carolyn chatted, trying to appease my anger. Finally, I stood up, said that I expected the room to be done by August 31 at the latest, and asked them to leave.

Over the next few weeks Robert managed to fit in a few days of work on the room, and by mid-September Nancy moved into my room, and I took the shed. There was still some finishing work to be done, but I knew it was as finished as it would ever be. Carolyn had not come to help Robert, and I did not hear from her for the next few months.

I focused my energy on trying to be more realistic about my schoolwork. I would have to get through the year without expecting to write women's history for all my sisters. Because of the meager offerings in the history department and the rules prohibiting graduate students from taking courses in other departments, I was forced to take courses that neither interested me nor had any focus on women. Joyce Berkman, who had taught the one women's history course the department offered, was not teaching anything I could take, since her field was British intellectual history, and I was interested in American history. I had also begun to feel that my advisor was not being totally honest with me. His evaluation of my major paper for his course the previous semester had been ambivalent. After praising my effort for its insight and thoroughness, he ended the evaluation with a question about whether I could "professionalize" my work. I was confused by the praise that ended in such an enigmatic question. Wasn't professional historical scholarship insightful and thorough? When I asked him what he meant, he replied that he didn't know if I had serious scholarly potential or if I had only a "B- mind." I decided it would be wise to stay away from him as much as possible.

By the middle of the semester I had to decide whether to apply for the doctoral program. After weeks of thinking about it, I opted to get my master's and get out. There were few jobs for Ph.D.s in history, I knew, and, though I had enjoyed some of my research and even some of the writing, I also thought too many more years in this history department might destroy me. I felt at once defeated and relieved.

Martha forced another decision that year. Our relationship had been developing beautifully, the only major problem being finding enough time to spend together. Although I tried my best to put some limits on the time I spent on my courses, I was obsessed with trying to learn as much as I possibly could—to fill in the blanks of all the history I didn't know. I also tried to spend as much time with the children as I could, but it never seemed to be enough to assuage my guilt about not being a "supermom." Martha's time was also limited since she had a full practice, was finishing a master's degree, and was in training with a Jungian analyst in Connecticut.

Early that school year we had decided that Martha would eat with us a few times a week, but, although she spent most of her free time at my house, I knew that arrangement would not last too much longer. She did not feel that the small apartment she had rented temporarily was really a home, and I knew she would soon want to find another place. When she did I was sure that she would not be as willing to spend most of her time at my house. But I tried not to think about all of that because I knew I'd have to face a decision I did not want to make.

I was afraid of living with Martha. After losing what little sense I had of myself in my marriage, I was afraid of what might happen to our relationship if we shared the same space. Living together, I thought, was more than I could handle. I would probably become very dependent on Martha and make all kinds of assumptions about her role with the children. I was sure I would grow to resent her for not being everything I wanted, although the rational side of me knew that no one could be all that I wanted. In our present arrangement I didn't expect her to do anything with the children, and if she did I was pleasantly surprised. Living together would change all that. As soon as it became clear to me that our relationship would be more than a brief affair, I had made Martha promise she would never ask me to live with her. She smiled, but agreed. One day toward the middle of the semester we decided to take some time for ourselves. Martha cancelled her clients, and I cut my classes. After a lovely day of being together alone, Martha broke her promise. She looked at me and very innocently said, "Let's live together." I was upset. She had promised she would never utter those words, but, even as I yelled at her, I knew that it was inevitable that I would agree. It was clear to both of us that we were making a life together, and for us that would mean at some time sharing a home. Nonetheless, I was a wreck.

When I recovered, we began the long process of talking about our fears, mostly mine, and the various possibilities. We thought about buying a two-family house. Martha would have one side, and the children and I the other, but that seemed kind of silly. We would be living together but not really living together. Because of my conviction that our relationship would be destroyed if we lived like a nuclear family, I suggested that we live with a few other people. I had wanted to try to live communally for some time and had approximated that kind of arrangement in Ithaca when Tony and Lanni lived with me. Martha, who was a person who valued her privacy, was not thrilled with the prospect of living in a large household. She was also quite intent on our owning the house ourselves. For a few weeks it seemed as if we would not live together at all, and I was relieved and disappointed. Finally, one evening after dinner Martha said she really did want us to live together. She had thought about it, and if she had to live with other people to live with me she was willing to do that. She was insistent, however, we buy the house.

I was surprised at how delighted I was by her decision. Despite all my fears about living with Martha, while we were discussing the various options I realized that it might be quite wonderful to live with her. We would really share a home in a way that Tom and I never had. Martha seemed happy, too. We stayed up half the night talking about the kind of houses we liked.

The next week Martha got a call that threatened our plans. She had been asked to take the position of staff psychologist at the Country Place, a residential treatment center for schizophrenics. It was a wonderful opportunity to work closely with Dr. Renee Nell, the Jungian analyst she had been studying with for more than two years. We were both overwhelmed. The position required that she live at the center—a two-hour drive from Amherst.

Martha's initial reaction was to say no, but, as we talked about it, she was less certain. I was very ambivalent. I could hardly stand in the way of what was clearly an important experience for Martha, but I wanted us to start our life together. And the thought of her living two hours away was awful. She had told the executive director of the center that she would have to think about their offer for a few days, and we did little else during that time.

To my great relief, Martha was not considering taking the position on a permanent basis but hoped they would hire her for a few months. I worried that they would convince her otherwise, but she came back having gotten just what she wanted. They'd agreed not only to take her for only four months but had also promised her most weekends off so that she could come back to Amherst regularly.

I was relieved but still unnerved by the sudden turn of events. I thought it might be better if we put off our plans to buy the house for another year. By then she would have reestablished her practice in Amherst, and I would know what my financial situation would be. Martha was adamant that we go ahead as planned. She had lived in a makeshift way for one year and didn't plan to do it for another. She was not interested in waiting. I could look at houses that came up for sale during the week, and she would be back in Amherst almost every weekend.

I called a realtor to see what was available and to get some indication of what the market was like. I thought I'd try to sell my house on my own, but I wanted an estimate. The news was not encouraging. Amherst's economy was closely tied to the vicissitudes of the university's budget, and, since there were rumors of an impending spending freeze, nothing was moving. There were no large houses for sale at that time near the center of town. In the country we could probably find something very nice and at a much better price. I was, however, not interested. It was important to me to live where the children could walk to school and downtown. The realtor was sure that the market would get better in the spring. There seemed to be little more that I could do but wait, and I was able to concentrate more fully on my schoolwork again.

I was in my last semester, and I'd had to enroll in courses, once again, that did nothing to expand my knowledge of women's lives. It was also frustrating to get so little help in the process of doing history. I'd been to a number of women's history conferences in which the question of how we should set about the task of learning about women's lives was crucial for the scholars, both young and established. There was no such talk about any kind of history in my courses at the university. Except for the course Joyce Berkman had offered during my first semester, the material consisted of lectures about the various periods, and we graduate students dutifully went to the library, collected information, and assembled it into thirty or forty pages of prose. The question of methodology arose only once in the form of a comment on one of my papers questioning what mine was. I would have loved to study questions of method but found it difficult to do that within a course that did not stress them at all.

It also seemed to me that I was being asked to do other unreasonable things in my papers. In one of my courses, American intellectual history, I chose to work on Emma Goldman. When I went to the faculty member for help with resources, he merely reached for *Notable American Women* and read me the citations. I then specifically asked him for help regarding material on anarchism, but he said he really didn't know of much. I gathered as much information on Goldman and her mentors and comrades as I could, as well as about her milieu, and wrote what I thought was solid analysis of her political philosophy. I was unable to relate her thought directly to the American scene, however, and got no help from the class. Not only were all the thinkers we studied men, but they were also all conservative or liberal. Socialism, feminism, or any of the other radical movements of the early part of this century were not mentioned, yet I was expected to make those connections with nothing in the primary or secondary sources to help me. Examining how radical movements overlap would have been a major undertaking in itself.

There was only one faculty member beside Joyce who did not seem hostile to my interest in women. He was a conservative who taught colonial history. When I told him I was interested in women's issues, his response was merely, "I don't care if you write elephant history as long as it's good history." I did a study on divorce in eighteenth-century Massachusetts, and he was extremely helpful with resources and even suggested me for a panel at a professional conference on the colonial period. It was a pleasant surprise to get this kind of help, and I thought about what some of my black friends had said and what I had read by black writers about how much harder it was to be in the North. I had expected only trouble from this man, and yet he was helping me. The liberals, on the other hand, led me to expect they were supportive of my interest but gave me a very hard time when I pursued my work on women. Although I knew their expectations were not appropriate to my stage in graduate work, my confidence was undermined nonetheless. I declined the offer to present a paper at the conference and thought only of the day when I would be out of graduate school. I hoped I could contain my rage for the few months I still had in the department.

My prospects at women's studies, on the other hand, were improving. The program was growing very rapidly, and the administration had agreed to fund more positions for the coming academic year. I was assured by the policy board that, if there was a staff position, I would have it. By May the spending freeze was imposed but it exempted nonprofessional positions. If I wanted it, I could have a half-time job with the program doing more of what I had been doing that year. Although the salary would be very low, I did not hesitate to accept the offer. There would be no better place to recover from my two years in the history department than women's studies. I would manage financially. I finished my courses and prepared for my comprehensive examination. I passed with distinction but felt little sense of accomplishment. I was only relieved that it was over.

The week after my exam Martha left for the Country Place. She had given up her apartment and would stay with me when she came back to Amherst on weekends. She would work until it was time for us to move. We hadn't found a house yet, nor had I found a buyer for mine. I expected that there would be some activity in the market once the semester was over. Just then I was too tired to worry.

I realized as Martha backed out of my driveway that I had not faced what it would mean to me not to have her in my everday life: It might be a very long four months. My acute sense of loneliness scared me. I sensed that I had already become very dependent on Martha and was disappointed in myself. If there was one thing I had learned from the women's movement, it was to be independent, and it seemed as if I had failed in that area as well as in all the others.

My belief that my life would dramatically change because of my new found consciousness had not been correct. Overall life was better. I was no longer someone's wife. I had forged a new life for myself, and I was surviving. There were, of course, problems with the children, but I felt less conflicted about how I was rearing them. Despite my feeling that I had failed because I had become dependent on Martha, I did love her very much, and the relationship was very important to me. But there had also been some very real pain. I questioned my intellectual abilities, and I had lost my two closest friends. As I sat in my kitchen that morning, I felt a profound weariness. My life had not been turned into a series of successes, but I was on the right road. It was, unfortunately, much rockier than I had allowed myself to believe it would be.

Chapter 20

*T*here were not many large houses for sale within walking distance to the center of town that summer, so my task of choosing houses for Martha and me to look at on the weekends was simplified. We settled on an old house that needed work but would, we thought, be quite lovely when the old and soiled wallpaper was removed and the walls painted. Two young women had agreed to move in with us, and, although I'd hoped we would live with women closer to our age, I liked Karen and Lisa. They seemed anxious to participate in running the household, and Neal and Hannah liked them. The rent they paid would certainly be important since money would be very tight that year. As Tom and I had agreed, my support payments were reduced because I'd finished school. My job at women's studies was half-time, and the salary did not make up the difference in my income. Martha was also anxious about money since she was starting a new practice.

Despite the low salary, I was glad that I had not refused the job at women's studies. I continued to feel that I was an integral part of a program that, for the most part, expressed my politics. I also knew that it would be possible to develop my own programs. When the rush of the beginning of the semester was over, I began to think about doing something for women in graduate school. The experience had been so painful and lonely for me that I wanted to find ways to alleviate the alienation and loss of confidence that seemed to be a part of the process of doing graduate work. After approval from the policy board I worked with Mary Lou O'Neill, a staff member at the U. Mass. Women's Center, who was herself a graduate student, to create support groups for graduate women. The first meeting was well attended, but the number of women dwindled at subsequent meetings. Despite the positive feelings among the women who came to the groups, it became clear that they were overloaded with work and often family responsibilities. I knew the feeling all too well.

We discontinued the meetings and planned a day-long conference. Optimistically, we'd reserved a large room for the conference, and, as we watched the seats fill, our feeling that graduate women needed support was confirmed. When the first speaker talked about the faculty in her department devaluing her work and the difficulties she experienced by being closed out of the professional and social networks among the male graduate students and faculty, I looked around the room and saw many heads nodding in recognition and agreement. The next speaker, a therapist, described her utter disappointment when she returned to school expecting to be treated like the adult that she was; the atmosphere was more like elementary school than college. She went on to say that the process was infantilizing and designed to make students, particularly women, feel stupid. I saw many women in the audience wiping their eyes. A faculty member who was the next speaker was as inspiring as we'd hoped she would be. While acknowledging the difficulties of graduate school for women, she discussed strategies for protection against the worst of the abuses as well as ways to manipulate the system to one's advantage. By the end of the day women crowded around us to express their thanks for the conference, and I was filled with emotion. The day had made it clear to me that my problems in graduate school were not unique. I felt sure that working with the women's studies program, which had allowed me to develop the conference, was where I should be.

There was one thing about the program, however, that was disturbing. Women's studies was almost exclusively white. While two faculty members from the Afro-American Studies department regularly listed their offerings on black women as women's studies courses, all the faculty, students, and staff who worked on our committees and made decisions about the direction the program would take were white. Occasionally, members of the policy board would lament the fact that our courses did not attract black and Third World students, but there was no discussion about incorporating material on racism or black and Third World women into the courses.

It seemed to me that women's studies had little to offer students who were not white. I wanted to change the situation, not merely to attract black and Third World women to our courses, but also for reasons that were central to our mission, at least as I had defined it. The simple fact that most of the women in the world were not white seemed ample enough justification for black and Third World women's lives to be a major focus of our courses as well as the research interests of the faculty associated with the program. If our goal was to study women, and white women were a distinct minority in the world, clearly it was incumbent on all of us not to limit our work to white women. I also felt that the study of racism, being a fact of life for the majority of women in the world, was crucial to any analysis of women. Though I sensed that white women were also affected by racism, the dynamics of that process were not clear to me. What was clear to me was that a women's studies program that did not address the issues of dominance and subordination however and wherever they existed would have only a limited vision of women's lives.

Although I strongly believed that a focus on black and Third World women was necessary, I was unable to articulate my reasons very clearly. Since it seemed that no one else in the program shared my perspectives—beyond hoping that black and Third World students would enroll in our classes—there was no opportunity for serious discussion of the issues I considered so crucial to the program's foundations. I also recognized that, beyond the limited reading I had done and what I had learned from Elaine, I was fairly ignorant about black and Third World women's lives and the role that racism played in the development of our society and on an international level. My education in the history department had been of no use but had, in fact, delayed my taking up these issues—the kind of history I had intended to study when I entered the department. For faculty in the history department, black people simply did not exist nor was racism a component of American history and culture. Even the historical fact of slavery was not discussed, except from the point of view of the abolitionists.

Racism, it seemed to me, continued to be a powerful force in all of our lives. I thought it would be useful to the program if I began to educate myself on these issues and suggested to the policy board that I sit in on courses in the Afro-American Studies department. I would not only enrich the program with what I learned, but I'd make important liaisons with some of the black women on campus. I was gratified when the board agreed with my plan and confident that faculty would be as anxious to include the new material in their courses as I was to gather all the knowledge I could.

Luckily that spring Johnnetta Cole and Esther Terry were offering a course entitled "The Black Woman," and, although I had read most of the books they were using, I looked forward to hearing what professors Cole and Terry had to say about them. I also wanted very much to hear the discussions among students. I made the decision before going to the class that I would listen and take in as much as I could rather than participate. I wanted to hear what black people had to say: to get a sense of how they would approach the works and to hear what issues were salient for them. I arrived early the first night in order to introduce myself and to ask if I could sit in on the class. I told the professors I was from women's studies and that I had been authorized by the policy board to educate myself by taking their class. Their response was affirmative but reserved. I went to the back of the room and took a seat, and, as I watched the students come in, I was glad to see a few other white faces. My experience with Elaine and her friends had made me sensitive to the reality that discussions in an interracial group were different from what occurred when whites were not present. The self-imposed limitations were not unlike what happened when women's issues were discussed in front of men.

The class was more than I had hoped it would be. Professors Cole and Terry were not only very knowledgeable but also excited by their subject. They also seemed perfectly balanced to team teach. Professor Cole's flamboyant style contrasted with Professor Terry's quiet intensity, and the combination drew in the shyest as well as the most vocal students. I kept my seat in the back row, apart from the class in some very real ways, yet feeling that I had come back to something very vital in myself. Although there was much in the discussions that related to me as a woman, it was also clear that the experience of living as a black woman in a racist society, a basic fact for the authors of the books as well as the black women in the room, was not part of my life. I was aware, too, that the black students, the faculty, and the authors shared a culture that I knew only from the perspective of an outsider. Yet I felt inexplicably closer to both the authors and the black people in that room than I did to most of the white women I knew. I was confused but absolutely certain about one thing: It had been very important to me to take that class, and I would definitely sit in on another class the next semester.

I could not articulate the meaning that the class had had for me, and I was even less sure of what I could say to my colleagues in women's studies. Beyond reading lists and the possibility of developing a working relationship with professors Cole and Terry, there did not seem to be a way to convey what I had learned. Partially, I was sure, the difficulty lay in my inability to understand clearly its importance to me. I hoped the benefits to women's studies would be more concrete the next semester.

There were no other courses on black women offered by Afro-American Studies, but I was beginning to understand that it was crucial to learn more about the culture that informed the lives of black women. I was delighted when I saw a course on black music in the listing for the next semester. It was taught by Archie Shepp, the jazz saxophonist, who had been very outspoken during the Black Power movement. I vaguely remembered reading an article in the *Village Voice* about a heated debate in which Shepp had been reported to have expressed an antiwhite attitude. I wondered if I would feel as comfortable in his class as I had in the one I had taken from professors Cole and Terry, but I was anxious to learn more about the music I'd loved for so long: I was also intrigued by the title of the course, "Revolutionary Concepts in Afro-American Music."

It was with some trepidation that I approached Professor Shepp on the first day of class to introduce myself and ask if I could sit in on his course. His response was a relief. He actually seemed pleased and thought I would be particularly interested in the section on Bessie Smith. He had thought, he said, of devoting an entire course to the great blues singer and asked if I thought women's studies might be interested in listing it. I assured him we would, and, as I sat in the back of the room, I wondered about the report I had read about Professor Shepp. Had his attitude toward whites changed, or had the report in the *Voice* merely been another case of white overreaction to black people asserting themselves? My thoughts were interrupted by Professor Shepp's voice saying that the course would begin with a discussion of African music, which was the foundation of all of Afro-American music—gospel, the blues, rhythm and blues, and black classical music, his term for jazz.

The subject for this class as well as the style of the instructor was very different from "The Black Women." A course on music is by its very nature less personal than the material evoked by literature and biographies of women's lives, and Professor Shepp's style of teaching, with its heavy reliance on the lecture, did not invite much discussion from the students, yet I felt the same sense of excitement hearing about Afro-American music as I did about black women. It also was wonderfully familiar to be in New Africa House, the building in which the Afro-American Studies department was housed. "The Black Woman" had been held at night when the building was empty except for the few other night classes. This course was in the morning, and the atmosphere of the building was like nothing I had experienced at any college. It was very noisy. People yelled down the hall, and, when I heard people screaming up to the classrooms from the street, I knew why New Africa House felt so much like home. It was like my old neighborhood in New York City. My friends and I always called to each other from the street— even to Thalia, who lived on the sixth floor. The people at New Africa House did not impose the conventionalities of "proper" or "professional" behavior on themselves, and it felt wonderful. I knew, however, that there had to be more than a nostalgia for my old neighborhood to explain my feeling of ease in that building. Despite the incontrovertible fact of my whiteness, part of me felt I belonged in New Africa House taking courses in the Afro-American Studies department.

My emotional response to the material was also confusing. Early in the course Professor Shepp outlined the basic elements of African music and showed how they had formed the basis of not only the field holler and work songs of the slaves but also the work of black musicians in 1975. The strength of African culture, its ability to survive the Middle Passage, and the trauma of slavery were not only amazing on an intellectual level; they also evoked in me a profound feeling of respect and even joy. Along with these positive responses toward African and Afro-American culture and people came a revived fury at Western culture and whites. I had never before thought of Africa as a place from which black Americans had come—never considered it to be the homeland of anyone but the "natives" I'd seen in *National Geographic*s I'd leafed through when I was a child looking for pictures of naked breasts and bare bottoms. This course affirmed the African heritage of black Americans through the close connection between traditional African music and contemporary Afro-American music. I was stunned at how thoroughly I had been socialized. I had never before thought of black Americans as having a heritage other than slavery, yet I'd known that slaves were brought from Africa.

Most of my colleagues and friends seemed only mildly interested in what seemed so cataclysmic to me. Worse than the disinterest of my associates was what had begun to happen to my relationship with Martha. She listened to what I was learning, but, when I began seeing racism everywhere and venting my rage at whites, it was clear that she did not share my feelings. We started to have terrible fights, and I found myself censoring myself to avoid them. I was beginning to feel very alone. My new knowledge was a kind of an obsession. I also knew that my feelings were very important, and I was compelled to go on with my quest.

The next semester, on the advice of Johnnetta Cole, whom I occasionally saw at various university committee meetings, I took "Introduction to African Studies." It was a new course team-taught by four faculty including Johnnetta. Because the faculty were well aware of the ignorance of most students about Africa, they began the course with a geography lesson. Africa, we learned, was a huge continent containing many countries, cultures, ethnic groups as well as many different kinds of climates. It was not, as I had thought, wall-to-wall jungle. Looking at the map, it seemed clear to me that my sense that Africa was all the same was more than ignorance. The huge continent dwarfed the United States, and it seemed only logical that it would contain as much or more variation than this country. Every class revealed something else about Africa that challenged my basic assumptions about the continent and made me question where they had come from. Somehow I'd learned to think about Africa as monolithic and backward, yet there was incontrovertible evidence that great African civilizations existed well before nation-states were established in Europe.

I had, of course, learned at Columbia about the great artistic achievements of ancient Egypt, but I had never considered Egypt to be part of Africa. I had certainly never thought of Greek civilization as having been influenced by Egypt, but I learned in the course that Socrates had been educated in Africa—"our" Socrates, the philosopher whose ideas, everyone knew, were at the very foundation of Western civilization. The Greek pantheon of gods, in fact, had African roots. What did it mean, I wondered, for a culture to deny its origins? Could we in the West know who we are if we don't know the origin of basic assumptions? As the course progressed, I learned that Western nations had not always considered Africa to be the "dark continent." African kings had been honored in European courts, but that had been before the slave trade and before colonization. In order to justify the buying and selling of African people, Western scholars had revised their assessment of the continent. If the reality of the great pyramids of Egypt could not be denied, then Egypt could be taken out of Africa.

Every week I told Martha what I had learned and vented some of my rage at whites—those who had perpetrated the brutal hoax that Africa was a backward place, who had bought and sold Africans, and who had imperialized and colonized the continent as well as whites who refused to see what had been done. Our fights intensified and were very painful for both of us. I began to understand that, when I attacked whites, Martha felt I was attacking her, and I was confused. I didn't feel attacked when I was in the class, nor had I taken Elaine's rage at whites personally. Though I did feel that I was a racist and that knowledge was difficult and painful to accept, I somehow did not feel that I was personally responsible for what had hurt Elaine and other black people. Elaine often told me that I wasn't really white, and I had argued that I had been raised as a white girl with all the privilege that accrued to someone with my skin color. My parents certainly thought of themselves as white and taught me that black people were inferior. Now I heard Elaine's words coming from Martha, but this time they were screamed at me in rage. I screamed back that I was as white as she but I had realized what it meant to be white and was trying to overcome my own racism. Even as I yelled this to Martha I wondered what she and Elaine meant. It was true that I did feel very different from all the whites I knew, but I also knew that I wasn't black. I was beginning to wonder who I was after all. One thing was very clear—I felt alone.

By the end of the semester Martha and I were fighting most of the time, and most of our arguments began with a disagreement that focused around race. When she made blanket statements about men I felt myself stiffen, even though I could easily have said the same thing myself when the women's movement first touched me. But when Martha said them I would sometimes quietly and sometimes loudly respond that all men were not the same. Some men— black men—did not have the same power as white men. The discussion quickly became an argument that was never resolved. One day, when we had been yelling at each other for some time, I heard myself saying that my grandfather's power had been very limited. There was no doubt in my mind, I said, that he had oppressed my grandmother, but he had been killed by the Turks nonetheless. I screamed my uncle had been put into a camp because he was an Armenian, and had my grandfather been alive he would have had no more power to save his son than my grandmother had had. I continued, now through my tears, to say that I understood the oppression of a people and that oppression had an impact on patriarchy. I was well aware that Armenian men were *male chauvinist pigs*, and it was impossible for me to live near my family because of the way women were treated, but there was something about our common pain that would always connect me in some profound way to Armenians, women and men.

Slowly, over the next few months, Martha and I began to understand where our respective backgrounds had put us, how they had informed our different reactions to oppression. The genocide— that story my grandmother had told me when I was fourteen, the tale I did not want to hear, the events of her life that no one else in the family acknowledged, that story that I had not thought about for years—had come back into my life. This time, however, I wanted to know more. What had happened in Turkey? Was my grandmother's experience unique or typical?

During this period my mother sent me a book written by an Armenian, as she occasionally did. I usually did no more than leaf through whatever it was she had sent and then put them away. This time I was intrigued. The book was *Passage to Ararat* by Michael Arlen, an autobiographical account of Arlen's attempt to come to terms with being an Armenian. Until I finished it, I spent every free moment I had reading that book.

Arlen's father, also a writer, had been raised in London. When he reached adulthood he changed his name from Dikran Kouyoumjian to Michael Arlen, emigrated to the United States, and became an acclaimed writer of romantic novels. The son described his father's writing as devoid of any reference to his Armenian ancestry. The omission was no surprise, according to the son, since, except for an occasional derogatory remark about Armenians by his father, the son had grown up with no indication that his parents were Armenian. The son questioned neither the omission of ethnic references in his father's life and work nor his own ethnic background until he was in his forties and both his parents were dead. Arlen was asked by an Armenian organization to give a lecture on contemporary writers. That invitation was to have a profound effect on his life:

My own identity as an American seemed to me fairly definite—at least on the surface. I had an American wife and American children—a satisfactory American career and life. Then, one day, out of the blue, I was asked by an Armenian group in New York to come down and give a talk about writing. I was surprised and flattered by the invitation—for my lecture services were not in great demand—and I said yes.

I can remember the evening vividly. The talk was given in an auditorium of the Armenian Cathedral, on Second Avenue—a place I had never before visited. The audience sat before me on little chairs—middle-aged Armenian men and women, for the most part, the men generally stocky, the women wearing old fashioned flowered dresses. What I said was undistinguished, but all of a sudden I myself felt greatly moved. I remember standing at the lectern gazing into the rows of clearly Armenian faces—more Armenians than I had ever before seen together—and experiencing an extraordinary pull. My eyes told me that these people were different from me, but I knew that they were not so different. I didn't know what else I knew.

Afterward an old gentleman with thick white hair came up to me. "An interesting talk," he said. "Although you didn't mention any Armenian writers. It's too bad we never saw your father here."

"I don't think he thought of himself as Armenian," I said. And as soon as I had said it I realized that it was untrue.

"Of course he was Armenian," said the old man. "You are Armenian. It is not such a strange thing to be Armenian. Come have some coffee."

I think I thought something like, You can go forward here, or stay where you are. And so I went with him and had some coffee.

Such small beginnings. That evening, for the first time, I met Armenians on my own. Armenian women who laughed and asked too many questions. Thick-chested men who seemed to have their arms around each other. Too many cups of coffee and small, sweet cakes. I was *there*—wherever *there* was. It was an uncertain beachhead, for I kept fighting off the desire to bolt. Never let them get too close! But I also knew that a corner of some missing piece had briefly become visible.

As I finally made my way toward the door, a voice called out, "You will come back!" I couldn't tell whether it was a statement or a question.

"I will," I said. The journey had begun. [1]

---

[1] Michael Arlen, *Passage to Ararat* (New York: Farrar, Straus & Giroux, 1975) 13–14.

Even though our experiences growing up as Armenians were opposite—I had been raised as an Armenian within an Armenian community, while he had virtually no sense of his ethnicity—there was so much, even in Arlen's first encounter at the church, that spoke to me, particularly his feeling of connectedness and his desire to "bolt." I read on eagerly as Arlen described his difficult journey. I understood his ambivalence. He was both compelled and reluctant to explore his identity as an Armenian; I had grown up knowing all too well that I was an Armenian, yet it seemed clear as I read this book that my own ethnic identity was a "missing piece" for me as well.

I had not felt such excitement since reading Doris Lessing. Martha Quest and Anna Wulf had become part of my life because their lives, as Lessing had shaped them, mirrored mine in a fundamental way, despite the obvious differences. Lessing had articulated essential truths about my life as a woman which I had vaguely felt but been unable to bring to consciousness. Now Arlen's book had evoked the same kind of response. I was not the only Armenian who had ambivalent feelings about my ancestry. He, too, resisted learning about the 1915 genocide despite the repeated urging of Sarkis, a character who become a guide on Arlen's journey back to Armenia—to Ararat.

While I was reading, I tried to tell Martha about it—to convey what it meant to me—but my attempts were not satisfying. I needed to find a way for her to know as much as she could, not only what Arlen wrote but what it meant to me. She agreed to read the book, but I was still not satisfied. Then it occurred to me that if we read it aloud to each other she could see and feel the impact of the words on me and I would also have some sense of what they meant to her.

We began to read and it was clear from the first few chapters of the book that it would help us bridge our differences. Martha laughed with me when Arlen's description of Armenian behavior so clearly described that of my relatives or even, I was embarrassed to admit, my own. We both fell silent when we read about the nineteenth-century obliteration of Armenian villages, atrocities committed against Armenians by the Turks and, finally, Arlen's account of the 1915 genocide.

There was no question that Martha had been deeply moved by *Passage to Ararat*. I wondered, however, how she had reacted to Arlen's exclusive focus on Armenian men. His journey was to Ararat and to his father, an attempt to discover who he was as an Armenian and to understand his father. While I had occasionally been annoyed by Arlen's inability to see Armenian women, the book had meant so much to me that I was able, for the most part, to ignore his omission. Martha had said nothing about this aspect of the book, and when I raised it she merely said it didn't matter. I was relieved, feeling that through sharing the book Martha had finally heard what I had been screaming about for months, though I had not been so clear myself about what was happening to me.

Chapter 21

Shortly after Martha and I had finished reading *Passage to Ararat*, women's studies sponsored a lecture by Andrea Dworkin, "Women and the New Right." Since I was interested in the topic, I decided to go, and Martha joined me. The large auditorium was almost full, but we found two seats near the stage. Shortly after we sat down Dworkin was introduced, and when she rose to the podium the audience responded with thunderous applause. She began her talk with general comments on the oppression of women and finally focused on Anita Bryant, who had just begun her campaign against gays and lesbians. To my great surprise, Dworkin asked the audience to empathize with Bryant—to see her as a woman, like ourselves, a woman oppressed by patriarchy. As Dworkin continued her litany of the wrongs perpetrated against women by men, I grew more and more uncomfortable. I looked around the room and saw some of my colleagues and many of our students in the audience. None of them seemed to be disturbed by Dworkin's endless recital of the powerlessness of women. I wondered if I was unable to accept the reality of my oppression as a woman.

I began literally to squirm in my seat, and I knew from the look on Martha's face that she was also disturbed. I leaned closer to her and heard myself whisper, "Not my grandmother." Even as I spoke I wondered what I meant, but Martha calmly nodded in agreement. I wanted desperately to leave, but that was impossible. The audience was spellbound, and we were seated in the middle of the row. I waited for Dworkin to finish, no longer hearing her but thinking about my grandmother and trying to contain myself.

The lecture was over, at last, and Martha said, "Let's get out of here." While the audience rose to applaud Dworkin, we almost ran to the door. The cool night air felt wonderful. I took a deep breath and vented my fury. She wasn't talking about me. I was not a total victim. I could act. I could change my life. I did have responsibility for my actions, and I most certainly held Anita Bryant responsible for what she did. Finally, the phrase that I had uttered in the auditorium came out again—not my grandmother. I would have to hear her story again.

I decided to tape the stories of my mother and aunt as well as my grandmother and was excited and terrified. The distance I'd maintained for so long from my family and my ethnicity had seemed to be necessary for my own survival. I'd desperately needed to be as American as possible and also to be as independent of the considerable demands of my family as possible. After I became a feminist I understood, too, that to stay within the family would have meant either adhering to the rigidly circumscribed roles for women or constantly fighting against them. Now, at the age of thirty-five, I wondered if I was threatening a relationship that had become fairly comfortable. But I had no choice. I had to hear my grandmother's story again.

I asked Martha to come with me when I went to New Jersey to do the taping. I honestly felt that I could not attempt the project without her support and was grateful when she agreed to join me. We arrived at my mother's house armed with sheets of questions I'd prepared. I had come to tape the story of my grandmother's survival, but I thought it was important to also get a sense of her role as a woman as well as some idea of what her economic status had been before the genocide. As I asked her what her wedding had been like, the kind of house she'd had, and who did the cooking and cleaning, my grandmother seemed uninterested and even irritated. Her memory of her early life was dim, and she seemed confused. The situation was not helped by my Armenian, which was worse than rusty. I could barely understand her, and she tried to speak in English, which had gotten worse than I remembered it. I called Aunty Ars into the room to help translate, but the situation did not improve. I looked closely at the small woman who sat before me. Perhaps, I thought sadly, I had waited too long. My grandmother looked very old. Her eighty-nine years seemed to have finally taken their toll.

With my aunt's help, I got some sense of Elmas Tutuian's early life. She was two years old when her mother died and her father sent her to live with her older sister Turvanda, who was married and whose daughter was just Elmas's age. Turvanda and her husband Arakel were wonderful to her, she said, just like parents. When she was seventeen years old Hampartzum Tutuian, a friend of Arakel's, asked for her hand. Elmas did not know him, and she thought he was too old for her, but Arakel convinced her to marry him, saying he was a good man and would take care of her just as he had. Before I could ask her another question she said in English, "I was seventeen years old. He was twenty-eight. At twenty-seven they took my husband. Berj was two years old, Ars seven, and Ashot four. I have three children. They took us out of the house—the Turks. My husband was a soldier. I have three children." She then turned to my aunt and told her to "tell about us. Tell about the Turk."

Aunty Ars began the story: "Christmastime they exiled all the men and boys fifteen and over. And then Eastertime we went to church and came back from the church our doors were all—what do you call—they locked it and had their stamp on it—only the dining room was open. No kitchen—nothing. And what we had on, we were left with that. And my mother went to the police commissioner who was very friendly with my father."

My grandmother seemed relaxed for the first time since I began asking her questions. The story was being told, and she was content to add her comments from time to time.

Aunty Ars continued: "My mother went to him to say that's what they did to our house. What are we going to do? And he said, 'It's going to be very bad. They are going to exile everybody. Why don't you become a Turk?' And my mother says, 'My husband is in the army, how could they exile me?'"

My grandmother broke in and corrected my aunt. "I told them, if my husband heard I became a Turk, he would go to his grave. And then he said it's going to be very bad. You'll be sorry. I told them what my nationality is—I'll be the same." She sat back and told Aunty Ars to continue. When Aunty Ars diverted to tell us something about her husband's family, my grandmother said, "Ashot's story, Ashot's story." Aunty Ars turned to her and told her not to skip ahead. My grandmother sat back and listened as her daughter told us that the police commissioner had arranged to allow them to use a few more of the rooms in the house.

One day an Armenian man who had somehow escaped being exiled with the other men in the town came to the door. He begged Elmas to hide him. Refusing at first, she finally relented. Yet she knew she could not keep him for long in the three rooms of the house that had been opened for their use and went to tell his wife and mother that they had to find another place for him. While she was gone Ars, Ashot, Berj, and their one-hundred-and-ten-year-old greatgrandmother were alone in the house. The man was hiding in a closet.

Aunty Ars went on: "They came, gendarmes . . . with the *muchdar*—was like sheriff . . . and he says, 'I said, we don't hide anybody—and the man is in there . . . where the wood is.' I was trembling. And my greatgrandmother had a cane. They took her cane—going like this [waving her hand around]. My heart was throbbing. And the sheriff says, 'Have you got a match?' We haven't. Berj says—how old was she—two or three years old—says 'yes.' I took the match from her and said, 'No, we don't have a match.' . . . So they went.''

When Elmas came home and was told what had happened she realized the man had to leave immediately. His wife and mother had been taken in by a Greek family, and their house was surrounded by Turkish police. Her solution was to dress him like a Turkish woman and send my aunt, who would appear to be his child, with him. Aunty Ars described their walk across the town:

> Turkish women wear a veil. Their face is closed. My mother brought it. He wore that and what belongings he had in a handkerchief. My mother sent me with him. You know it was quite a far way. I'm going from the front and he is following me . . . When I reached his house all the gendarmes, police, you know, all around. So he says, let's go from the back. They have searched the house. So he got in. I came back. I said never again. I was trembling. . . . But my mother was so—there was no fear with her. She didn't know what fear was. So Easter came after Easter. They sent us. We were the last ones to be exiled. . . Visim's family, they were four, no they were three. Verzin, three, five with my mother and my greatgrandmother . . . and we had a distant cousin, she had two daughters—eleven people. They put us on those cars that ox pulled it. Whatever we had they took us . . . far, far away.

My grandmother interjected, "No Armenians or nothing." And as my aunt tried to remember how many days they'd traveled, my grandmother impatiently said in English, "Wait a minute. We go over there. The man came over and said in Armenian, 'They don't want you in our town.''' Aunty Ars disagreed, and they began to argue about the sequence of events. My grandmother sat forward in her chair and said, "Let me say it in Armenian." She looked very different than she had a short while ago when I had been asking her about her early life. Her eyes were bright, and she seemed to be fully engaged in what was happening. But Aunty Ars continued the story:

> That man, that gendarme—everybody was crying . . . he starts crying with us. He was such a nice person. Anyway, third or fourth day, it was raining, it was dark. In the evening somebody came . . . like a sheriff or something. He said, "I have to leave them over here." He said, "Government told me to bring them here, and I'm going to leave them here." He said, "I don't have anyplace." And there was one room. And there was one room. . . He says, "What's that?" He says, "That's the school." He says, "Where's the key?" He says, "the *khoja*" the teacher they call the *khoja* "he's gone home in another town." You know what he did, the gendarme, he gave one kick, broke the door. He took us all up there, eleven of us, you know, small room. We don't have a door up there. And the people start coming. To Armenian they used to call *gavors*.* And they are coming and looking from the door. Young men about eighteen, seventeen years old. They're saying, "Let's see what the *gavors* look like." Anyhow, maybe an hour later, big tray of food came. See there were two Agas, two brothers, one had gone to Istanbul, you know, had come back, he fed us.

She turned to my grandmother, who had been listening to her intently, and asked her how long the brother fed them. My grandmother replied, "He said, 'For a week you are going to give them their meals'. . . And later they came for Ashot." My aunt told her she was mixing up the story. She said they had come for Ashot later, and for a few minutes they argued, and my grandmother finally sat back and waited for my aunt to continue. She told us about the food the brothers provided for them, and finally she said, "One day they came. They sent somebody, and we have to go someplace. We

---

* Turkis perjorative for Armenian

all went. They are taking the boys." My grandmother sat up and said in Armenian, "I will tell that." Although my aunt tried to interject from time to time, my grandmother would not be stopped. She spoke rapidly but this time I understood everything she said:

The police came and saw us, and the two brothers were sitting there. They [the police] wanted to know how many boys there were there. They said two, there are two boys. Visim and Didi. [Didi was what the children in our family called our Uncle Ashot.] And then he said—he looked and said—"That one is too small. I am going to take this one. I am taking this boy."

"Where are you going to take him?"

"They are collecting the boys."

I said, "This boy's father is a soldier. You are not taking this boy. He is my boy. I won't give him to you. He is mine. He is mine."

He said,'"He is not yours."

I said, "He is mine."

And we were screaming in Turkish, "I won't give him." The brothers were listening. "This boy is mine," I said, "and his father is a soldier," I said. "Soldier, do you understand?"

"I am going to take him."

"You can't," I said. "I won't give him," I screamed. "I won't give him," I screamed. "I won't give him. You can't," I said. "Who are you to take my boy?" I said.

He screamed at me. Then he said, "You are doing too much."

I said, "You are doing too much. Do you understand?" And how he screamed. "You cannot take my boy. He is my boy."

He said, "He is the king's boy."

"No," I said, "he is mine. I won't give him to you. Understand this," I said, "you know if there is a God in heaven, this boy will not stay with you. If there is no God... Day and night," I said, "I will pray that when the English come" (already when you say "English" the Turk trembles) and take your child from your wife's arms, and you will know what I am feeling. Do you understand? Night and day I will pray. If there is a God, he will come and do that, if there is no God, do what you want. But I will not give my son, understand that." And I was crying. I looked at the brothers and said, "I will pray that the English come and take your wife's child away from her. If there is a God, know this."

He said, "All right. Let me take your son."

I said, "I won't give him to you. Take me with him. I'll go. Take me with him."

"No," he said. "I am telling the brothers to bring you tomorrow. I will take this child now."

I said, "Very well, if you are going to take us tomorrow, I will bring my son with me. I will bring my son."

"No," he said, "I am going to take your son."

"I won't give him," I said. "I will bring him."

He turned to the brothers and told them to bring the rest of the family the next day, that he was going to take the boy then.

"Very good," I said, "I will bring my son with me."

He said, "You are making this too long."

My sister-in-law said, "Please let them take him and we will go tomorrow."

He told the men again that they were to bring the rest of the family to Dadai.

He took Ashot away. Arsenic was crying, "First, I lost my father, and now I am losing Ashot." She was crying. "Quiet," I said. "We are going tomorrow too. Quiet." She kept crying saying that she had lost her father and now she lost Ashot.

My sister-in-law said, "It's all right, tomorrow we will go." The next day we went to the brothers and said, "We are ready. When are you going to take us?" The man laughed.

I said, "Why are you laughing?"

"He fooled you," he said.

"He took your son. He told us later that you are going to stay in this village."

"Oh. Is that how it is," I said. "You wait and see." After the children went to bed, I told my sister-in-law. I called her sister. We loved each other. "You know what I am going to do? I am going with the villagers." I wrapped my head up and I am going to Dadai with the villagers to get Ashot.

Early in the morning the two of us wrapped ourselves up, my sister-in-law and I. I said, "If I come, I will come. If not, take care of my children." I wrapped myself up and started my journey. I started and came to a mountain. No people. No road. Nothing. By now it is around five o'clock in the after-

noon and dark. I am alone on the mountain. I looked in front
of me and saw someone coming. I said, "If you love your God,
stop." I screamed, "If you love your God, stop." I want to
go with him. I ran after him and held the horse. I begged him
to take me to his house.

He said, "I can't. I am not going there, my girl. I am going somewhere else."

At that point I broke in to ask if the man was a Turk, and Aunty
Ars answered quickly, "Turk. Turk." My grandmother continued:

He said, "Where are you going?"

I said, "I am going to Dadai. What is the way to Dadai?"

"Go down this way," he said. "There will be a mountain
in front of you. There is a road on that mountain. If you stay
on that road, you will reach Dadai."

I was still holding onto him, and I said, "If you love your
God, take me with you."

"I can't," he said. "I am invited somewhere else, and I
can't take a young woman with me." The man said, in Turkish, "Let God be with you. I am showing you the right road."

I got on the road and climbed the mountain. I am in the
mountain. Mountain. Big trees. I sat under a tree. It was dark.
I sat under the tree and said, "Jesus Christ, if you are there,
help me, help me. I am doing this for my child." I sat there
until it was light, awake all the time. I haven't eaten anything
yet. When the birds started to cheep, I got up. The man had
told me the road to Dadai. I went a little further, and there
were people there. I ran to them. Three women were sitting
(it is before my eyes as I am saying this)—three women were
sitting and two men. They were taking food to the soldiers.
The man said, "what do you want? Where are you going?"

I said, "I am going to Dadai."

The man felt sorry for me. He said, "I will take you to
Dadai. We are going there too. We are taking food to the
soldiers."

I said, "No. Show me the right way and I will go to Dadai
myself."

Because the Derderians had become Turks and were living there, I said no. "I have relatives there. I will walk."

The women started to laugh and were speaking in Turkish. *Aman,** the man let them have it. "Look at this woman's face," he said. "Aren't you ashamed of yourselves? Why are you laughing? Shame on you!" He got angry at the women.

I said, "Don't get mad at them. I am going to Dadai." I went to Dadai, understand? I went to Dadai to Vahram's house and they welcomed me. I am crying. "They took my Ashot."

He said, "Yes, they have collected all the boys, and they are here. They are in the school. That is why our friend came and made us Turks. They had a ceremony so they won't take our son."

Then Vahram's mother said, "Now they are having breakfast. After they eat they are all out in the garden. It is a large school with a large garden."

I said, "Very well. Please get me some coffee. After coffee I will go. I will not stay." To see my son! I was trembling all this time. I drank my coffee and went to the school. They said it was two blocks away. I went the two blocks. There were mothers outside. They took all the boys, and many of these mothers were there.

Aunty Ars broke in to explain that the Turks intended to raise the Armenian boys as Turks. "They were going to do a circumcision so they did become a Turk then, see. That's how they think."

My grandmother waited for her to finish and continued her story. "Ashot saw me and come running," she said. " 'Mother, save me. You save me.' I said, 'That's why I came to save you. I am going to save you. I won't leave you in the hands of these Turks. Don't worry.' He went upstairs crying. I thought about the police commissioner who told me, if you are in trouble, come to me."

I was confused and asked who this police commissioner was, and my aunt explained it was the one in Kastemoni, where they had lived before the exile. She said he had told her mother that he would help her if he could. She explained that he had been very friendly with her father. "His great grandmother was an Armenian, see. He said, 'I have Armenian blood in me, too.' He was a very nice man." She went on to say that my grandmother had walked from Dadai to Kastemoni, a walk of three days. "When she went, her feet were swollen. They said my mother's feet were swollen."

---

* an Armenian exclamation meaning "Oh, my goodness"

She told us that there were some Armenians in Kastemoni who had become Turks to avoid being exiled and that my grandmother had gone to their house. As soon as there was a pause in the conversation, my grandmother went on:

> I went to their door and knocked on it. I was dressed like a Turk. They said, "Please come in." When I got there I was numb. When I knocked on their door, I was numb. It was as if I was going to go crazy. I couldn't go in. They said, in Turkish, "Come in. Come in, madam." I opened my face,* and they started to scream, "Oh, Elmas." They all came and we hugged each other.
>
> 'What is it?" they asked.
>
> "They have taken Ashot," I said. "They took Ashot. I am going to the police commissioner." But I couldn't walk for three days.

My grandmother paused, and my aunt said, "Yeah, for three days she couldn't walk. You can imagine what's happening to us, back there. Because they came, and they want to know where is my mother." My grandmother said, "They put my feet in hot water and rubbed salted butter on them." Then she described her meeting with the police commissioner:

> It was early Friday morning. He had just come downstairs to wash up. It is in front of my eyes now. He said, "Please come in," in Turkish. The rest of the family was upstairs. I closed the police commissioner's door and opened my face.
>
> "Oh my, Elmas. Where did you come from? What has happened?"
>
> I said, "They took my Ashot. They took my Ashot."
>
> He said, "I told you to become a Turk, and you didn't do it."
>
> "You know best," I said. "I beg you, save my Ashot."
>
> People upstairs noticed that there were two people talking. His wife looked down from upstairs.
>
> "Oh my, Madam Elmas," she said. "Come upstairs."
>
> I cried, "They took my Ashot." I am crying.
>
> The police commissioner came and said, "Don't cry. I'll see

---

* removed her veil

what's what. Don't cry."

"If I don't cry, tell me what it is I have to do to save him.
I have to save him. I have to save him."

He said, "Today I am going to see my superior. I will speak
to him and see what can be done... But don't tell anyone you
are here. There are some Turk dogs, who if you say Armenian, they will cut your throat."

Within a short period of time the police commissioner arranged
for my grandmother to formally renounce her Armenian ancestry
and become a Turk. She was also able to do the same for her children, including Ashot, and all the other relatives who were still in
exile. He had also arranged to bring them to Kastemoni, but Ashot's
release took a longer time. After four months, the whole family
was reunited.

Aunty Ars began to talk about what it was like. "We came to
Kastemoni," she said. "And we used to live, all of us in—I don't
know how many rooms. We had houses, but we didn't have it anymore. And we were Turks... We had like a small apartment. My
aunt and cousins—all together. We used to sew burlap bags. That's
how we survived. And then one night, I never forget that night,
two men, they're going to break our door."

My grandmother broke in, saying in English, "Wait a minute—I
am talk," and began again in Armenian:

My sister-in-law and I are like sisters. We were sewing bags
for the soldiers. The children went to bed. I said, "Get up and
go to bed. I will finish this one, and tomorrow I will take
them." She got up and went to bed.

Then she got up and ran to me, saying, "Sister, sister, sister, they are breaking the door down."

I said, "Don't worry. It's nothing."

She said, "No, no. It's not what you said, get up."

I got up. I got up and saw that they were going to break
the door. They were going to break the door down and come
in. What were we going to do?

Ars said, "Mother, throw me out the window." I said,
"How can I throw you out the window?"

"Whatever you do, throw me out the window," she said.
"Throw me out the window."

Suddenly I had an idea. I said, "Let's open the windows,

and all at once let's all scream fire. Save us. There is a fire."
All of us were yelling out the windows. After that we noticed
that there were soldiers in the street. The superior of the soldiers said, "This is not a fire, it is a rape."

Soon after that we noticed that they went away. Then the
police came. They knocked on the door. We said we won't
open the door. They said, "We are the police." They came
in. They asked what happened. And how did I get that idea
to yell out the window?

In the morning they took us to the police commissioner.
He said, "What happened?"

We told him, "We were sleeping, and my sister-in-law
woke me up saying that they are going to break our door. They
were going to break it and come in."

The police commissioner said, "What neighbors do you
have there?"

"The Aga's son, the shoemaker's son, and another person's son. That's all. No one else."

I was sitting there, and they brought both of them. When
they saw me, they turned pale.

The police commissioner asked where they were last night.
They said they were home.

I said, "No, you were the ones who were throwing rocks
at the door and were going to break it."

The police commissioner got up and hit them both.

My grandmother said, "Do you know what? When I am in trouble, I am never afraid. When I went to Turkey they made terrible
trouble for me." I remembered then that she had gone to Turkey
when she was in her late seventies. She told us what happened:

I signed a paper saying that I was going to leave, and the official said it was forged...

The mayor came and said, "They want you." I went.

He said, "Go over to that man." I went there. He said,
"What do you want?"

I said, "I don't want anything. You said you wanted to
see me and so I came so you could see me."

And the place was full of people...

He asked, "Who signed this paper?"

I said, "I did."

He said, "No you didn't."

I said, "Give me the pen." I took the pen and signed my name.

"That is my signature." He saw it was the same. I opened my mouth in the government office and said, "Aren't you ashamed of yourselves? Shame on you doing these things. No one can sign my name. Only I can make my signature. Look at me and look at my hair. Such a woman doesn't do such things. Shame on you."

In the government office—everyone was sitting there. No one made a sound. I am never afraid. When I have something to say, I say it.

The man came and took me to my relative's house. "Oh," he said, "you are like an *aslan.*"

I asked her what *aslan* meant, and she told me it was a lion woman.

We had been taping for close to an hour, and, thinking that my grandmother must be very tired, I suggested that we stop for a while. She assured me that she was not tired at all, and my aunt seemed anxious to finish their story. When I agreed that we would continue, my grandmother sat back and listened to my aunt tell us what happened after the night their neighbors had tried to break down the door.

We moved to where the Greeks lived, where there was an Armenian church and school. We moved there after that affair.... My mother and Araskin, *Der Hayr's** wife, she had a son and daughter; we lived in one room and they in one room. And my mother was going with a few other women— they were going from town to town selling needles and thread, this and that, packs on their backs, you know. . . Mother took me. We went to one town. It was night. Some young boys came, you know, and they're saying, "If we kill the *gavors* no one will know." And nobody could know it.

And then from far away, I suppose it was their parents, they came and said, "Shame on you people, these are people." And they told us, "You people better go to the next town and stay there." So we went.... Coming back, some town,

---

* an Armenian priest

some farm, they chased the dogs after us. All the dogs are around us. I was going crazy, crying, yelling. Finally, all the people came and chased the dogs away.

After that I got sick. . . . My mother came. She got sick. She had the typhoid fever. And the doctor saw me and said, "Who is going to take care of her?" [Arsenic was about ten years old at the time.]

I said, "I am."

He said, "You know you have to wet the sheet in cold water, wrap her in it." All night long I had to do that . . . and wash the sheet, boil it. I used to do all those—and I was a little girl. All night long, she is burning, you know. I got cold water, put the sheets, wrap her in.

I must have dozed off. All of a sudden, she says, "Arsenic?" You know, my name. She says, "I'm all right. I saw your father in my dream."

After telling us about her own bout with typhoid, my aunt told us how my grandmother managed to get her family to Istanbul.

All the English had come. . . They were taking captives. English soldiers, they came to Kastemoni—all generals and things, you know. They had their guides and things. One night, our door was ringing and ringing. They wanted to come in. Do you remember [to my grandmother] the English?

The next morning my mother went and talked to their superior. She told them what happened and said that they were not that kind of people over here. They wanted to get in. . . . English came with an Armenian interpreter. They were going to take all the orphans to Istanbul.

So my mother went and saw the interpreter and said, "I have children. I want to go to Istanbul and maybe from there—I have relatives. My sister is in America. I have to go there."

He said, "I will take you to the captain." He took her to the captain. He said, "We can't do it. We can only take so much and no more."

And my mother said, "I'll be their mother. They need a mother, these orphans."

And that's how we came to Istanbul.

It would be years, however, before they were able to leave Turk-

ey. Turvanda and Arakel had gone to New York just before the genocide began, but they were unable to raise the money for Elmas's
passage. Aunty Ars described how they lived: "In Istanbul when
Armenian people came from America they used to bring old clothes.
Mother used to work there. We used to sew the burlap bags . . .
the man, that I saved his life, Armenian man, he was doing that
business. He used to give us that work."

My grandmother broke in to say "I all the time worked."
I asked if they had been very poor, and my aunt responded,

> Very poor. And we had one room. That was our bedroom, in
> an apartment, you know. We had the ground floor. One room.
> That was our bedroom, living room. . . . It was bad. . . . We all
> worked, otherwise we can't—we used to go to the fields and
> pick perper [a wild green] and something else . . . no meat,
> you know. We didn't have sugar. You know, during the war
> [World War II] nobody had it. I mean when they rationed
> everything over here. . . .
>
> One day I went to the A&P and here was a big line. I said
> to the manager, "Why is there such a big line?"
>
> He said, "Today they're giving away coffee without a
> coupon."
>
> I said, "Well, I do without it. I'm not going to wait for that
> line."
>
> He said, "Why?" I said , "you know, I've seen it—that
> I could do without it. There is no panic about it."
> We have everything over here.

I asked if she had been hungry a lot, and she answered, "Oh
yeah. Sometimes we have an onion and sometimes apples for dinner. Whatever we find."

Finally, my grandmother located a nephew of hers who was
working for a rug exporter in Iran. She wrote and told him what
they had endured and how difficult their lives were. He sent the
money for their passage, and they left Turkey for New York City.

My aunt and grandmother began to reminisce about their lives before the genocide, but I was too exhausted to listen anymore. I was
relieved when my mother knocked on the door to say that dinner
was ready. We rose to leave my grandmother's room. I wanted to
say something to her—to convey some of what I was feeling. I had

been deeply moved but was unable to think of something appropriate to say. Telling any of the members of my family what I really felt was something I had not done for years, and my relationship with my grandmother had been marked by hostility since my brother's birth. My aunt and Martha left the room, and I waited for my grandmother to get out of her chair. I held her arm and thanked her for telling me her story again.

I spent the remainder of the weekend listening to and taping the memories of my mother and Aunty Ars, and Dodo, an older cousin—this time without my grandmother. My mother remembered very little about the exile and had no memories of her father, who was gone by the time she was three. She talked about being hungry in Turkey, about the darkness they had to endure at night because they could not afford fuel for lights, and about the disease and starvation which ravaged the tent city in Istanbul where the majority of Armenian refugees lived. Most of what she remembered took place after they came to New York when she was eleven. Dodo, whose family had left Turkey before the genocide, told me in vivid detail about the relatives who came to live with her family when they arrived in this country. Aunty Ars's focus was on the various jobs she had had before and after she was married.

I was interested in what they had to say, though I experienced none of the emotional intensity I had felt when I listened to my grandmother. I was still filled with her story and was anxious to get home.

Chapter 22

Over the next few months I began to feel that my grandmother's story had had a powerful effect on my life, though I was not at all clear about it. I decided to transcribe the tapes, to write the story down, in an attempt to understand it. I also wanted to write it down for my grandmother. Now I realized that twenty years earlier, when she'd said, "Tell it to the world," she had charged me with insuring that her story did not die with her. I had no idea how to tell it to the world or even if I wanted to, but at least I could put it on paper for her. The gesture would be highly symbolic, since she could not read English.

For weeks I spent my spare time translating and transcribing the tapes, and, as I heard over and over again how the Turks had come for Ashot, how my grandmother had screamed again and again that they had no right to take him, that he was her son, I wept. For the first time I felt connected to her pain, to the pain of my mother, aunt, and uncle, and, by extension, the Armenian people. I also now understood why I had cried, often with wrenching sobs I could not control, when I read about the separation of black children and parents during slavery. The rage I'd felt against whites and Western civilization for what had been done to Africans and African Americans now included Turks. In both cases, my anger turned to fury because the horrors were not acknowledged. Africa remained the dark continent, and the Armenian genocide was still forgotten.

There was more to the story, however, than pain and rage. As I pieced together my grandmother's early life from the little she'd remembered and from the few things my aunt told me, one thing was very clear: My grandmother had not been raised to take care of herself, even in normal circumstances, yet she had managed to survive the genocide virtually alone. She had gotten her son back and arranged for the return of all of the eleven people from her family who were in exile. Back in Kastemoni, then in Istanbul, she had managed to find housing for her family and had kept them from the starvation that had killed thousands of Armenians.

Now I understood her story was about survival. Not only had she overcome her circumstances, but she had resisted victimization as well. The high point of her story was when the Turks came for Ashot and she said no—that they had no right to her son.

The same woman who had taught me to defer to men, whom I had grown to dislike after the birth of my brother because she so obviously favored him, was also the woman who taught me, through her story, that woman were strong. It had been the knowledge of my grandmother's resistance and survival that had made it impossible for me to accept a feminist politics that focused only on women's victimization. Unwittingly, she'd taught me that, even within a strict patriarchy, women were not rendered helpless.

I was amused at the irony of my grandmother making possible both my openness to the women's movement and my dissatisfaction with it. Her story had lain dormant in my psyche for twenty years, but its influence had been profound. It had provided soil for the blossoming of the feelings behind my politics. I now realized that it would not, could not, be denied. I finished the oral history, had a copy bound for my grandmother, and felt satisfied as I looked at the title in gold letters on the blue leather binding: *Elmas Tutuian— Lion Woman.*

My grandmother would never know what her story had meant for me. By the time I finished it, she had had a stroke, and my parents had made the difficult decision to move her to the Armenian Home for the Aged. She was not often coherent but when she was she railed at being in the home, being incapacitated, being alive. She prayed for the Lord to take her, she told me, and with a spark in her eyes said she wanted her body to be burned. The time was past, when the recording of her story mattered.

I had given a copy of the oral history to my parents, Dodo, and Aunty Ars, and after I heard nothing about it for a few months I asked my parents if they'd read it. Perhaps, I thought, they had been too preoccupied with my grandmother to have had the time. They responded that they had, of course, read the story. The said there were many inaccuracies. My father complained that the dates could not be correct, and my mother, that there was too much about Aunty Ars, who, she said, had gotten everything mixed up. I said I could make changes but I had wanted at least to get the story on paper. They said nothing. The fear that my relationship to my family might change was groundless after all. We would remain as distant as we ever had been.

But I was changed. I now consciously identified as an Armenian. I also understood some of the origins of my politics but was unsure at the same time, where my new sense of self would lead. I longed to talk to other Armenians, but my relatives, most of whom I saw very rarely at large family gatherings were the only ones I knew. My last attempts at serious conversation with some of my cousins had been in the 1960s when we had been polarized on opposite sides of the political spectrum. I was anxious to meet Armenians who were not family members for other reasons, too. I didn't know what it meant to be an Armenian and wondered if what I had identified as "Armenian" was merely what my family did.

With the hope of learning about other Armenians, I subscribed to an Armenian weekly newspaper published in Boston. Every week I glanced at articles on the activities of church dignitaries, news of various Armenian organizations and their ladies auxiliaries, and announcements of trips to Armenia. I was not enlightened, and from what I could see in the paper there was nothing in the Armenian community for someone like me.

One day, during my usually quick perusal of the paper, I spotted a small announcement of a day-long workshop on the psychological and social effects of the genocide on the children of survivors. The workshop, which was being organized by two Armenian psy chiatrists, was for people whose parents or grandparents were survivors. I sat with the paper in my lap and realized with a bit of a shock that I was both the granddaughter and daughter of survivors. I'd known, of course, that my mother had gone through the genocide, but the focus had always been on my grandmother. She had told me the story, while my mother never talked about Turkey. I knew from taping her words that she had few memories of what had happened to her family but now I saw that, regardless of her specific memories, her life had been shaped by the genocide. She had, no doubt, known terror and hunger. I was the child of someone who had experienced that pain, and now I knew there was a part of my psychological history I had not previously thought about.

What had been the effect on my life of being the daughter and grand-daughter of survivors of the genocide? I remembered an article in the *New York Times Sunday Magazine* that Tom had given to me years ago. It was about the children of survivors of the Holocaust. Now I vaguely remembered that I'd been fascinated by the article and meant to get the book it was based on, but never had.

Clearly, I would have to attend this workshop, but it was with some trepidation that I sent for a registration form. Did I really want to go into a group of Armenians? What would they be like, and, more troubling, how would they respond to me? I was as far as one could be from the image of the good Armenian woman I had grown up with and which was, I was discouraged to see, still well represent-ed in the Armenian weekly. Women were absent from the impor-tant committees but appeared as organizers and cooks for the various fund-raising events. I worried, too, about what other Armenians would think about someone like me whose daily life included vir-tually nothing Armenian except for what was on the dinner table.

The workshop was held near my parents' house, and since it began early Saturday morning I decided to stay with them that Fri-day night. I wondered how they would react to my attending such a workshop, but they said little about it. I would tell them more about it when I got there,I thought. Still they seemed uninterested. My father asked who the psychiatrists were, and, when I told him, my mother said that one was the grandson of one of my grandmother's friends. Didn't I remember Mrs. Boyajian from the old neighbor-hood? I said I didn't and tried once more to engage them in a dis-cussion about the effects of the genocide but stopped when my mother said that I should not talk about such things when my cou-sin Dodo came. She, Uncle George, and Aunty Ars would be over for dinner very soon. I had to remember that Dodo's mother had been Turkish, she said, and talking about the genocide upset her. The evening was spent, like so many others, eating and talking about the family.

When I got to the workshop the next morning I was pleased to see a group of about forty people, including many who looked my age. After a brief introduction we were assigned to small groups where we would spend the bulk of the day. Each group of ten to twelve people would have two psychiatrists as leaders: an Armeni-an and, to keep some objectivity they said, a non-Armenian. The psychiatrists introduced themselves, and I noted that all the non-Armenians had Jewish names. I wondered if any of them had written the book about children of the Holocaust which I had never read.

Optimistically, I walked to the room that had been assigned to my group, but my high hopes for sharing feelings and experiences with other children of survivors were quickly dashed. The discussion focused on Armenian politics. It began with a statement by a man that we needed to get the Turkish government to admit what it had done to the Armenian people. Another man said we needed the land. We Armenians could not rest until we had Armenia back from the Turks and the Russians. Someone else, also a man, quickly responded that Soviet Armenia was what we had, and we had better understand that. We would not get anything else. He had been there many times, and those of us who had not should plan a visit soon. It was important to go for as long a period as possible, he said, because only then could we know what it was like to be in an Armenian country controlled by Armenians. His comments sparked a lively debate about whether Armenians did, in fact have control. How could we be content, a man asked, with an Armenia behind the "Iron Curtain"? We could not rest, a woman said until we had a free Armenia.

Though I found the debate interesting, it was not what I had come to hear. I wanted to know what other people felt about being Armenian. Had they had the same feelings as I had growing up? What had it been like for them to be raised by a survivor? I waited for a break in the discussion to ask those questions, but when I did only one woman responded. Her eyes filled with tears as she recounted some of what her father had told her of his experiences. He had been a young man when the Turks came to his village. They had taken all the men to the outskirts of the village and beaten and shot them. Somehow her father had not been killed but had been left for dead by the Turks. When she recalled how, every day of her childhood, he had shown her the scars on his head from that beating so that she would not forget what had happened to the Armenians, she broke down and could not continue. To my surprise, her revelation did not encourage others to tell their stories but only served to heat up the political debate. One man slammed his hand on the table, saying that the world has forgotten and that we must make Turkey pay. The man who had urged us to go to Armenia disagreed. Armenians had to do all we could to support Armenia. Only the Armenians there were in a position to preserve the language and the culture. Only they could insure our future.

The non-Armenian psychiatrist broke into the discussion to ask if people could talk about their feelings about the genocide. In his work both with survivors of the Holocaust and their children, he said, he had found that many survivors experienced guilt for being alive, and they had transmitted that guilt to their children. The room was silent until one of the men finally said that only when Turkey was made to pay would we be free. The psychiatrist said that those who worked with Holocaust survivors had noted that the guilt survivors felt had not dissipated even after the Nuremberg trials, when the world community had formally held Germany as well as individual Germans responsible for the Holocaust. His attempt to get the group to talk about their feelings was, however, completely unsuccessful.

Toward the end of the day the psychiatrists left the room to confer with their colleagues, and I suggested that we go around the room and tell each other what we had expected from the day and what we had gotten. Once again the room was silent. People seemed puzzled by my suggestion. Finally, the woman who had cried about her father asked me to tell them what I had wanted. I took a deep breath and decided to tell the truth. I explained that I had had a hard time growing up Armenian. Even in Washington Heights, which I had learned in the discussion at lunch was *the* Armenian community in New York City, I had felt different from everyone else. The effect of the genocide on my life was something I had only recently, at the age of thirty-five, begun to consider. I had come to the workshop with the hope of sharing my feelings and questions with others who had had a similar experience in order to learn more about myself. I said I had been very disappointed, and I thought that the day had been a lost opportunity. Breaking the silence that followed my remarks, one of the women said she was glad I was coming back to the Armenian community. Once I did, she said, I would feel much better. Confused, I asked what she meant and realized from her response that she had misinterpreted what I'd said about wanting to reclaim some of Armenian culture for a desire to become part of an Armenian community. I told her that the two things had been very separate for me. I did not believe that I ever would live within an Armenian community. She asked why with such sincerity that I responded honestly. I said I could not live my life as an adult woman within the confines of an Armenian community where there was no room for me to be who I am. To my surprise, she said she knew what I meant, but she did not elaborate. No one else spoke.

It was soon time to return to the large group meeting where we would hear about the issues raised in the other groups. Perhaps the group I was in was unique, I thought, but was discouraged to hear that none of the groups had discussed the day's topic: the psychological and social effects of the genocide.

I left quickly when the workshop ended. My expectations that the day would give me some insight into what it meant to identify as an Armenian American had probably been unrealistic, but I was disturbed that, once again, I had learned only that I felt different. I was an Armenian. I was the child of survivors, but what did it mean that I could find so little common ground with others who shared my experience? What did it mean that I could not accept so many of the traditions of Armenians because they were rooted in male dominance? Could I be an Armenian and challenge patriarchal traditions? What did it mean that I did not participate in the ancient Christian church of Armenia—the religion my grandmother had refused to renounce, the reason for her exile. I had not agreed with the man in the workshop who said that the culture was being maintained only in Soviet Armenia, but what did it mean that I no longer spoke the language and had not consciously passed on any of the Armenian tradition to my children?

I was in a state of utter confusion about being an Armenian and was relieved to finally get home. It was wonderful to see Martha and to be able to talk with her about what I'd experienced. It was also a comfort to be back in an environment where I could be myself. I had told the woman in the workshop the truth: I never could live in an Armenian community where my politics, values, and lifestyle would not be accepted. I had struggled to become an adult woman who was defined not by marital status and number of children but, rather, by my ability to function independently and to believe in myself. I had work that I thought was important and a commitment to try to do what I could to change the world. Martha and I were building a life together that was based on mutual respect. The struggle to acknowledge and accept our differences had been worth the pain of our battles. Being an Armenian was important to me, but I had no intention of giving up any other part of my life.

I felt pleased with the directions in which my life was developing and wondered how my new Armenian consciousness would affect my future. Finally, I had received my grandmother's legacy, but it would be years before it was incorporated into who I am.

Afterword

In the spring of 1984 Arlene Avakian and Martha Ayres came to California. For a week they lived with me, my lover, Kate Miller, and our daughter, Jenny. We had a fabulously good time. We ate our way through every favorite recipe each couple could devise on alternating nights. We agreed that it was lucky for all of us that we lived on opposite coasts. Were we to spend more than an occasional week with each other, we would soon be unable to waddle anywhere. Whatever Kate's and my cooking skills, there was no doubt that Arlene was an absolute culinary genius. In reading this memoir, I could smell and savor the foods Arlene described. More important, I came to understand the emotional significance of food in her life: of its careful and artistic preparation, its patient, sensuous consumption. Food has been an essential link for Arlene, a means of traveling among cultures and a way for her to connect with women of different racial and ethnic backgrounds. These scenes of chopping, cutting, tasting, pounding, and storytelling are reminiscent of many kitchens over many generations.

Like the smells from her kitchen, Arlene's voice was present for me as I read: its solid New York base, its thickness, and its resonating sarcasm ("Even the Pope didn't look like our archbishop," she complained of her family's Armenian church). Her narrative rings with the zest of Arlene's personality, the power of her presence. There's no pretense here either, no watered-down, sanitized version of experience, dressed up for publication. Her rage is raw, emotions palpable, and her tone periodically edged with guilt and anger. If this anger is understood in context—as coloring only her particular view of "what happened"—much information about personal relationships and the formative years of women's studies becomes available to us.

For example, in personal relationships, Arlene's intense emotional presence sometimes caused people to withdraw from her: either they backed away from her anger or withdrew to a fixed oppositional camp. I attribute this emotional presence at least in part to her cultural experience, especially when she is relocated to the iceland of Manitowoc and Sheboygan, where her "difference" (read ethnicity, volatility, and a dark complexion) most contrasted with a white, middle-class culture. At different times, conflict erupts as Arlene passionately seeks a way to be herself with others and demands the same honesty from them. Throughout the memoir, there is much pain, self-doubt, and a dogged will to go on, and there were times when it felt to me that Arlene was Lion Woman herself.

Nowhere is this courage more evident than in her struggle for the life of her son, Neal—her effort, as she wrote, "to help him develop to his potential, whatever that was." It is typical and shameful of our society, not only that Arlene had to do this entirely alone, but that she was often blamed for his condition, and her story is an important addition to a growing feminist literature analyzing psychiatric, social, and childcare services. Yet, Neal never stopped growing, changing, and "developing to his potential" because Arlene never stopped believing in him.

Ultimately, as the memoir tells us, the confluence of feminism, her recognition of an Armenian cultural heritage, and the acknowledgment of a lesbian identity allows Arlene to find a garden she can call her own. Her process of discovering connected identities may be emblematic of that shared by many other women of her generation. At first she resented the women's liberation movement because she thought it had come too late for her. Yet, stirred by young women in their twenties and the promise of another way of being in the world, she shook off the conventional structures of marriage and motherhood—who said it was too late?—and struck off for Amherst, "a new frontier." In reading Arlene Avakian's story, I was reminded of this paragraph written by her contemporary, Joan Lester, in "Letter to My Younger Sisters," August 5, 1979:

> How the decade of the sixties ripped open our hearts, and in the upheaval of our anger, we were transformed as we began to transform world history. All of us in that wave of fire were changed and a new determination forged to fundamentally

alter our notion of our relationship to the world as women. We began to widen the space in which we lived. That widening of space meant, first, for virtually all of us, the ending of our marriages, the clearest, most immediate confinement. And the beginning of struggle to create new lives with new forms for new content. We whose commitment to struggle was forged in the early civil rights battles brought the struggle home, and set out then at twenty-five or thirty to recreate ourselves and history.[1]

Through both women's recollections, we are witness to the emergence of a movement that allowed women to claim themselves with self-determined purpose and direction. For Arlene Avakian, it is not always a smooth course; she doesn't always know where she will land or how she will get there. The point, however, was that she—like so many women of this time and place—would walk under her own power.

Arlene Avakian's introduction to women's liberation converged and collided with her participation in the movement to create women's studies. Like her struggle for identity within personal relationships, her description of debates, quarrels, and losses within women's studies speaks to widespread and long-lived tensions. Should "female studies," as it was called then, be a compensatory program intended to integrate women into the mainstream curriculum and dissolve after three years when it was presumed this integration would be accomplished? Or should this new area—with its new methodologies, pedagogy, and texts—see itself as a transformative field, deeply connected to the women's liberation movement? Versions of this debate are still at the center of many discussions in women's studies, as are problems with a Eurocentric curriculum and the predominance of white faculty. And there are new variations on these themes. As women's studies has become increasingly institutionalized—awarded departmental status and tenured positions—so have pressures been keen for scholars to replicate patterns of theoretical obfuscation typical of academics in traditional disciplines. There has also been pressure to sublimate or lose entirely the relationship between scholarship and feminist activism. Quite correctly, many faculty have also pointed out that significant theoretical illumination has come from feminist adaptations of Marxist, Freudian, Lacanian, and postcolonialist theories. Still, struggles over what African-American literary critic Barbara

Christian has called "the race for theory" also reveal the extent to which theory itself, as it has been constructed and privileged, is profoundly male-centered and Eurocentric.[2] The richness of these discussions has placed women's studies at a critical edge of intellectual life in which many of the frameworks governing such disciplines as history, political science, literature, psychology, and anthropology, for example, have been challenged, particularly by Third World feminist scholars. Women have become, in the words of one Chicana critic, "their own ethnographers."[3]

One may read Arlene Avakian's personal story as such an ethnography, an articulation of evolving consciousness and a tool with which to map a deeper understanding of our collective experiences as women and to understand how ethnicity, race, class, and sexuality define who we are.

A crucial moment in this quest for self-consciousness came on the night that Arlene Avakian and Martha Ayres attended Andrea Dworkin's lecture "Women and the New Right." Feeling that Dworkin dwelled only on women as victims rather than acknowledging their strengths and resistance, Arlene began muttering under her breath, "That's not my grandmother!" By the end of the evening the mutter had become a defiant cadence: "Not my grandmother!" The story Arlene had heard and sublimated when she was fourteen years old, retold in her memoir with such dramatic effect, crashed into her consciousness and reframed her personal history. In particular, her grandmother's story helps explain Arlene's identification with the civil rights movement, her dissatisfaction with a feminism that affirmed universal sisterhood while erasing differences of race, class, and ethnicity, and her deepening sense of alliance with African-American women.

Through Arlene's narration, we see the extraordinary strength, will, and determination of the women in her family and their paradoxical, often frustrating subordination to men. Her aunt Lucy's story, in particular, is a complex weave of resistance, defiance, and subordination. "Though she lived in America for more than fifty years, she refused to speak one word of English," Arlene says, recollecting that for Lucy, in her apartment with its wall-to-wall Persian rugs, "her house was her country. She hadn't wanted to emigrate, and she would keep as close to her own ways as possible."

I am reminded here of Judith Ortiz Cofer's narrative of her Puerto Rican childhood, *Silent Dancing*. She describes her mother's similar resistance to assimilation:

My mother never adopted the U.S.; she did not adapt to life anywhere but in Puerto Rico, although she followed my father back and forth from the island to mainland for twenty-five years according to his tours of duty with the navy. She always expected to return to *casa*—her birthplace. And she kept her fantasy alive by recounting early years to my brother and me until we felt we had shared her childhood.[4]

Again, in her partially autobiographical essay "The Cult of the Perfect Language: Censorship by Class, Gender, and Race," Mitsuye Yamada recounts the story of her mother, whose silence emerges both from resistance to humiliation and internalized beliefs about her class and immigrant status. Yamada's mother spoke the dialect of her rural prefecture, the "standard," middle-class, Tokyo dialect, and English. "Here is a woman," Yamada writes, "with incredible stories to tell, who is capable of speaking and writing in three different languages, but whose stories will never be recorded in any of those, because she herself has judged them flawed in some way."[5]

Arlene Avakian's memoir is part of, and enriches, a new genre of women's writing typified by Cofer and Yamada. Informed by a feminist class, racial, and ethnic consciousness, this work is part of a process of reclaiming personal histories and maternal legacies. The reclamation has been a source of enormous pride and has provided ways of knowing no longer circumscribed by traditional scholarship. This writing also provides a link between generations of women, allowing us to envision, in Marge Piercy's loving words, a "worked jigsaw / of the memories of braided lives."[6]

In the years covered by Arlene's autobiography, women's movements and struggles flourished, forming a broader context in which to place her life's momentum. Activists staged marches to "take back the night" and for lesbian and gay pride; concurrently, they created shelters for battered women and their children, centers for women's health, and telephone lines to counsel rape survivors. Others fought for legislation protecting rape victims during cross-examination at the trials of their alleged assailants and for a host of affirmative action guidelines. Consciousness-raising groups, women's bookstores and coffee houses, women's presses, newspapers, journals, newsletters and broadsides, music festivals, and cultural events of every imaginable variety proliferated. Black feminists organized their first national conference, while Chicana feminists caucused in La Raza conferences and Native American women rose to the forefront in struggles for land rights, health services, and reproductive rights, and against government relocation schemes. Workers organized the Coalition of Labor Union Women, and a few years later clerical workers at Yale shook the foundations of that venerable bastion of patriarchal authority (and incidentally split some women from each other along class lines).

The way in which Arlene chooses to relate how she and Martha fell in love reveals how far the feminist movement has come since the early seventies when homophobia ripped it apart. Arlene and Martha's story is told here without defensiveness, pretense, or apology. It is told with humor, radiating love, and the power of their commitment to each other. Arlene describes her relationship with Martha as "the healthiest relationship I had ever had in my life." Martha wasn't afraid of Arlene's anger. Knowing that emotions, like thoughts, are in constant flux, together they find a process that allowed for resolving or living with differences. It is an encouraging, even inspiring, model, with both personal and broadly political implications. Despite proclamations of a postfeminist era, women's movements affected millions of lives and shaped the perspectives of a whole generation. These movements also fundamentally and personally affected the decisions Arlene Avakian was able to make in her life. They provided counsel, community, and life-affirming validation that her feelings were not the ravings of a "mad housewife" but the clear-sighted perceptions of one very smart and very brave woman.

Bettina Aptheker

Notes

1. Joan Lester, "Letter to My Younger Sisters," *Valley Women's Voice,* September 1979. (*Valley Women's Voice* is a small women's publication in Greenfield, Massachusetts. A reprint of the letter was given to me by the author.)

2. Barbara Christian, "The Race for Theory," *Feminist Studies* 14, no. 1 (Spring 1988): 67–80. A related essay is Maxine Baca Zinn et al., "The Costs of Exclusionary Practices in Women's Studies," *Signs* 11, no. 2 (Winter 1986): 290-303.

3. Alvina Quintana, "Expanding a Feminist View: Challenge and Counter-Challenge in the Relationship between Women," *Revista Mujeres* 2, no. 1 (Enero/January 1985): 12. (*Revista Mujeres* is published at the the University of California, Santa Cruz.) See also Judith Stacey and Barrie Thorne, "The Missing Feminist Revolution in Sociology," *Social Problems* 32 (April 1985): 301-16; Susan Hardy Aiken et al., "Trying Transformations: Curriculum Integration and the Problems of Resistance," *Signs* 12, no. 2 (Winter 1987): 255-75; and Ellen Du Bois et al., *Feminist Scholarship: Kindling in the Groves of Academe* (Urbana: University of Illinois Press, 1988).

4. Judith Ortiz Cofer, *Silent Dancing: A Partial Remembrance of a Puerto Rican Childhood* (Houston: Arte Publico Press, 1990), 38–39.

5. Mitsuye Yamada, "The Cult of the 'Perfect' Language: Censorship by Class, Gender, and Race," in Mitsuye Yamada and Sarie Sachie Hylke ma, eds., *Sowing Ti Leaves: Writings by Multicultural Women Writers* (Multicultural Women Writers of Orange County, 6151 Sierra Bravo Road, Irvine, CA 92715, 1990), 117.

6. Marge Piercy, "Looking at Quilts," in Marge Piercy, *Living in the Open* (New York: Knopf, 1974).

New and Forthcoming Books from the Feminist Press

The Captive Imagination: A Casebook on The Yellow Wallpaper, edited and with an introduction by Catherine Golden. $35.00 cloth, $14.95 paper.

Eva/Ave: Woman in Renaissance and Baroque Prints, by H. Diane Russell. $59.95 cloth, $29.95 paper.

Here's to the Women: 100 Songs for and about American Women, by Hilda Wenner and Elizabeth Freilicher. Foreword by Pete Seeger. $49.95 cloth, $24.95 paper.

I Dwell in Possibility, a memoir by Toni McNaron. $35.00 cloth, $12.95 paper.

Intimate Warriors: Portraits of a Modern Marriage, 1899-1944, selected works by Neith Boyce and Hutchins Hapgood, edited by Ellen Kay Trimberger. Afterword by Shari Benstock. $35.00 cloth, $12.95 paper.

Long Walks and Intimate Talks. Stories and poems by Grace Paley. Paintings by Vera B. Williams. $29.95 cloth, $12.95 paper.

Margret Howth: A Story of Today, a novel by Rebecca Harding Davis. Afterword by Jean Fagan Yellin. $35.00 cloth, $11.95 paper.

The Mer-Child: A Legend for Children and Other Adults, by Robin Morgan. Illustrations by Amy Zerner and Jesse Spicer Zerner. $17.95 cloth, $8.95 paper.

Now in November, a novel by Josephine Johnson. Afterword by Nancy Hoffman. $29.95 cloth, $10.95 paper.

On Peace, War, and Gender: A Challenge to Genetic Explanations, edited by Anne E. Hunter; Catherine M. Flamenbaum and Suzanne R. Sunday, Associate Editors. (Volume VI, Genes and Gender Series, edited by Betty Rosoff and Ethel Tobach.) $35.00 cloth, $12.95 paper.

Women's Studies International: Nairobi and Beyond, edited by Aruna Rao. $35.00 cloth, $15.95 paper.

Women Writing in India: 600 B.C. to the Present, edited by Susie Tharu and K. Lalita. Vol. I: 600 B.C. to the Early Twentieth Century. Vol. II: The Twentieth Century. Each volume $59.95 cloth, $29.95 paper.

For a free catalog, write to The Feminist Press at The City University of New York, 311 East 94 Street, New York, NY 10128. Send book orders to The Talman Company, 150 Fifth Avenue, New York, NY 10011. Please include $3.00 postage/handling for one book, $.75 for each additional book.